CHINESE WORKERS OF THE WORLD

CHINESE WORKERS OF THE WORLD

Colonialism, Chinese Labor, and the Yunnan–Indochina Railway

Selda Altan

Stanford University Press
Stanford, California

Stanford University Press
Stanford, California

This book is published with financial support from the Association for Asian Studies through its AAS First Book Subvention Program.

Printed in the United States of America on acid-free, archival-quality paper.

Library of Congress Cataloging-in-Publication Data

Names: Altan, Selda, author.
Title: Chinese workers of the world : colonialism, Chinese labor, and the Yunnan-Indochina railway / Selda Altan.
Description: Stanford, California : Stanford University Press, 2024. | Includes bibliographical references and index.
Identifiers: LCCN 2023044749 (print) | LCCN 2023044750 (ebook) | ISBN 9781503638235 (cloth) | ISBN 9781503639331 (ebook)
Subjects: LCSH: Railroad construction workers—China—Yunnan Sheng—History. | Industrial relations—China—Yunnan Sheng—History. | Railroads—China—Yunnan Sheng—History. | Investments, French—China—Yunnan Sheng—History. | China—Foreign relations—France. | France—Foreign relations—China.
Classification: LCC HD8039.R3152 C523 2024 (print) | LCC HD8039.R3152 (ebook) | DDC 331.7/62510095135—dc23/eng/20231204
LC record available at https://lccn.loc.gov/2023044749
LC ebook record available at https://lccn.loc.gov/2023044750

Cover design: Lindy Kasler
Cover photograph: One of the numerous stages in the construction of the Hekou–Kunming railway line, taken at 413 km near the capital city of Kunming, China between 1903 and 1910 (Mulhouse Municipal Archives/Cité du Train—Patrimoine SNCF).
Typeset by Newgen in Sabon LT Pro 10/15

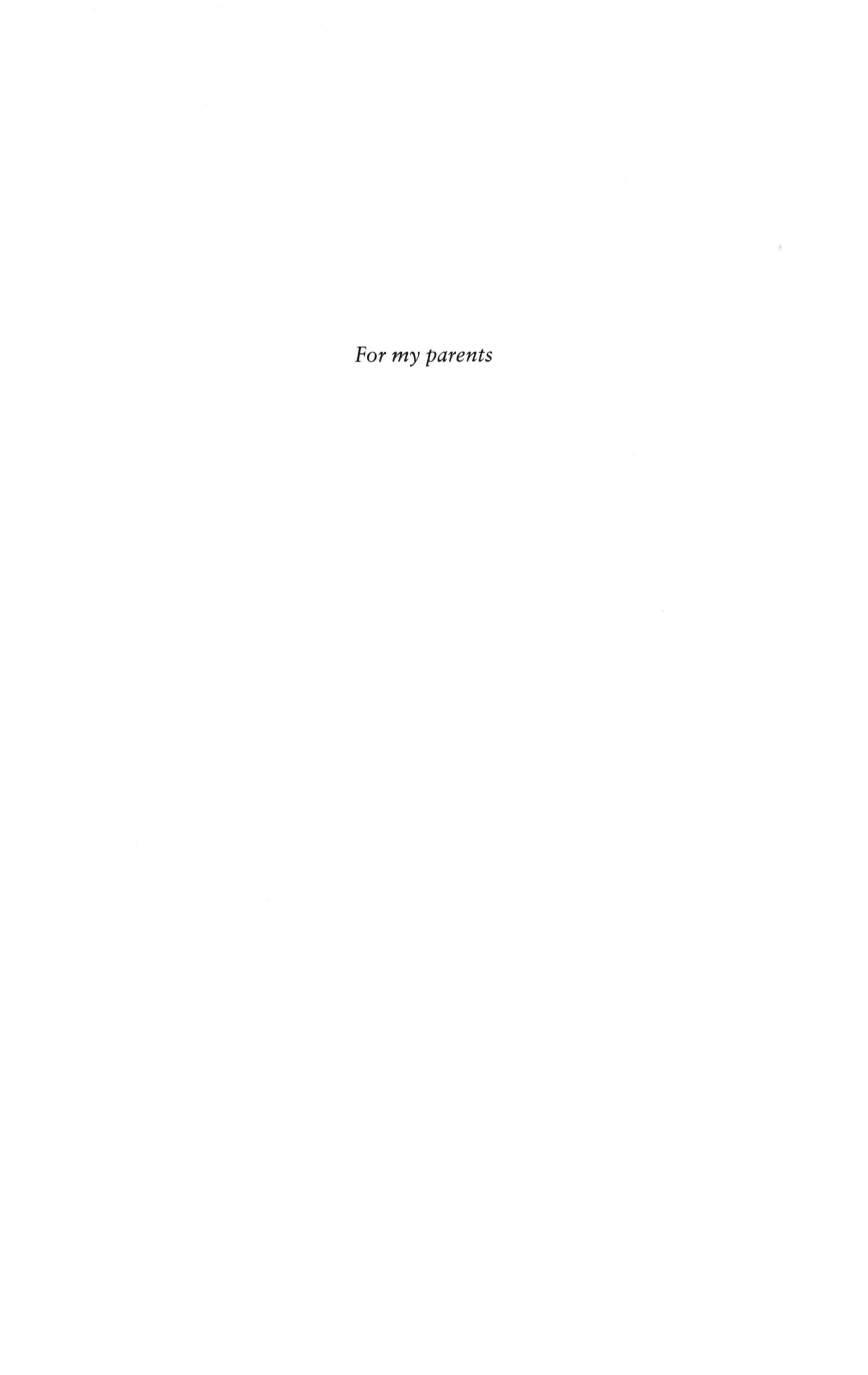

For my parents

Contents

Acknowledgments

There are moments in life that bring profound happiness, and few are more gratifying than witnessing the fruition of your perseverance and hard work. I embarked on the journey of this book a decade ago. This process has accompanied me through the most important moments of my life. Without the support and guidance of mentors, friends, and family, this project would never have taken its present form.

My primary advisor, Rebecca E. Karl, has always been more than a mentor. She not only taught me the importance of posing meaningful questions as a scholar, but also guided me toward a fulfilling academic career. I am deeply indebted to her for her unwavering belief in my abilities, even in times of intense self-doubt. At New York University, I had the good fortune to know Marilyn Young, a prolific storyteller, fervent political activist, and exceptional teacher. As an academic mentor and compassionate friend, Marilyn supported my project until the end of her life. In her absence, Frederick Cooper's intellectual breadth and careful guidance reassured me that my work was in capable hands. His continued support as I worked on this book has been invaluable.

I owe thanks to David Ludden for his assistance throughout my graduate studies, and to Manu Goswami for being a role model in intellectual depth and articulate writing. Joanna Waley-Cohen has enriched my understanding of Chinese history and Mikiya Koyagi offered fresh perspectives and valuable feedback on this project.

The research for this project spanned vast geographies. My stays in Shanghai and Kunming were eased by Ni Lan (Shanghai University) and Joanna Waley-Cohen (NYU Shanghai), along with Pertia Wang. Öznur Kuzu welcomed me into her home in London and Caroline Battistelli was a gracious host and guide during my numerous stays in Paris. My New York years were enriched by the intellectual companionship of

Roslynn Ang, Maggie Clinton, Robert Cole, Mirela David, Anatoly Detwyler, Mara Yue Du, Katherine Grube, I-Yi Hsieh, Myung-Ho Hyun, Jeong Min Kim, Uluğ Kuzuoğlu, Soonyi Lee, Jenny Lee, Andrew Liu, Julian Suddaby, Qin Wang, Meng Wei, and Qian Zhu, to whom I extend heartfelt gratitude.

As I developed my research into a book, I benefitted from the insights and encouragement of mentors and colleagues at various universities. Selçuk Esenbel, İsenbike Togan, and Meltem Toksöz at Boğaziçi University; Farid Afzar, Megan Brown, Timothy Burke, and Ahmad Shokr at Swarthmore College; and Michelle Campos, Jessica Harland-Jacobs, Nancy Rose Hunt, Matthew Jacobs, Sheryl Kroen, Emrah Şahin, and Louise Newman at the University of Florida helped me view the project from a broader angle. At Randolph College, I received enormous support from History Department Chair Gerry Sherayko and Interim Provost Elizabeth Perry-Sizemore for my research and writing commitments. My colleagues Chelsea Berry, Suzanne Bessenger, John D'Entremont, Crystal Howell, Connor S. Kenaston, Justina Licata, and Kelsey Molseed have modeled productive and collegial scholarship. The support from my colleagues at Randolph College, as well as my neighbors on Wedgewood Road, provided a sense of an extended family. Special thanks go to Jeong Min Kim (University of Manitoba), whose companionship saved me from the isolation of solitary writing and infused our meetings with enthusiasm.

I must acknowledge Joshua H. Howard's meticulous reading and feedback on the manuscript, which helped me navigate its structural challenges. Thanks also go to David Atwill (NYU Shanghai) for his encouragement and to my editor, Dylan Kyung-lim White, along with the staff of Stanford University Press, for their investment in this book.

The research for this book was made possible by multiple grants and the assistance of librarians and archivists with whom I had the pleasure of working. I acknowledge financial support from Randolph College, New York University, ACLS/Henry Luce Foundation Fellowship Program in China Studies, and China and Inner Asia Council Grants of the Association for Asian Studies.

Finally, I extend my love and deepest gratitude to my family. My sister-in-law, Müzeyyen Coşkun, has been a steadfast caretaker for my daughter during my numerous research trips. My sister, Sema Kara, has offered unwavering support. Her glowing praise for my work provided the motivation I needed to complete the project. My dear Ayda learned to entertain herself while I was immersed in writing, and for her understanding, I will be forever grateful. My husband, Hakan, has been a pillar of patience and support through the stormy seas of my academic life, always standing by my side and showering me with unconditional love. Though my father could not see the completion of this book, I take solace in knowing that my parents, Sevgi Özdelice and Zekai Altan, never doubted my resolve and determination. I dedicate this book to them in recognition of their love and support.

CHINESE WORKERS OF THE WORLD

Introduction

ON A SCORCHING SUMMER DAY in June 1906, a Sichuanese named Li Chengfa left his hometown with his eighteen-year-old son. They were two of the many Chinese workers recruited to toil at the construction of a foreign-built railway in the neighboring Yunnan province. They had signed work contracts with a French recruitment company on recommendation from the Catholic missionaries in their village.[1] Along with the wadded blankets, blue work jackets, and bamboo fiber hats they had received, they were also given expectations and dreams of opportunity, soon to be tested by dangerous and challenging conditions.

It was a time of complex international politics. On April 10, 1898, the Qing central government had signed a treaty with France. In compensation for German colonial acquisitions in northern China, the treaty granted the French Indochinese government the right to build a meter-gauge railway from Haiphong, Vietnam, to Kunming, China, the capital of the southwestern border province of Yunnan.[2] With the French parliament ratifying the convention on June 20, 1901, and the establishment of a private company, the railway's construction began in earnest by 1903. Yet, the execution of this ambitious project proved to be riddled with challenges. The undertaking became a monumental engineering feat, particularly with a considerable portion of the 466-km Yunnan section constructed in the inhospitable and disease-ridden Nanxi valley. Ascending from 76 km in Hekou to 2,030 m in Kunming, the railway's path demanded the creation of 158 tunnels, 22 iron bridges, and 108 stone bridges as it wound through mountainous terrain and across turbulent rivers.[3] These engineering challenges were compounded by a series of problems, including the railway company's austere labor

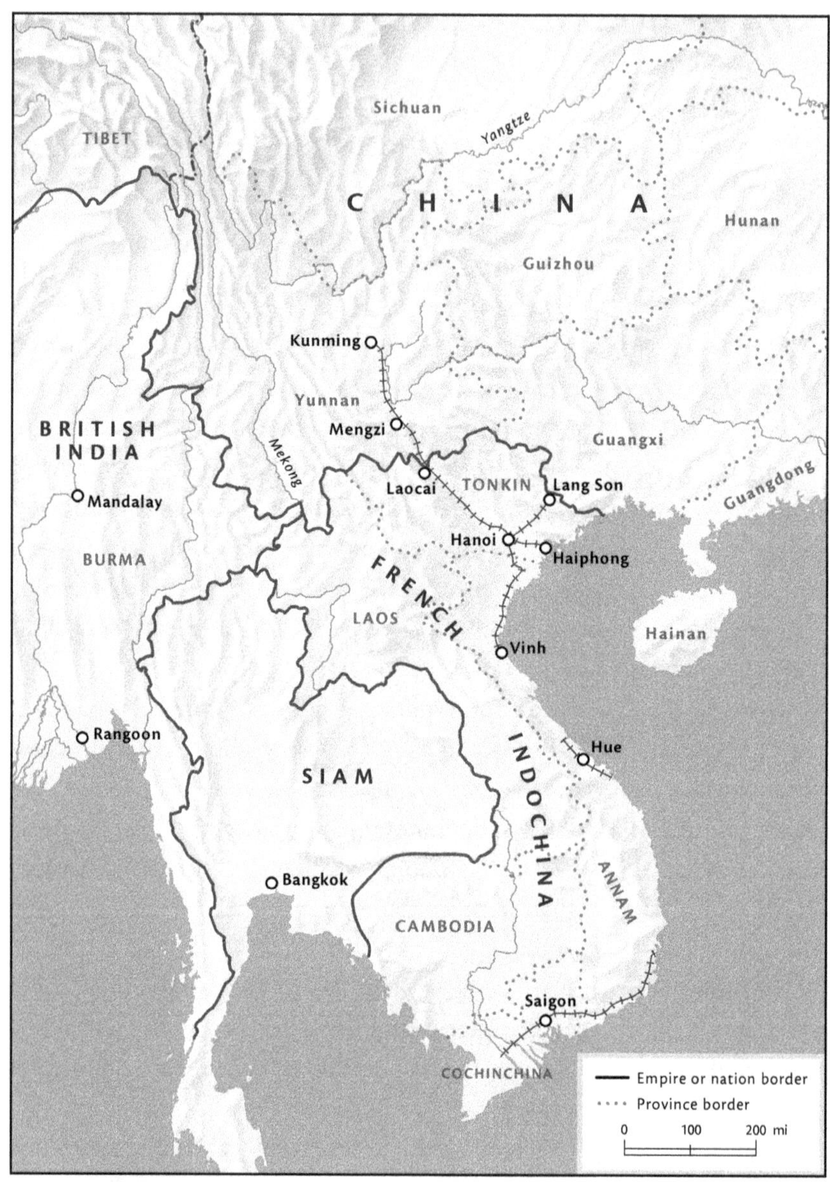

MAP 1 Map showing French Indochina and China's southwestern provinces in the early twentieth century.

management, the recklessness of Italian contractors, persistent worker resistance, and a bourgeoning nationalist sentiment in the region. As a result, contentions, rebellions, and a fatal crisis involving thousands of Chinese and Vietnamese workers turned what initially seemed like a promising venture for colonial expansion into a symbol of imperialist misadventure.

Amid this turbulent backdrop of conflict and failure, the experiences of ordinary laborers like Li and his fellow workers take on profound significance. Their story illustrates a conflict, rooted in changing production relations and work ethics, between Chinese traditional labor practices and French industrial expectations. Upon their arrival, Li and his son were tasked with shoveling a large trench and building the embankment at the entrance and exit of the trench, using the soil drawn from it. The task was difficult for the men who were not used to working with the peculiar Western tools. The workers quickly overcame their clumsiness in using the shovel, but the wheelbarrow seemed outlandish.[4] What was the point of using that contraption instead of a shoulder pole, which left their hands free for smoking?

To French employers, practices like the use of shoulder poles and frequent breaks for smoking were the root causes of inefficiency. Workers' acts, including smoking or absenteeism due to illness, were scorned as "pretexts for them [the workers] to stroll and idle around."[5] Any restriction on their individual "prerogative" would be condemned and lead to "nothing less than a strike or a mass desertion of the worksites."[6] The journalist who detailed Li's railway work experience stated that due to the strength of trade guilds in China, which zealously defended the rights of their members, any disagreement over the implementation of the contract terms or the enforcement of work discipline would cause strikes or mass desertions, albeit temporarily resolved by prompt interventions.

To satisfy the expectations of their workers, whom the French journalist labeled as "self-indulgent," the railway company's managers had to organize the work in such a way that the workers labored for appropriate durations, depending on the season, and had enough breaks for

FIGURE 0.1 Workers using wheelbarrows at 214 km of the railway. ©Archives Cité du Train–Patrimoine SNCF.

meals, naps, and observance of significant holidays such as the Chinese New Year, Lantern Festival, Dragon Festival, Autumn Festival, and the Festival of the Emperor. Every month, the company granted the workers a two-day respite to partake in nearby markets and fairs, as documented by the journalist. These holidays did not include the harvest season, during which Li and his fellows were reported to have increased their income by working on local farms rather than the railway. Owing to traditional work methods and frequent recesses, the output of a Chinese worker amounted to "only a quarter of the work that a good European worker would have done in a shorter time."[7] When considering the added costs of compensation for work-related accidents, allegedly caused by the workers' ignorance, along with salaries and other benefits, the notion of cheap Chinese labor was a mere fantasy. In the words of the French journalist, "the fate of these [railway] workers was more worthy of envy than pity."[8]

Contrasting the French reporter's self-serving narrative that painted a rosy picture of the working conditions, Swiss engineer Otto Meister's

(1873–1937) memoirs tell a starkly different story. Both local workers and recruits from other provinces were faced with numerous difficulties immediately after they arrived at the worksites. The region to the south of Mengzi was plagued by fever, cholera, and dysentery. While the European staff enjoyed a diet of chicken, beef, veal, mutton, and various vegetables, even indulging in cakes and tarts baked by Vietnamese cooks (though they had to pay for bread), the contractors hoarded worker provisions due to the logistical challenges of transporting food supplies to the worksites. Many workers were reduced to subsisting on nothing but rice and tea.[9] Medical clinics and ambulances were stationed at certain intervals along the railway, but corruption was rife among the medical personnel, who often sold medicine to sick workers at exorbitant prices, despite the company providing medical supplies for free. In Meister's chilling words, "the coolies were dying like flies."[10] He was tragically correct: by the end of construction, at least 12,000 of approximately 65,000 Vietnamese and Chinese workers had succumbed to malaria, work-related accidents, and fatal conflicts with their employers or Qing military forces.[11]

While these accounts may appear to be contradictory, they both contain elements of truth. Particularly in the early years of construction, the company and non-Yunnanese worker recruits were caught off guard by the region's malarial climate. Once the harsh reality was uncovered, workers did not hesitate to abandon the worksites to preserve their lives. These mass desertions, often misinterpreted by Europeans as a cultural distaste for hard work, were only part of the story; unexpected was the widespread worker resistance to harsh working conditions and the contractors' ruthlessness. Despite the legal advantages held by the European staff, Chinese and Vietnamese workers were unafraid to pursue their interests through both official channels (petitioning and court appeals) and defiant acts (mass desertion, absenteeism, rebellion, theft, and even homicide). While some of these actions might seem unconventional when viewed through the lens of European histories of class struggle, they were indicative of a sophisticated understanding of acceptable work and the growing awareness among Chinese workers of changing production relations and labor market dynamics in an industrializing world. This phenomenon highlights a relatively unexplored dimension of European colonialism in China, namely, the formation of new class identities.

Building Class Identities: A Transnational Analysis

Li was the third child of a prosperous merchant-landowning family from Sichuan, one of China's largest and most prosperous provinces. The province's climate was so exceptional and the soil was so fertile that, even with primitive methods, farmers enjoyed bountiful harvests garnering wealth and comfort. Yet, the longstanding tradition of partitioning lands into smaller lots among family members, in adherence to progenitorial rights, had gradually reduced income from agriculture. Historically, the Li family had relied on the trade of silk and vegetable tallows to manufacture soap and candles. But Li's parents had made a series of unfortunate investments that diminished the family fortune. The financial downturn deepened when the family's conversion to Catholicism—an unpopular decision within their community—led to social ostracization.

On a larger scale, Li Chengfa's personal story is intertwined with China's sweeping socioeconomic transformations at the dawn of the twentieth century. Militarily defeated by European powers and Japan in several wars from 1839 to 1900, China found itself burdened with crippling financial sanctions and a lack of industrial production.[12] It had to open its borders to foreign powers for railway projects, mining, and other industrial investments while simultaneously suffering from a parasitic, British-imposed opium trade that caused a steady depletion of Chinese silver reserves.[13] The influx of foreign investments in treaty ports, which the Qing government attempted to offset by sponsoring enterprises in nearby locations, served to undermine traditional handicraft industries in the interior. Shanghai, for instance, emerged as a hub for cotton textiles, silk reeling, candles, and soap, largely at the expense of small-scale rural production. By 1907, the only industry in which the Li family remained involved was the home-based production of straw sandals, commonly worn by impoverished Chinese citizens. From 1895 to 1913, Sichuan saw the inauguration of a mere nineteen manufacturing and mining enterprises, a figure still higher than the five native-capital enterprises founded in Yunnan during the same period.[14]

The confluence of foreign capital, popular rebellions, and administrative reforms in China instigated a series of structural changes, the effects of which were not uniformly distributed across the country's diverse regions or even within individual provinces. For instance, population increases since the eighteenth century varied in magnitude, leading to dissimilar outcomes in rural interior regions compared to the more commercially developed eastern cities. Similarly, modifications to administrative regulations in the tenancy system enhanced the living standards of farmer-tenants in some provinces, whereas in others there was a trend toward higher deposits and payments in silver instead of copper or payment-in-kind, as in Chongqing, Sichuan.[15] The situation in Yunnan, where mining was the main economic activity and diverse ethnic groups populated border areas within a nearly autonomous rule, presented a completely different story. The province consistently ranked among the lowest in the Qing provinces in terms of population size, cultivated land, and rice yields.[16]

The establishment of treaty ports and the augmented presence of foreign investors and missionaries in peripheral economies created opportunities for peasants needing supplementary income to subsist in an increasingly monetized economy. Li Chengfa's decision to convert to Christianity, for example, was influenced in part by the church's role as a safety net, offering immediate help in times of need. In the absence of missionary aid, the Li family lacked the resources to endure recurrent famines. In this evolving economic context, where cash wages became an essential source of income for the average person, Li saw the rationality in working on the railway to earn cash and send it home to pay for the hired labor on the family's land. Although economic historian Bin Wong posits that Chinese peasants became only semiproletarian due their continued connection to the land—thus differing from their European counterparts—the overall trend was a significant increase in the number of Chinese peasants engaging in wage labor.[17]

The proletarianization of Chinese peasants became particularly conspicuous in the southern port cities that emerged as hubs of the global coolie trade in the 1850s. In dire need of cheap labor after the abolition of slavery, European colonial powers, led by Britain, looked to the densely populated regions of China and India to fulfill the labor requirements for agricultural production and infrastructural development in their colonies. In this context, the term *coolie*, originally employed to describe unskilled day laborers, came to signify a particular category of South Asian and Chinese workers who were mass-recruited under contractual agreements stipulating the terms of employment and imposing penal sanctions onto workers for violations of those terms.[18]

For the male population of certain southern Chinese provinces, such as Fujian and Guangdong, seeking employment abroad in Southeast Asia had long constituted a conventional means of livelihood.[19] In the nineteenth century, Dutch and British colonizers in Southeast Asia capitalized on this stable labor source in competition with regional labor "gangs." Meanwhile, within China, where there was still a sovereign government, Britain used unequal treaties to "liberalize" the Chinese labor market so that it could be freed from the Qing government's central control. This maneuver facilitated a more flexible and exploitative labor environment, aligned with the interests of foreign powers.

The Treaty of Nanjing, signed in 1842 after the First Opium War between Qing China and Britain, marked an initial step in the transformation of the Chinese labor market. This treaty dissolved Chinese intermediary companies (*hongs*) by allowing British merchants to "carry on their mercantile transactions with whatever persons they please" in the treaty ports of Xiamen, Fujian, Ningbo, Shanghai, and Guangzhou.[20] Immediately after, the Qing government signed similar treaties with other foreign powers, freeing commercial transactions of various kinds. These treaties enabled foreign and Chinese dealers to dispatch mass coolie shipments to French Réunion, Spanish Cuba, Brazil, and Peru, despite a continued government ban on foreign travel. The Beijing Convention, ratified in 1860 after the Second Opium War, affirmed the autonomy of Chinese individuals in engaging with British subjects and "shipping themselves and their families on board any British vessel at any of the open ports of China."[21] An addendum six years later saw the Qing government pledge to end illegal coolie recruitments while also acknowledging the legitimacy of voluntary labor contracts. It even promulgated regulations concerning the conditions of coolie employment abroad. In sum, by 1866 a "free" labor market was created in southern China, which attracted dislocated rural populations to overseas work opportunities.

The same process through which Chinese labor's circulation expanded across a larger area, from the Americas to Australia and South Africa, whether through free migration or indenture, sparked the development of a global race theory, commonly known as the "Chinese question" or "yellow peril." On one hand, the theory portrayed the "docile" immigrant Chinese labor force as a menace to the white working classes in the West because trade union leaders contended that Chinese workers lacked the political maturity to cultivate class consciousness and advocate for higher wages.[22] On the other hand, there was a recognition of the indispensability of inexpensive Asian labor during a period when it was vital for building the infrastructure of Euro-American capitalism. Still, the Western bourgeoisie campaigned against Chinese immigration. Their concerns centered on the potential threat posed by the success of "Asiatic races" in accumulating capital owing to their unrivaled standing in the global labor supply chain.[23] Historian Mae Ngai traces this white anxiety to the gold rushes in the US and Australia, when Chinese gold seekers emerged as successful miners and merchants in the West thanks to their cooperative and egalitarian work arrangements.[24]

Conversely, Chinese overseas workers' exposure to diverse labor regimes contributed to their self-definition, enriching their perspectives and interest-seeking actions. Since many Chinese workers viewed these overseas excursions as temporary arrangements to improve their living standards back home, an analysis of Chinese working-class identities would be deficient without considering the insights and experiences returned by these overseas workers.[25] Additionally, many Chinese immigrants supported the revolutionary movement in imperial China by sending funds and providing a platform for republican propaganda. Their engagement extended beyond mere financial support, forming an intricate link between the diaspora and the mainland. If we recognize the Chinese republican revolution in 1911 also as a diaspora movement, it is equally crucial to consider the profound impact of Chinese overseas workers in shaping and contributing to the emergence of working-class identities in China.[26] Given the interconnected nature of these labor phenomena, this book examines labor recruitment processes for the Yunnan railway within the context of the global coolie trade and Chinese emigration.

Labor and the Limits of Politics in Late Imperial China

Yunnan is known for its long history of uprisings, influenced by the dynamism of its vast miner population and ethnically diverse communities that historically experienced a degree of semiautonomous rule on the fringe of the Qing Empire.[27] Right before French incursion into the region, Yunnan's Muslim miners had revolted against Qing imperial authority and declared their independent sultanate in 1856, an ethnic state that endured until quelled by Qing forces in 1873.[28] Prompted by escalating ethnic tensions and foreign intrusions in border regions, the Qing state in the 1870s hastened a program aimed at curtailing the autonomy of native chieftains, a continuation of the policy initiated during the Yongzheng emperor's reign (r. 1722–1735), in preference for direct administration.[29] As part of this plan, the central government tried to consolidate its rule over Yunnan's ethnic communities by taking a proactive role in economic modernization. Historian C. Patterson Giersch categorizes these governmental initiatives as the initial stage of what he terms "disempowered development," alluding to the flourishing of the government-backed Han enterprises to the detriment of minority populations.[30] Although these policies came to fruition only in the Communist period, they laid the groundwork for viewing the economy as a pivotal factor in state consolidation and national cohesion.

Simultaneously, rising nationalist propaganda emanating from China's eastern treaty ports found its way to Yunnan with a reimagined conceptualization of national sovereignty. These antidynastic nationalists, akin to Qing officials, posited the economy as the bedrock of sovereignty in the modern age. Nevertheless, in their view, the state's legitimacy was not derived from the emperor's divine mandate but rather hinged on achieving a satisfactory growth rate and augmenting citizens' purchasing powers through industrial output and international trade. The Qing government, conversely, had failed in forestalling foreign domination over the Chinese market and in cultivating a key prerequisite for a robust national economy: competition. In essence, the recognition of a "subject of right," an individual endowed with civil and political rights before the state, was insufficient to confer the state's legitimacy.[31] Rather, the formation of a "subject of interest" was a requisite, an individual who would vie in the national market, ideally with international competitors, under equitable circumstances as reconstituted by the state—a condition disrupted by foreign imperialism in China.[32]

The Qing government was cognizant of its new role in the competitive age of modernity. Following the defeat in the First Sino-Japanese War of 1895, the imperial court initiated a reform program with an emphasis on military modernization, but the undertaking was thwarted by a coup masterminded by conservative factions of the ruling elite. The outbreak of the Boxer Rebellion in 1899 and its suppression by foreign allied forces deepened the conflicts between those xenophobically opposed to foreign methods and those who perceived Western modernization as the sole avenue for the nation's salvation. Within this latter contingent, divisions persisted over whether to lead change from above or below, from the state or the people. Even among nationalists who advocated for direct action and mass mobilization as their political modus operandi, there was a preference for fostering an elite interest group independent of the state, even if it meant marginalizing lower classes or minority groups. This stance was predicated on the assumption that capital accumulation by national elites (subjects of interest) necessitated a consistent and inexpensive labor supply. Consequently, they opted to circumscribe the lower classes to the status of the "subject of rights," rather than elevating them to the role of "subjects of interests" within their nation-building project.[33] That is, within the nationalist paradigm, Chinese workers (along with ethnic communities) were entitled to recognition of their civil rights but were not envisaged as a constituency with conflicting interests to the national bourgeoisie (to the Han majority in the case of ethnicities), at least until the creation of fair competition within the national market.

The nationalist project, as conceived, was self-contradictory at its inception. On one hand, it proposed an inclusive nation-state as a guarantor of the equitable distribution of sovereignty across the entire population. On the other hand, the definition of the nation as an ethnic category, combined with the confinement of politics to deliberate actions fostered through capital accumulation and political activism, effectively marginalized non-Han and uneducated sectors of society from participatory decision-making processes. Government-driven attempts to modernize the administrative system also amplified the disparity in power among various social groups. Bereft of the right to vote in newly constituted local elections, the lower classes, predominantly peasants and workers, were consigned to a supposedly apolitical realm, characterized by a perceived lack of national consciousness. Simultaneously and somewhat paradoxically, both revolutionary and constitutionalist intellectuals designated these same groups as essential elements in the realms of territorial defense, economic advancement, and national reproduction. Within this complex scenario, rife with ambiguity and overdetermination, workers had to navigate their path into self-empowerment.

Labor historians who studied the origins of the Chinese working class and the labor movement have often defaulted to a nationalist commitment toward the creation of a national bourgeoisie, focusing their inquiries on whether Chinese workers developed an autonomous movement that could be cast as class struggle. For example, historian Jean Chesneaux identifies at least 152 strikes occurring between 1895 and 1918 as protests against low wages and deplorable work conditions. Still, he posits that the Chinese working class "had not yet taken action on its own behalf" before 1919, but rather "merely provided support for movements directed by other social classes."[34] Similarly, he documents that worker organizations founded prior to 1919 were predominantly mixed associations, cofounded by employers and employees to advance national industries through vocational training and mutual aid in competition with foreign entities.[35] Thus, while Chesneaux acknowledges the emergence of a bourgeois class during the waning years of the dynasty, he contends that the imperative to develop the national economy, coupled with the enduring dominance of traditional guild mentality, inevitably undermined the surfacing of class conflict. This, in turn, impeded the formation of trade unions and typical labor actions such as demands for an eight-hour workday or May Day celebrations, all of which are considered to be manifestations of class consciousness.

This book advances two interrelated arguments that contribute to our understanding of working-class subjectivities in late Qing China beyond the categories of class consciousness and movement politics. First, it contends that the emergence of the Chinese working class is not confined to archetypal labor protests but can be traced to contingent encounters and precarious transitions. Drawing inspiration from Ken Kawashima's exploration of unemployed Korean workers in post–World War I Japan, the book acknowledges that the transition from peasant to proletarian is not linear but unfolds through an insecure process of contingencies.[36] In these transitory moments, such as entering or leaving the labor market, worker identity is born, extending the scope of worker subjectivity beyond the traditional spheres of workplace encounters to include the very beginning and end of the employment process.

I frame the Yunnan railway workers' refusal to work—whether by not signing the contracts offered by recruiting companies or deserting the worksites after seeing abominable working conditions—as political with the help of Marx's discussion of the realization of labor. In *Grundrisse*, Marx writes that "the use value which the worker has to offer to the capitalist, which he has to offer to others in general, is not materialized in a product, does not exist apart from him at all, thus exists not really, but only in potentiality, as his capacity."[37] This capacity is realized only when the capitalist puts the worker to work. Contrary to the "objectified labor" or labor "present in space," in the form of commodities and exchange value, the notion of "labor as subjectivity" or labor "present in time" provides an avenue to consider resistance to capitalist subsumption that precedes the materialization of class conflict at the production site.[38] This resistance begins with the worker's refusal to realize his productive capacity in the service of capital. In this sense, Chinese workers' intuitive rejection of labor contracts on terms that deemed unacceptable stands as political as their decision to strike in protest against low wages or deplorable working conditions. Similarly, workers' decision to withdraw their bodies from a deadly capitalist operation can have dire consequences for the capitalists, as seen in Yunnan. This reframing thus provides a nuanced understanding of the cognitive dimensions of identity formation that transcends conventional categories of class consciousness or labor movements.

Second, the book proposes a shift in understanding the space where class identities emerge. Instead of focusing solely on national contexts, it extends its inquiry to transnational encounters by integrating the overseas experiences of Chinese indentured workers with the interactions between Chinese workers and European employers, especially in the peripheral setting of Yunnan, where economic forces were less pronounced and social classes were less distinct than in the treaty ports or colonial territories. Drawing inspiration from Cedric Robinson's theory of racial capitalism, which argues that capitalism is an inherently racialized system of profit making, the book illustrates how Chinese workers were racialized both in overseas colonial territories and within China through extraterritoriality, consular courts, and European medical facilities.[39] European builders of the Yunnan railway dismissed Chinese workers' acts of desertion, theft, and murder by racializing them as mere crimes originating from cultural characteristics. Yet, these defiant acts and day-to-day struggles were far from trivial. They not only spotlighted labor exploitation in Yunnan as a racial and moral question but also facilitated the birth of a Chinese worker identity in a universal sense. This universal identity was rooted in the shared knowledge of the nineteenth-century overseas work experiences but transcended those experiences in ways unforeseen by Chinese nationalists and foreign colonists. Early twentieth-century Chinese workers skillfully leveraged colonial competition for cheap labor to improve their employment conditions, juxtaposing contract terms from different colonial powers before lending their labor to foreign employers. It was this globally shaped cognizance that rendered them receptive to the calls of communism in the subsequent decade.

It is ironic that Li Chengfa had to move from the prosperous province of Sichuan to poverty-stricken Yunnan, one of the country's three provinces sustained through government aid. He was rational enough to leave his hometown to escape creditors who would have condemned him to destitution. The French journalist complimented Li for his rational decision, depicting him as an enterprising individual (subject of interest) who would utilize his capital (labor/capacity) to maximize revenue. He exhibited this same rationality in converting to Catholicism without totally quitting significant Chinese customs, such as ancestor worship. The portrayal of Li as a rational actor sharply contrasts with the stereotypical Euro-American image of the Chinese worker as an inassimilable, crafty Oriental. The coexistence of these contradictory depictions of the Chinese worker in Western colonial discourse complicates efforts to understand how Chinese workers perceived themselves in a globalized world. Still, the following chapters will elucidate how they discerned the value of their labor in the face of racial stigmatization or underestimation by various political and economic actors.

Chinese and French Historiography on the Yunnan–Indochina Railway

At the time of its construction, the Yunnan–Indochina railway sparked intense controversy within French political circles as the nation was trying to set the best course for their country, either through colonial expansion or protectionist developmentalism. In the postcolonial period (Ho Chi Minh declared the independence of Vietnam in September 1945), French historiography gained a monolithically critical tone in seeing the railway as a failed project of French imperialism. In 1963, Michel Bruguière, emphasizing the Franco-British rivalry in East Asia, argued that the exploitation of China's abundant resources was dependent on the creation of a solid colony, not on obtaining "artificial and revocable concessions."[40] Thus, the fierce colonial competition in the region rendered the railway economically unviable within the broader French colonial project. In a more recent work, Jean-François Rousseau contends that the Yunnan–Indochina railway exemplified a typical imperial railway venture, failing to achieve its military, geopolitical, and economic objectives. Particularly noteworthy is the stark disparity between the substantial financial and human costs incurred and the railway's hasty abandonment during World War II.[41] The recent proliferation of publications featuring personal memoirs from French diplomats, business figures, and railway employees further reinforces this argument of failure.[42]

In contrast to French scholarship, Chinese historiography on the Yunnan–Indochina railway has exhibited notable fluctuations. Until the late 1990s, the railway was constantly portrayed as the Trojan horse of French colonialism, and the local uprisings between 1898 and 1910 were purported to be manifestations of Chinese anti-imperialist nationalism against foreign colonizers.[43] According to these accounts, the economic activities of France and Britain in Yunnan also fueled the emergence of a nascent local working-class movement, thereby transforming the province's class structure in a capitalist direction.[44]

During the early 2000s, Chinese scholarship underwent a radical shift in perspective regarding the Yunnan–Indochina railway. While the emphasis on the imperialist nature of the railway project remained a background theme, a new interpretation that emphasizes the railway's positive contributions to Yunnan's socioeconomic development and modernization has become commonplace.[45] These positive perspectives culminated in the official centenary celebrations of the railway on March 31, 2010, which saw the participation of representatives from France, Vietnam, and China. The celebration ceremony was not only a commemoration but also part of China's broader plan to revitalize commercial and diplomatic ties between China, France, and Southeast Asian nations, later to be connected to a Silk Road revival project.[46] During the ceremony, Chinese official representatives highlighted how the Yunnan railway had contributed to the modern development of the ethnically diverse and economically underdeveloped province. This new emphasis served to underscore the railway's significance in driving progress and connecting the province into a larger regional economy.

In parallel to this change in official standpoint, Chinese scholars have produced a nostalgic and even artistic portrayal of the Yunnan railway since 2010. Through these visually captivating works, these scholars illustrate the railway route's aesthetic landscape, prominently featuring railway stations with distinct architectural characteristics while also evoking collective memory by sharing personal accounts of railway employees and villagers along the railway tracks.[47] Anthropologist Wu Xingzhi explores the Yunnan railway within the framework of Arjun Appadurai's theory of "things of events," and extensively examines its place in collective memory as a signifier of the province's colonial past.[48] In 2018, acclaimed novelist Fan Wen published a novel titled *Bisezhai*, centered on the Yunnan railway's construction process.[49] The narrative revolves around two Greek brothers who, in their pursuit of Oriental riches, find themselves in the service of the French railway company as section overseers. In addition to depicting the hardships endured by Chinese workers, the book delves into the psychological impact of colonial power dynamics, akin to George Orwell's exploration in "Shooting an Elephant." Complementing these scholarly and literary endeavors, a multitude of art exhibitions and museum showcases in China and France further contribute to our comprehensive understanding of the railway. These collective efforts, in a postcolonial spirit, expand the discourse beyond mere economic analysis, shedding light on the broader sociocultural implications of colonial encounters intertwined with the Yunnan–Indochina railway.

Chapter Overview

I have structured this book to portray two sides of the Sino-French encounter. The first four chapters, relying mainly on French sources, illustrate how French colonial agents approached the railway and labor conflicts in Yunnan. The last two chapters emphasize Chinese perspectives and analyze how Chinese nationalists and officials deliberated the relationship between labor/class and Chinese state building.

The first chapter lays out French motivations for initiating the Yunnan railway. When southwest China became a backyard to the French Indochinese colony following the Sino-French War of 1884–85, debates about the desired Yunnan railway project centered on whether to frame it in terms of British-inspired free-trade expansionism or neomercantilist protectionism. The railway received parliamentary approval in 1901 only because it promised to be labor intensive rather than requiring large capital investments. The chapter discusses the significance of the Yunnan railway for the economic restructuring of France's Indochina colony, notably with the creation of the Indochinese opium monopoly. The latter part of the chapter examines the foundation of the Yunnan railway company as an extension of Indochinese railways and analyzes the Yunnan–Indochina Railway Treaty, highlighting French shortsightedness about China's labor-market dynamics.

The second chapter continues discussing French economic aspirations in Yunnan, specifically in mining. As Yunnan's mineral deposits attracted nineteenth-century French travelers, laying the foundation for the "Yunnan myth," they also enticed French protectionists to invest in the Yunnan railway. But when French colonizers secured mining rights in Yunnan, they faced overwhelming challenges due to local miners' resistance, which was amplified by the Qing government's aspirations to use mining revenues as the basis of its consolidation over Yunnan's ethnic minorities and Chinese nationalist propaganda depicting mining as the epitome of China's industrialization. They then turned to a relatively marginal project: using Islam as a nexus to connect Yunnan's marginalized Muslim communities with Middle Eastern Muslims living under French rule. To the dismay of French officials and investors, none of these endeavors gave France a solid ground to establish itself in Yunnan.

The third chapter examines how French officials racialized disobedient railway workers as "undisciplined" "Orientals." Facing the labor shortage in Yunnan, the railway company agents had to recruit workers through the intermediary of foreign companies involved in the overseas coolie trade. While the railway company tried to eliminate government interventions in recruitment to minimize labor costs, the supply-demand dynamics of the Chinese labor market gave the workers the upper hand in negotiating the contract terms. The chapter argues that Chinese workers' skillful market manipulation was part of a global movement toward labor awakening and that their large-scale exodus from deadly worksites brought attention to the cruelty of colonial developmentalism.

Chapter 4 explores French strategies, mainly in medicine and security, to control the defiant labor force. In response to mass mortality among workers, France expanded medical facilities along the railway and recruited doctors from its colonies, but they failed to either forestall worker casualties due to malaria or override workers' preference for traditional Chinese remedies. French security enforcement also fell short despite the existence of consular tribunals, a French-operated prison, and Vietnamese railway guards from Indochina. The chapter argues that medical racialization and the utilization of extraterritorial rights to the advantage of French citizens were part of a larger French biopolitical scheme, seeking to expand French colonial influence by subjugating the laboring body.

In chapter 5, the focus shifts from the constitution of French biopolitics in Yunnan to an analysis of Chinese nationalist approaches to the use of Chinese labor in colonial railway projects. The chapter analyzes several pieces in the Japan-based revolutionary periodical *Yunnan Journal* (云南杂志) to understand why Yunnanese nationalists, affiliated with Sun Yatsen's Revolutionary Alliance, did not theorize labor when forced labor was a significant characteristic of French colonization in Indochina. Instead, the alliance focused on improving land value and relegated labor to a secondary position in their broader nation-building project.

Chapter 6 discusses the nationalist movement in Yunnan in its two major episodes. First, it analyzes nationalist arguments for the retrocession of the Yunnan railway, situating them in the campaign for railway nationalization. The chapter asserts that the Yunnan branch of the movement eventually failed due to the Yunnanese gentry's economic weakness, even when French officials were prepared to negotiate the railway's sale, which they deemed a financial disaster. The latter part analyzes the failed Hekou rebellion, organized by Sun Yatsen with assistance from the Revolutionary Alliance located in Vietnam. The group's condescending attitude prevented them from mobilizing workers and local ethnic groups for their antidynastic cause. The chapter concludes that nationalist activism's limited outlook in Yunnan confined worker struggles into a racialized discourse rather than viewing them as building blocks of a dynamic economy.

CHAPTER 1

French Imperialism and the Yunnan–Indochina Railway

"Without labor, the riches of the colonies become an onerous burden for the mother country."[1]

EARLY RESEARCH ON FRENCH COLONIAL activities in China and Southeast Asia viewed the Yunnan railway as a byproduct of the nineteenth-century political rivalry between Britain and France in Southeast Asia. Michel Bruguière, for example, described Franco-British rivalry in Yunnan as "flag imperialism," arguing that the railway's construction was "less an economic necessity than a mental requirement."[2] Robert Lee, emphasizing the eventual triumph of economic imperialism in France's China policy, suggested that the primacy of the economy over politics was the inevitable result of "mattress diplomacy," a term he used to describe French prudence in avoiding potential military conflicts with Britain while increasing their influence in Yunnan.[3]

In contrast to state-centered perspectives, John F. Laffey characterizes the efforts of the Lyon Chamber of Commerce to advance French business in China, especially during the Lyon Mission in 1895, as "municipal imperialism."[4] The term suggests that diverse agents and interest groups, rather than a unified government strategy, shaped French colonial policy in this period.[5] Although recent scholarship assigns equal weight to economic and political factors, earlier debates continue to haunt the scholarship, leading to futile efforts to define a uniform policy that consistently guided French colonization in Africa and Asia during the Third Republic.[6]

This is not to deny the existence of common patterns and structural dynamics in late nineteenth-century French colonization. In particular, the *Transindochinois* and uncompleted *Transsaharien* railways bore striking similarities in terms of their initiation, financing, advocacy by interest groups, and labor employment systems. A consortium of business magnates who harbored mostly unrealistic financial and commercial expectations from the construction and operation of these railways initiated both. The initiators obtained parliamentary approval only after active lobbying by French business elites and their political cronies. Metropolitan campaigns touted these railways as potent "military instruments" and harped on the promise of political gains as much as economic rewards. However, once the contracts were signed, political expectations lost their purported value and the builders or financers were often at loggerheads with government representatives in the field.[7] And, finally, both projects utilized diverse recruitment strategies including contract labor, corvée labor, and wage labor, all of which turned out to be a byword for workers' misery and exploitation.[8]

The similarities of the two infrastructure projects were grounded in the larger French project of empire building, which arose from a desire to restore French national grandeur vis-à-vis British colonial activism in Asia and German hegemony in Europe in addition to the needs of nineteenth-century French capitalism. Nevertheless, railways were not simple business operations in the service of the empire. On the contrary, they were the driving force for colonial expansion into unconquered territories. The Yunnan railway is a case in point.

The idea of building a railway from Tonkin to southwest China was part of the French colonial agenda throughout Tonkin's pacification in the 1880s. Similar to the French railway lobby advocating the economic potential of penetrating interior African markets, the proponents of the Yunnan railway contended that French colonization in Indochina would be worthless without an overland connection to Chinese markets. Early French explorers and merchants enthusiastically lauded Yunnan as the most prosperous province in southwestern China, brimming with inexhaustible mineral deposits and high-quality tea, silk, and opium.[9] This remote border province became so popular among foreign Orientalists that from 1864 to 1893, at least 456 visitors traversed the province despite its challenging terrain, rudimentary transport infrastructure, and disease-prone subtropical climate.[10] Over time, the fanciful allure of "the Yunnan myth" was displaced by sobering accounts of pervasive poverty, but Yunnan's economic backwardness neither invalidated its strategic location as a pathway from Indochina to more affluent Chinese markets nor eclipsed the potential financial rewards of constructing and operating a railway.[11] The Yunnan railway thus became the catalyst for the formulation of French colonial policy in northern Vietnam and southwest China.

The Third Republic's ideological reorientation from protectionism to liberalism, alongside French merchants' leadership, fostered an environment where the Indochinese and Yunnan railways evolved from contentious ventures into alluring opportunities. Whereas French industrialism and its neomercantilist appeals characterized the first three quarters of the nineteenth century, the last quarter was dominated by liberal economists who rescinded their professed anticolonialism and contended that "free colonization" should be promoted against the state's onerous conquests.[12] In other words, late nineteenth-century political discourse in metropolitan France resolved the expansion debate and moved on to discussing the roles and limits of state involvement in empire building.[13]

Railways proved instrumental in harmonizing liberal values with the interests of neomercantilist industrialists. As much as they opened new venues for free trade, railways' construction also ensured substantial orders from French heavy industry.[14] A similar consensus arose concerning the expansion of France's stake in the China market, although debates persisted as to how and in which parts of the Celestial Empire France could exert its influence without risking an international conflict.

Until the early 1890s, relations between China and France were under the shadow of the Sino-French War of 1885–87, which resulted in the severing of northern Vietnam from Chinese control. In 1897, French diplomats and capitalists were able to secure some projects in northern China, such as building Port Arthur and the Beijing–Hankou Railway, but the French presence in the south, adjacent to its Southeast Asian colony, was almost negligible. On June 20, 1895, France and China signed a convention authorizing the French company Fives-Lille to build and operate an extension of the Indochinese line from Langson,

Vietnam, to Longzhou, Guangxi, but the project remained unrealized due to doubts about the railway's profitability and conflicts between the company managers and French diplomats.

Similar divisions overshadowed the Yunnan railway project. Diplomats like Frédéric Haas (Sichuan) and Jean Marie Antoine Louis de Lanessan (Indochina), and merchants like Ulysse Pila (Lyon) were enthusiastic about the potentials of a Tonkin-Yunnan route into China, but others like Paul Cambon (1843–1924), the ambassador in London, and Gaston Doumergue (1863–1937), a metropolitan politician who would become the minister of colonies in 1902, advocated vigilance regarding the expansion of French activities into the Chinese interior. Similarly, Maurice Dejean de la Batie (1863–1933), then consul in Fuzhou, was critical of the inefficiency of French businesses and believed that France should look for prospects in the treaty ports before dreaming of invading the inner parts of the Qing Empire.[15]

The assessment of cautious diplomats and metropolitan politicians was accurate. French economic activities in China were limited compared to the British, whose merchants practically monopolized trade in the southern regions around the Yangzi River. In 1902, France's share in foreign investments in China was 11.6 percent while Britain's and Russia's each exceeded 30 percent.[16] A major portion of this investment was in the form of railway loans, as French business investment constituted only 5.9 percent of the total foreign business investments in China.[17] Even in Fuzhou where French engineers built an arsenal, which became the flagship of the Chinese fleet with almost a quarter of Qing China's total naval investments, France failed to establish its presence, lagging behind other countries in maritime and other businesses.[18]

Among French businesses, the Lyon Chamber of Commerce developed a keen interest in China, especially after Lyon's silk industry was devastated by the silkworm disease, *pebrine*, in 1852. In their search for a cost-effective alternative to Italian silk producers, the silk merchants of Lyon turned to China. In the 1850s, Lyon's silk imports from China grew so rapidly that by 1860, China supplied half of France's total silk consumption. In the following decade, French merchants purchased half of Shanghai's and a third of Canton's raw silk exports.[19] Since silk imports from China constituted the most substantial portion of the trade deficit between the two countries, silk merchants took the lead to shape France's China and Indochina policies.

Ulysse Pila (1837–1909), a Lyon-based silk producer who would acquire fame as the "viceroy of Indochina," pioneered the inflow of French entrepreneurs into China and France's Southeast Asian colony. In 1867, he founded his silk company in Marseille with a branch in Shanghai and later moved his headquarters to Lyon after the crisis of Marseille's silk industry. Seeing Indochina as a springboard to balance France's trade deficit in the silk trade with China, he founded a branch of his company in Tonkin along with a steamship line between Haiphong and Hanoi.[20] In 1884, the Lyon Chamber, of which Pila was a leading member, commissioned Paul Brunat (1840–1908), an engineer with expertise in the silk industry, to explore how Tonkin's commercial prospects connected with China's southwestern provinces. Brunat was one of the first people who suggested a railway line to China as an alternative to the unnavigable Red River.[21]

Even in the absence of a railway connection, Pila worked relentlessly to develop cross-border trade between Tonkin and Yunnan. To his dismay, rampant banditry in Tonkin, the colonial government's inefficiency in subduing Tonkin rebels due to constant changes in policy and personnel, and wasted sources hindered the creation of favorable conditions for free trade. As if Tonkin's instability was not enough, French metropolitan industrialists had enforced a general tariff in colonies. The trade ban on opium, the second most valuable item of exchange between Tonkin and Yunnan, further compounded the problem by encouraging smuggling and depriving the colonial government of revenue.[22]

Contrary to the neomercantilist wing of French politics, the Lyon Chamber had long been "one of the most active temples of French liberalism."[23] Nevertheless, after numerous disappointments in Tonkin, Pila had to present Tonkin as a low-cost production site and a market for French machinery to entice French industrialists. At the same time, he advocated for a robust colonial government in Indochina, which would pacify Tonkin, support infrastructure ventures, and instill confidence in external investors, thereby attracting more French capital to the colony.

As French merchants laid the groundwork for deeper French military and economic involvement in the area, the Ministry of Foreign Affairs instigated an opportunistic policy along the China borders. China's southwestern provinces were still unexploited, and no global power seemed troubled by France's potential economic expansion in that area thanks to the "Open Door" agreements stipulating the equal sharing of benefits between France, Great Britain, Russia, and Germany. Since no consensus existed in Paris regarding how to increase France's influence in the Far East, maintaining the balance of power between the competing countries was the most practical strategy. With these considerations in mind, French policy in Yunnan was defined as economic penetration or "pénétration pacifique" [peaceful penetration], at least until Paul Doumer (1857–1932), the new governor-general of Indochina, decided to restructure the Indochinese economy by taking bolder steps to subdue neighboring Yunnan.

Paul Doumer: How to Develop a Colony?

Doumer, the son of a railroad worker, was a math teacher in France before he met Gabriel Hanotaux (1853–1944), the future Minister of Foreign Affairs. A member of the Groupe Colonial, Doumer ascended to the position of Minister of Finance in the cabinet of Léon Bourgeois (1851–1925) in 1895. However, in an attempt to remove him from political debates in Paris, Doumer was appointed as the Indochina governor at the suggestion of Jules Méline (1838–1925), the president of the Customs Council, a protectionist and an ardent opponent of Doumer's national income tax.[24]

Paul Doumer adeptly united the Lyon-based entrepreneurs' liberal aspirations with his colonial ambitions by reconciling French protectionist industrialism and liberal expansionism. On one hand, he prioritized the interests of metropolitan industries over economic development in colonies. Colonial development was desirable for Doumer as long as it did not cause "an unsustainable and disastrous competition" for metropolitan industries.[25] On the other hand, he asserted himself in his dealings with China to secure exclusive trade opportunities for France in China's southwest provinces. In short, despite their ideological differences, Doumer and the Lyon Chamber shared the objective of advancing French colonial businesses across Chinese borders, particularly via Yunnan.

Unlike the economically motivated merchants, Doumer approached French colonization in Indochina from a broad perspective, seeing it not only as a project to exploit local markets but also as a conduit for spreading French influence in the Far East through cross-border commercial and cultural endeavors.[26] This strategy aimed to benefit metropolitan industries and showcase the value of expansion to opponents of the imperial project. Upon arriving in his new post in Indochina, Doumer specified the most urgent tasks to be accomplished in the colony: remedy the financial situation and develop an economic model appropriate to the local customs, pacify rebellious groups in Tonkin, reorganize the government structure, reform the administrative system, provide the necessary means and equipment for economic development, increase the production and commercial capacity by facilitating French colonization and native work, and, finally, extend French influence into the Far East and especially into neighboring countries.[27] Without doubt, Doumer was the governor Pila had long been dreaming of.

At the time of Doumer's appointment, the Indochinese economy depended on agriculture and the rice trade, characterized by primitive farming methods and dominated by a few landowners and merchants.[28] Locally produced rice was exported to China and other countries in the region mostly through Chinese merchant intermediaries. The colony was rich in mineral resources, especially coal, but only a few French companies exploited these assets. Inadequate inland transportation and the reluctance of French industrialists to invest in the colony confined the colonial economy to small-scale local businesses.

Having taken the reins of the colonial government, Doumer expeditiously instituted state monopolies in salt, alcohol, and opium to ensure the colony's fiscal autonomy. Liberating the colonial economy from the metropole would mitigate arguments that the colonies imposed a burden on the French economy. Another rationale for implementing the *régies* was to empower the central administration vis-à-vis the regional authorities, which had the prerogative to collect direct taxes.[29] By turning indirect taxes into the central state's primary source of revenue, Doumer planned to provide funds for the proliferation of public works that would serve both economic and political ends. These works, particularly railways, would unify the colony, bolster the economy, and invigorate metropolitan industries through the utilization of French manufactures in construction. Within this grand design, the Yunnan railway was envisioned as an artery to enlarge the French colony's social, economic, and political reach.

Yunnan Opium: A Source to Finance Indochinese Railways

Doumer did not require exceptional insight to grasp the significance of opium in the regional economy. During the initial stages of French colonization in Indochina, it was clear to many observers that cultivating poppies and producing opium were crucial for building a strong colonial economy in Southeast Asia. De Lanessan (1843–1919), part of a government mission sent to the colonies to prepare for the 1889 Exposition Universelle, detailed the economic potential of the region in 1886. His report suggested that in addition to Tonkin rice and French cotton cloth and thread, opium and tobacco were among the most valuable commodities to be traded between France, Indochina, and China. With a French colony now in the region, he stated, "nothing would be easier than introducing poppy cultivation and production of opium into our Indochinese province."[30] De Lanessan also commented on China's substantial consumption of opium, which he compared to tobacco use in Europe, arguing that opium smoking was neither better nor worse than smoking tobacco or drinking alcohol; it was just harder to satisfy.

However, despite French optimism about the opium trade's potential in Indochina, the Southeast Asian colony lacked the ideal attributes for opium production. Poppies required higher altitudes and "first use" of the land, meaning they would not grow well on previously cultivated lands.[31] Their seasonal cycle could also disrupt the cultivation of other crops. Chinese communities, due to a lack of interest from native Indochinese farmers, dominated opium production in many parts of Southeast Asia, forming secret societies or officially recognized congregations.[32]

In 1861, the new French administration of Cochinchina introduced a tax farming system to break the Chinese merchants' monopoly. Still, two French businesses were given a de facto monopoly, which increased opium smuggling. In the south, the quality of Saigon opium was so poor that it was hardly sold in the Annam or Tonkin markets.[33] By 1881, the Cochinchina administration had established a state monopoly on opium and collaborated with Cantonese businessman Wang Tai (1828–1900) to refine opium exported from India.[34] Opium *régies* were created in Tonkin and Cambodia in 1893.

These efforts were significant in bolstering the colonial budget, but the trade would not thrive without China's involvement, either as producer or consumer. The southwestern Chinese province of Sichuan was the biggest producer of Chinese native opium, although British opium from India was also popular among the urban populations and elites of Sichuan. Yunnan, the second-largest producer of native opium, exported most of its production into adjoining provinces and Southeast Asia.[35] Positioned on Indochina's immediate border, Yunnan's opium offered a high-quality alternative to opium produced in Indochina.

Much to the frustration of colonial officials, the reality of international settlements in China did not align with French expectations. British treaties with China created significant barriers to entry, making it almost impossible to break the British opium monopoly in the Chinese market. The Tianjin Treaty of 1885 stipulated that France's opium trading would be limited by special regulations even while France gained significant privileges in many other fields. The Sino-French commercial treaty of June 26, 1887, allowed France to export Chinese opium to Tonkin through the southern cities of Longzhou, Mengzi, and Manhao, on the condition that an export duty of 20 taels was paid per *picul*.[36] Yet, upon reentering Chinese borders, French merchandise was subject to import tax, equaling its cost to foreign opium.[37] The price became even higher after the implementation of the consolidated tax, *tong shui*, in October 1906, which amounted to 115 taels per *picul*. Thus, even if France gained rights to trade Yunnan opium in more locations, it was impractical to try to sell native Chinese opium back to consumers in

China, whereas the wholesale purchase of Yunnan's opium for the Indochina market remained a profitable option.

On February 7, 1899, Doumer conferred monopoly rights for the purchase, production, and sale of opium in the colony to the Department of Customs and Excise.[38] Initially, Tonkin and Annam were supposed to buy only Yunnanese opium, while Cochinchina was to be supplied with Indian opium. In time, regional specifications were mixed to unify supplies all over the colony.[39] Then came Doumer's second step to break the British monopoly: replacing Indian opium in the Indochina market with cheaper opium from Yunnan with the help of Chinese merchants rather than enriching British merchants. His successors enjoyed the fruits of his strategy as the share of Yunnanese opium in the Indochina market increased from 38 percent to 70 percent in 1904–8.[40]

In 1900, the opium monopoly generated 21.5 percent of the colony's general budget. Thereafter, it averaged a 25 percent contribution, making it the most important state-controlled commodity from 1899 to 1922, despite the global anti-opium campaign's negative impact after 1906. Once the costs of running the *régies* were factored in, the actual profits from the opium, alcohol, and salt monopolies may not have been very significant. Still, their revenues were sufficient to stimulate the colonial budget and facilitate the issuance of the first government bonds in 1898.[41] Even politicians who criticized Doumer's administrative and military centralization in the colony were impressed by the outcome of his economic reforms.[42]

Opium's role in increasing colonial revenues enhanced the perceived value of the Yunnan railway among French bureaucrats and politicians. In his 1901 report, Charles Marie Guillemoto (1857–1907), the director of the Indochinese Department of Public Works, estimated that 120,000 kilograms of opium were exported from Yunnan. He anticipated that, upon the completion of the railway, opium traded from Yunnan to Guangxi and Guangdong would be transported via train, given the existing route's length and dangers. Also, transporting opium through Tonkin would render many local routes previously used for the opium trade obsolete.[43]

Similarly, Henri Brenier (1867–1962), the vice director of the Indochinese Department of Agriculture and Commerce, believed the official figures from the imperial customs registers did not accurately represent Yunnan's actual opium production. A significant portion of the local production was consumed within the province itself. In 1899, the value of opium production in the province reached 53,400,000 francs, which Brenier interpreted as indicative of the province's high purchasing power.[44]

On the Chinese side of the border, Yunnan's opium export dues in 1901 constituted 17 percent of its customs revenue, while tin accounted for 80 percent.[45] According to the annual commercial report, 43 intermediaries managed the opium trade in Yunnan, with the majority of shipments going to Hong Kong and Tonkin. The Indochina administration supported the trade by promoting the use of Yunnan opium among the Vietnamese elite.[46] From 1897 to 1901, opium shipments to Tonkin reportedly increased from 525 to 1,751 *piculs*. It became 2,900 *piculs* in 1905, and 4,000 *piculs* in 1906 (all sold to Tonkin *Regié*).[47] By 1907, Laos was using exclusively Yunnan opium, and over 90 percent of the opium in Annam was from Yunnan.[48] In the Canton market, Yunnan opium was expensive due to its popularity, rivalling Indian opium. However, the majority of consumption occurred within the province itself, with an estimated tenth of the population using opium for medicinal or recreational purposes.

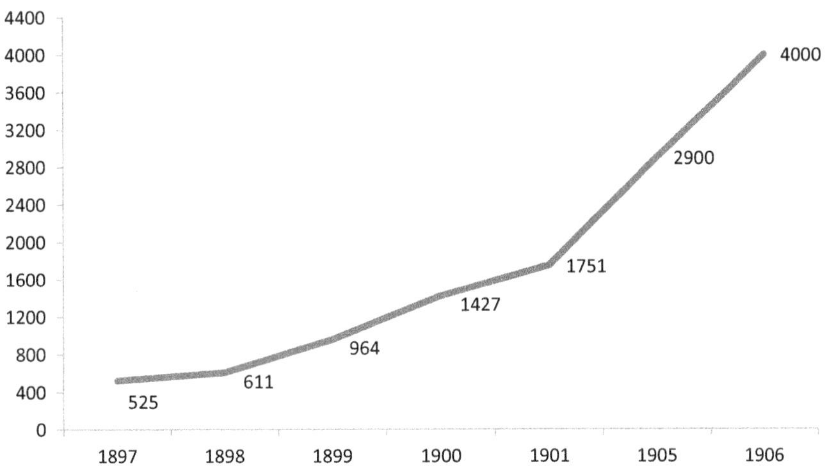

FIGURE 1.1 Yearly opium exports from Mengzi customs to Tonkin in *piculs*.

TABLE 1.1 Commercial Traffic Through Railway in Eastern Yunnan in 1906

Imports	Travel distance (Km)	Tonnage (T)	Unit price	Revenue (francs)
Ring-spun cotton (Laocai to Mengzi)	170	890	0.25	37,825
Ring-spun cotton (Laocai to eastern Yunnan)	400	5,337	0.25	533,700
Cotton fabrics	400	400	0.25	40,000
Various	400	4,373	0.15	262,380
Total				873,905
Exports				
Tin	170	4,000	0.25	165,000
Opium and tea	400	400	0.40	64,000
Others	400	400	0.15	24,000
Total				253,000

The financial returns of the link between Indochina and Yunnan extended beyond the profits generated by the wholesale purchase of Yunnan opium by the Indochinese *régie*. When the Yunnan–Indochina railway began partial operations between Laocai and Mengzi in 1906, France became the carrier of cotton fabrics, tin, opium, and tea (shown in Table 1.1). Although revenues from opium cargoes were not as high as those from tin or cotton, opium was the principal commodity that allowed France to outmaneuver British opium merchants in Indochina. The commercial traffic data in the table also suggests that even prior to the railway's completion, import trade had outpaced export trade, which contrasts with the balanced state of trade in 1900 and 1901.

While French Indochina was augmenting its revenues from trade with China due to the railway's partial opening, opium ceased to be a reliable source of income across the border after 1906. This was largely because China was shifting its ambivalent stance on the opium trade in favor of total eradication. Previously, Qing politicians, more concerned about opium imports' economic impact than the drug's harm to individuals and society, had condoned the production and consumption of native opium, especially in remote regions like Sichuan and Yunnan.[49]

Opium's role in the imperial economy was so substantial that after the Boxer Rebellion in 1899–1900, creating an opium monopoly appeared as a viable method to generate income to pay for the indemnity demanded by European powers. Although the project started with the mission of de Thévenard (1864–1906), an inspector from the Indochinese Department of Customs and Monopolies, in September 1901, a German delegation, which included representatives from Arnhold, Karnberg & Co., negotiated with Chinese officials for six weeks.[50] In pursuit of the prospect of $40 million in trade, it was reported that German representatives offered one million taels to foreign sympathizer Prince Qing to persuade the empress and bring the issue before the Grand Council.[51]

Paul Beau (1857–1926), the French minister in Beijing, astutely leveraged the discord within the Grand Council to his advantage. He reminded Zhang Zhidong (1837–1909), a prominent member of the council who strongly opposed foreign involvement in such sensitive business, that France had already put de Thévenard to his service to provide assistance on matters of constructing the monopoly, not with the intension of strengthening French businesses, but out of the belief that only a Chinese monopoly could prevent future conflicts among European powers. Even then Beau knew that the plans for an opium monopoly would likely falter due to the issue's complexity. In the end, the Qing government, having secured US support, chose to eradicate opium traffic entirely.[52]

On September 20, 1906, as part of the Chinese anti-opium campaign, an imperial edict introduced several restrictions on poppy cultivation and the opium trade. Backed by Yunnan-Guizhou Governor Xiliang's (1853–1917) determination to halt the trade, the new policy caused sharp declines in Yunnan's opium production.[53] French officials in Mengzi anticipated further decreases, as the edict was just the beginning of a long-term anti-opium crusade.[54] For 1907, Yunnan's annual opium production was reported to be worth 32,000,000 francs. In Mengzi, export values dropped from 6,500,000 francs in 1906 to 1,043,000 francs the following year. The area in Mengzi previously used for poppy cultivation covered nearly 100 hectares. With only eight licenses granted for opium cultivation in 1907, the French consul in Mengzi expected the cultivation area would not exceed four or five hectares after the new regulations.[55] These figures suggested that opium was on the verge of vanishing from Yunnan's economy.

As expected, Yunnan's opium exports plummeted from 4,730 *piculs* in 1906 to 638 *piculs* in 1907.[56] Although French officials hoped that the fully operational railway would create new revenues, the Mengzi consul remained uncertain about what item could replicate the value created by opium. Customs reports made no reference to the opium trade in 1910, despite continued cultivation by remote ethnic tribes and uninterrupted use by consumers in local opium dens.[57]

The restrictions on opium production in China dealt multiple blows to the expansion of French economic interests in the region. First, they caused significant declines in Yunnanese purchasing power, complicating the sale of foreign goods in the local market. Second, French expectations of profiting from opium cargoes proved futile. And finally, the downturn in opium imports to Indochina from Yunnan triggered a notable surge in opium prices in Indochina. Prior to the ban, French merchants paid 400 piastres for a box of Yunnan opium, but postban, the price escalated to 1,300 piastres. British opium was even more expensive. Contemporary journalists criticized the French colonial administration for not stockpiling opium in anticipation of future demand.[58] Ironically, French efforts to expand the Indochinese markets for Yunnan opium, by changing local smoking habits, ended up boosting British profits. Their Indian opium gained more value with the Chinese ban on opium cultivation and commerce. Pressured by the global anti-opium movement and dwindling supplies from Yunnan, the Indochina administration had to reduce its dependence on opium revenues.[59]

In sum, the Indochinese opium trade with Yunnan, systematized by Doumer in the late nineteenth century, played a crucial role in extending the French colonial economy into China until the Chinese opium ban of 1906. Ultimately, France was not able to break the British monopoly on opium trading and lost a major source of income with the ban.

Nevertheless, the revenues from the opium trade had already been used to finance numerous public works, including the Yunnan–Indochina railway. In this sense, opium contributed to the creation of the French empire in similar ways as it had served the building of the British Empire.

Formation of the French Railway Company

Governor Doumer's foreign policy was an extension of his vigorous economic planning. Unlike many metropolitan bureaucrats and politicians who gravitated to a more cautious and restrained attitude in international relations, he believed in the necessity of immediate and decisive action to prevent international debacles like Fashoda.[60] Luck was on Doumer's side as well. In 1897, Germany secured a base in Qingdao, located in eastern China's Shandong province, followed by Russian demands in Port Arthur and Dalian, in the northeastern Liaoning province. France's response was to ask the Qing government to affirm the inalienability of Yunnan, Guangxi, and Guangdong provinces in the south, to appoint a French citizen as the head of the Chinese postal services, lease a coaling station on the southern coast of China, and confirm the concession of a railway from Tonkin to Kunming, Yunnan's capital.

The Qing government found the demands acceptable as they did not involve territorial claims and recognized Chinese sovereignty over the southern provinces, thereby maintaining a power balance between the European powers. Whereas the Qing Foreign Affairs Bureau consented to many of these conditions, they pointed out that foreign staff were already heading China's postal services and maritime customs. Thus, French participation in this area was deferred until an independent postal system could be established. Besides, Qing officials requested details about the proposed railway route into Kunming and postponed the negotiation of specific aspects to a future date.[61] With these amendments in place, a preliminary railway agreement was signed on April 10, 1898.

After the signing of the preliminary railway treaty between Qing China and France, Doumer went to Paris in late 1898 to secure funds for his colonial ventures. Before taking the loan bill to the parliament, he met with the representatives from prominent financial institutions, including Société générale, Banque de Paris et des Pays-Bas, Comptoir national d'escompte, Crédit lyonnaise, and Crédit industriel et commercial. In this initial attempt, he managed to secure a loan of 200 million francs earmarked for the construction of five railway lines, including the Yunnan railway. Against his adversaries, who believed that the defense budget should supersede infrastructure projects in the colonies, Doumer made a case for the railway as a strategic military asset.[62]

Upon his return to Hanoi, Doumer dispatched at least six missions to Yunnan, mostly headed by military personnel.[63] If these missions' blatant disregard for local customs and the dignity of the local population were stark demonstrations of French impudence, Doumer's own visit in mid-1899, utterly ignorant of Chinese protocol, showcased his expansionist mindset. Local officials, alarmed by Doumer's audacity, asked for supplies for their troops in anticipation of a potential French incursion into the region. After Doumer's departure, local miners, disturbed by the intrusive surveys conducted by the Anglo-French Mining Syndicate, attacked foreigners and attempted to torch the customs office in Mengzi. In July, a crowd in Kunming besieged the pagoda leased to the French railway commission, accusing them of disrupting religious and commercial activities. In response to pleas from paralyzed French officials and staff in Yunnan, Doumer was preparing his troops for a march into Yunnan when the French Ministry of Foreign Affairs intervened, halting his plans. Seizing Yunnan would contravene the Anglo-French Convention of January 15, 1896. This agreement, designed to resolve the territorial disputes between Britain and France in Southeast Asia, stipulated that any privileges in the Chinese provinces of Yunnan and Sichuan be shared between the two powers.

Although Théophile Delcassé (1852–1923), the foreign minister at the time of these incidents, was an expansionist who worked diligently to establish the French colonial empire, he accepted full responsibility for the failure of the Fashoda crisis in 1898.[64] Without a doubt, he wished to avoid another conflict with Britain. French diplomats in China echoed this cautious approach from different angles. Stephen Pichon

(1857–1933), French minister in China, critiqued Doumer's actions in Yunnan for being overly political and detrimental to French economic interests. He prudently underscored the costs of a possible occupation of Yunnan, suggesting that the railway's commercial aim should take precedence over its political interest.[65]

Following these tensions, it was evident that the railway should not be left solely to the Indochina administration. Convinced of Pichon's proposal that the work be organized as a private business enterprise, the Ministry of Foreign Affairs decided to dispatch a consul to Kunming to act as a liaison between the Qing and French governments on matters of railway construction. Auguste François (1857–1935), the former consul in Longzhou in the neighboring province of Guangxi, arrived in Kunming on October 29, 1899.[66] In March 1900, Pichon traveled to Hanoi to meet Doumer, convincing him of the potential negative outcomes of a military intervention in Yunnan.

Even though Pichon opposed Indochinese expansionism, he endorsed the idea of attaining a French sphere of influence along the Tonkin border to counterbalance British dominance in the Yangzi valley. He did not believe that the open-door policy proposed by the US, whose business enterprises in China were thin compared to other powers, would benefit France. Nonetheless, Pichon's arguments were insufficient to convince the Ministry of Foreign Affairs of the necessity of the spheres of influence. To the officials in Paris, securing a sphere of influence in the south could jeopardize French economic interests in other parts of China.

In the meantime, US Secretary of State John Hay urged European powers to recognize the equality of all nations in China and expressed the US government's support for the open-door policy and the integrity of China, as opposed to dividing the country into territorial spheres of influence dominated by European powers.[67] Encouraged by American liberal attitudes toward China and informed by Paul Cambon, the French ambassador in London, who recommended business cooperation with Britain in Yunnan, French policymakers affirmed their commitment to a China policy driven by economic pursuits rather than territorial gains. Within this pragmatic plan, Doumer was a critical factor, as he was the only one who could guarantee funding for the Yunnan railway thanks to his influence among metropolitan financial circles dating back to his ministry days. At the same time, it was essential to maintain checks and balances. Ultimately, Doumer had proved too ambitious to be left to his own devices. Under the circumstances, transferring the railway construction to a private company backed by the Indochina government was a practical strategy that would limit Doumer's authority over the project without sacrificing his financial backing.

In 1901, when Doumer returned to Paris to negotiate the foundation of the consortium for construction with an offer of further concessions, Crédit Lyonnais and the Banque de Paris et Pays-Bas withdrew from the project, although they pledged to purchase shares amounting to one and a half million francs in the railway company.[68] Their disengagement was due to gloomy reports from Kunming Consul Auguste François about local insurgencies in 1899–1900. Engineer Léonce Guibert also reported that the actual cost of construction would be 107 million francs, far exceeding Guillemoto's original estimate of 70 million.

Parliamentary opposition to the proposed convention for the formation of the concessionaire company was twofold. The first issue, already addressed in the 1898 bill, was the transfer of construction in Yunnan to a private company. The Colonial Commission of the Chamber dealt with this issue by highlighting the unique challenges of the region. According to the commission, construction's "hazardous conditions" and its estimated high costs justified such a transfer. Given Yunnan's difficult topography, the estimated cost of 95 million francs was understandable, though obviously too high for the colony to undertake on its own.[69] The reporters also noted that the requirement to use French materials increased the costs. These factors, along with the concessionaire's credibility, were taken into consideration by the commission when approving the bill and its costs for the Republic. Since the creditors were deemed trustworthy, the vote was essentially about the project's potential.

The highly realistic commission report acknowledged that Yunnan was neither rich nor populous enough to yield quick economic returns. Yet, it was optimistic about the future use of mineral resources. The commissioners evaluated the potential to reach the prosperous province of

Sichuan via Yunnan. Interestingly, they believed that Yunnan's climate and sanitary conditions offered a "sanatorium" for Indochinese compatriots. Deputies were told—somewhat misleadingly—that the locals, mostly of non-Han ethnic origin, had always been welcoming and polite in their relations with French subjects, and thus no trouble was expected during construction. Overall, the railway was "a new outlet for metropolitan capital," promising "more than 100 million francs worth of industrial orders from France," in addition to new markets for French merchandise.[70]

The supportive tone of the report emerged in the special circumstances of 1901. In February, Eugène Etienne (1844–1921) founded the Committee of French Asia, declaring its purpose at the inaugural banquet:

> Europe, especially in Asia, will be called upon in the near future to assume a new task; an awakening of barbarism in China would be a peril for the whole world. From that task, we have to take our share. We want that France, thanks to the conquests it has already made, becomes a great Asian nation, as it is a great African nation.[71]

When the committee's official bulletin began publishing articles lauding Doumer's efforts in the Far East, many other periodicals followed suit, propagating investments in China and Indochina, particularly in railway initiatives. These publications helped Doumer involve a wider network of politicians, bureaucrats, and businessmen during his time in Paris.

The convention for the partial construction and operation of the Haiphong–Yunnan railway, signed on June 15 between the Indochinese government and Banque de l'Indo-Chine, Comptoir national d'escompte, and Crédit industriel et commercial, was presented to the French parliament on June 20, 1901. Despite the fervent criticism of deputy Gaston Doumergue, the bill passed with 415 deputies voting in favor and 103 voting against. The law was promulgated on July 5, 1901.

Via the convention, the parties agreed to establish a company with a capital of 12.5 million francs to be named the "Compagnie française des Chemins de fer de L'Indo-Chine et du Yunnan." The colonial government promised to build the Tonkin section of the railway by April 1, 1905, whereas the company was tasked with the construction and operation of the Yunnan section. The concession, generously bestowed upon the company, was valid for seventy-five years (Article 25), subject to the condition that the colonial government reserved the right to purchase it after fifteen years of operation (Article 27).

In terms of internal functioning, the company was free to use any means and methods to complete construction work (Article 5), but the outcome of their work was subject to technical inspection and surveillance by the Indochinese Department of Public Works (Article 14). During construction and thereafter, the company was required to report to both the Indochinese government and Paris on the progress and finances of the work and operations (Article 8). This enabled the colonial government to maintain control over the overall process. In return, the Indochinese administration guaranteed the company against any material damage caused by unrest, rebellions, and wars in Yunnan (Article 58). This provision was a clear signal and promise of growing French interest in the social and political stability of the province.

To ensure French control over the project, the convention stipulated that the company's administrative board be composed solely of French citizens (Article 3). Similarly, all materials necessary for train operations and railway construction were to be of French origin and transported under the French flag (Article 53) to reassure skeptics, vis-à-vis the value of colonization, that the interests of French industry would be protected. In addition to these general points, the convention did not cover the specifics of the Yunnan section. For instance, the colonial government could offer free land for the Tonkin section (Article 12), but no statement was made regarding Yunnan since the Qing government held sovereign power on the Chinese side of the border. The rest of the agreement mostly concerned postconstruction operations such as tariffs, rules, and regulations for transportation and cargo traffic, as well as the postconstruction issuing of bonds, purchasing of shares, and payments of the government subsidy.

With regard to construction, the agreement did not provide specifics, but Doumer was in contact with two companies. The first was La Société des Batignolles, headed by Jules Gouin, which was a branch of the widespread network of Gouin family businesses. Senator Eugène Gouin (1818–1909), who headed La Banque de Paris et des Pays-Bas, actively participated in negotiations for the Yunnan railway concession just as he did in other matters related to China. In 1900, he purchased 250 shares in the Anglo-French Mining Syndicate in Yunnan.[72] The second construction company in communication with Doumer was La Regié Générale de Chemins de fer, under the leadership of Count Georges Vitali (1830–1910), another notable businessman of Greek origin. He had built the Salonica and Smyrna railways in the Ottoman Empire and played an important role in negotiations between Deutsche Bank and the Ottoman Bank for the construction of the Baghdad Railway.[73] These two companies undertook the construction work in Yunnan.

The French Company in Yunnan and the Railway Agreement of 1903

With the approval of the convention by the French senate and the foundation of the consortium in 1901, a new phase of French activity in Yunnan began. The Indochina administration, led by Doumer, enthusiastically put forward plans to settle a large French population in Yunnan, including women and children, and to build public services like schools, post offices, and hospitals despite the metropolitan government's concerns that these secondary enterprises would harm relations with China and other powers.[74] As a countermeasure, the Ministry of Foreign Affairs urged the company to set up a branch in China without delay while simultaneously attempting to restrain the Indochina government from sending their own missions for preconstruction work. In October, the ministry, at the request of Qing authorities, refused to authorize the mission headed by Blim, an official from the Indochina Public Works Department employed by Doumer, to lay the groundwork for his larger Yunnan plan.[75] The most urgent task for Foreign Affairs was to send company agents to prepare a construction plan and acquire approval

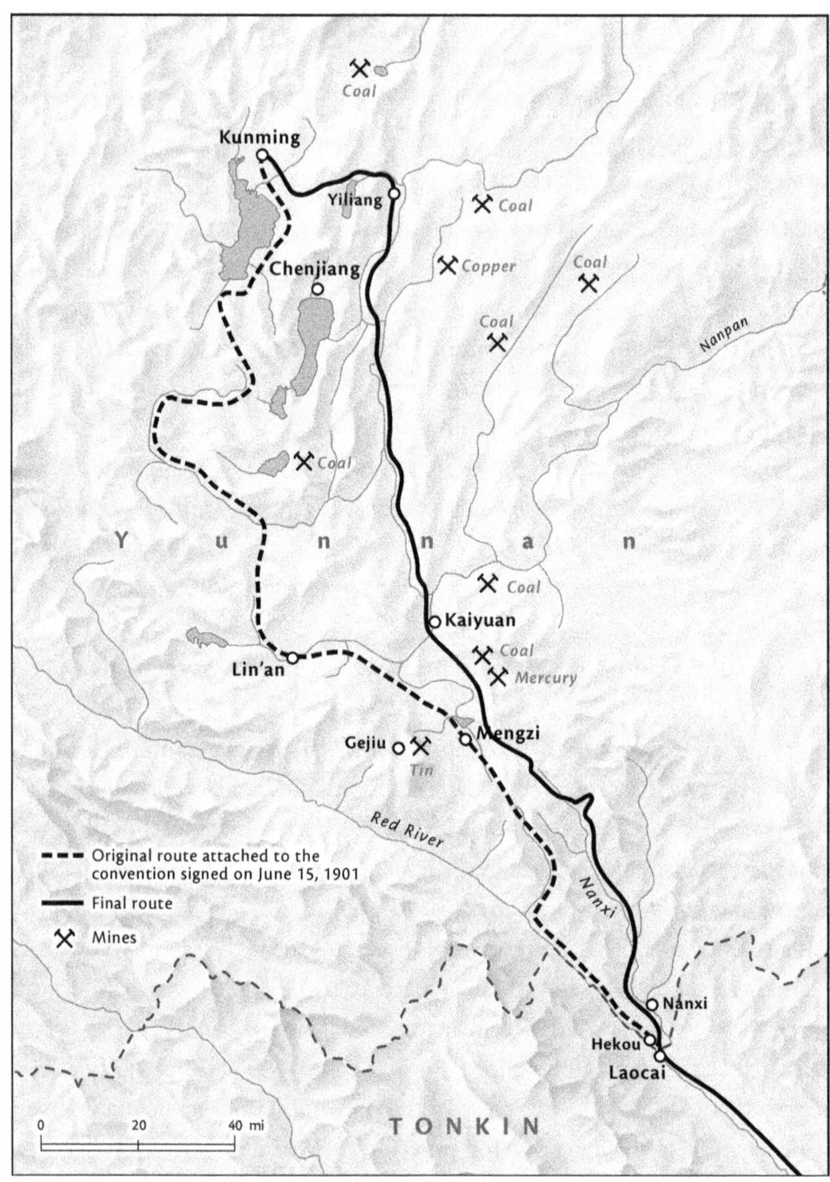

MAP 2 Map showing the original and final routes of the Yunnan railway.

from the Indochina governor, which might take months according to the convention.

When company agents arrived in the province in November 1901, new issues arose. First, the inspection teams discovered that the original route, though closer to the mining areas, was neither precise nor technically feasible given the difficult terrain. Instead, they selected another route via the Nanxi valley for the section between Laocai and Mengzi, and via Amizhou and Bose for the section between Mengzi and Kunming. This eastern route, it was claimed, was shorter and would be less costly. Second, the agreement signed in 1898 did not meet the expectations of the interested parties: for Qing officials, it was too vague and therefore easy for France to manipulate to its advantage. For the French side, its scope was too limited as the Indochina administration had a broader plan to increase French activities in the province's local life. The company directors urged Foreign Affairs to solve the land issue since the sole authority on this matter rested with the Qing government. It was crucial to assure everyone that land acquisition was strictly a civilian and commercial endeavor.[76]

In response to the needs of both France and China, a revised and detailed version of the agreement of 1898 was signed on October 29, 1903, after lengthy and exhausting negotiations between the two governments.[77] During the negotiations, Doumer was recalled to France due to François's persistent complaints on behalf of the company. François stated that the Indochinese missions sent by Doumer were causing issues with both Qing and French officials and, furthermore, obstructing the company's work on the railway. Immediately after the Hanoi exposition of 1902–1903, Doumer relinquished his position to Paul Beau, who was the French minister in Beijing at the time.[78] Thanks to this replacement, Qing officials continued treaty negotiations with more amenable French peers.

As clearly understood from the treaty draft presented by Interim Governor Lin Shaonian (1845–1916), the stakes for the Qing government were more than just a business deal; they were about China's sovereignty. As a result, the Chinese side insisted that the consulate, not the company, handle all the railway-related transactions with local officials. They sought to tightly control everything from land acquisition to construction materials, as well as labor recruitment and salaries. In this way, the Qing aimed to make the railway a profitable investment for the regional economy while effectively asserting Qing China's authority. The French side, on the other hand, had always conceived the project as an opportunity to benefit French industries, rather than as a long-term investment in the industrial development of southwestern China. Still, they agreed to buy construction materials from China, not France, with the help of local officials, and at fixed prices (Article 8). This article undermined the argument that railway construction might create a market for the French metal industry.

In the agreement, Qing officials conceptualized China's sovereignty through themes of land, labor, and foreign military intervention. For this reason, limiting French territorial expansion in the region by specifying the locations where land purchases or transfers would occur was a primary concern for the Chinese side. In contrast, the French side viewed land acquisition as a basic prerequisite for the beginning of the construction. The first eleven articles of the final agreement focused on route planning and land acquisition procedures. The Qing government agreed to deliver lands to the company for the confirmed railway route. Private lots had to be purchased by the local government before being handed over (Article 3). In determining the routes, the company was expected to avoid cemeteries, temples, residences, and agricultural fields as well as government offices and city fortifications (Articles 2 and 7), since these were critical for social stability and national defense. The company was allowed to build a parallel logistics road for transporting workers and materials, provided that private lands required for that road were leased by the company from the owners. Upon the completion of the project, the company was to return these leased properties to the original holders (Article 4). Buildings used by the company employees were subject to the same rule. With these measures, the Qing government aimed to prevent the French from taking root in the province.

For the Qing government, the second condition for preserving its sovereignty was to hold sway over the labor force. Having experienced the troubles of the coolie age, China had learned over the course of the nineteenth century the importance of protecting overseas Chinese workers for the sake of its national standing in the new global order. Even if China did not have a national labor law at the time, it asked for ethical treatment of Chinese workers in many mining and railway agreements signed with foreign governments. These treaty regulations empowered both local officials and workers employed in foreign projects. The Yunnan Railway Treaty was one of the early examples featuring treaty clauses directly concerned with the conditions of workers.

The Qing government insisted the company employ only local workers apart from technical staff, although they conceded that workers from neighboring provinces could be recruited if workers in Yunnan were insufficient or their salaries too demanding. Although French officials affirmed the ban on European workers, they broadened the geographical scope of recruitment to cover all of China as well as Vietnam (Article 12). Notably, Qing officials anticipated disputes over worker salaries and thus demanded that in the event of a worker strike, the local government would be in charge.[79] This was unacceptable to the company. Instead, the company redefined the local government's role to be an intermediary to prevent the officials' excessive interventions. They also reserved their right to recruit workers from abroad (the ban on Vietnamese workers was removed from the proposed text) if no solution was found to the problem of wage increases.[80] The French government showed its commitment to keeping labor costs at a minimum with this article. At the same time, the parties agreed that workers would be paid *fairly*, though the definition of *fairness* (*gongdao*) was not clearly stated. Interestingly, however, at this stage a labor shortage was not foreseen as a major impediment to the timely completion of construction.

From the Qing official perspective, workers could potentially pose a threat to the social order as some of them might be agitators or bandits, so Qing representatives deemed it necessary to keep a record of all recruitments by local officials (Article 12). Similarly, any issues that might arise among Chinese workers were to be referred to local authorities. In criminal cases, the company was expected to respect the verdicts handed down by Chinese judges (Article 14). Around this time, the Qing government was already dealing with radical groups such as nationalists or anarchists. It is understandable that they did not want to create another foreign concession area where these radicals would organize freely.

In another clause, it was decreed that all Chinese workers, craftsmen, and attendants were to be treated properly. In the event of an accident, injured workers or the families of deceased workers were to be compensated. Providing medical services to workers was also the company's responsibility (Article 13). Although company guards, whether recruited locally or from abroad, were authorized to quell any unruly actions at work sites, the company had no right to protect workers or intervene in official procedures once a crime was committed. If a social disturbance occurred, it was local forces that were tasked with responding, not any other military force. This rule also applied to the protection of the company's foreign employees, with no concession given for the intervention of a foreign army (Article 15). The same concern led to another article regarding official control of explosives used during construction. Article 24 stipulated that if China ever became embroiled in a war with a foreign country, the trains were not permitted to assist enemy forces, while it was guaranteed that Chinese arms and soldiers would be transported at half price.

Considering the imperialist impositions on Qing China in the late nineteenth century, it is often assumed that the Qing government was too weak to negotiate the terms of the agreement. To the contrary, China's delay tactics seem to have worked, as France conceded to many of the Chinese demands. Doumer was no longer in office to intimidate the Chinese side with military threats, while his agreement with the railway company, which held the French government accountable for the railway company's losses, was in full effect. Since territorial expansion was eliminated from the French colonial agenda, both the company and French diplomats became more focused on completing the work by the deadline set by the Convention of 1901.

Attaining an exemption on customs duties for construction materials and obtaining authorization to recruit as many workers as necessary were also crucial. In the final analysis, building a railroad was a labor-intensive task, impossible to accomplish without official support in labor recruitment. The Qing government pledged its assistance as long as their sovereignty was respected. What bothered Qing officials was not labor rights in and of themselves, but sociopolitical stability and economic development in the region. An influx of foreign workers, or any mistreatment of Chinese workers by foreign entities, could potentially jeopardize both. In this regard, the interests of the Qing and French governments were not entirely at odds: both wanted to complete the railway expeditiously without local disturbances. How could they have foreseen labor resistance becoming the main source of contention in a peripheral rural province?

Conclusion

In the wake of France's colonial consolidation in Indochina, Yunnan, seen as a gateway to the vast Chinese market, attracted the attention of French officials and merchants. However, due to ideological conflicts in the metropolitan center and colonial domains, French diplomatic missions lagged behind their British counterparts in establishing a foothold in southwestern China. Only when Indochina Governor Paul Doumer restructured the colonial economy to ensure its integration with Chinese markets through cross-border commerce and railways did French interests in southwest China intensify. Yet, French policy's oscillation between expansionism and protectionism, combined with the resistance of Chinese officials and the populace to French colonialism in Yunnan, soon revealed that the Yunnan railway would not materialize in the manner its industrial initiators had fantasized. While the silk and cotton trade continued to flourish between France and China, the most promising sectors of mining and opium had proven to be completely fruitless by 1906.

Amid arguments both for and against the railway, Doumer successfully convinced his metropolitan colleagues that extending Indochinese railways into Yunnan would serve the interests of French industries and colonial politics. More importantly, he managed to secure investment in the railway from French financial institutions by offering them excessive guarantees. However, these guarantees ended up weakening France's position during its negotiations with the Qing government. Pressured by the deadlines and responsibilities agreed upon in the 1901 Convention, French officials had to acquiesce to the demands of Qing China without much resistance. The same responsibilities motivated both parties to maintain social order and stability, especially by keeping the railway labor force under control. Having witnessed numerous uprisings by the vast mining population in the province, as well as the challenges of the global coolie trade, Qing officials knew that recalcitrant workers could serve as a lever to exert influence over France when necessary. For this reason, during negotiations for the railway agreement, they identified the workers, the country's land, and territories as the pillars of Qing imperial sovereignty.

CHAPTER 2

An Attempted Civil Conquest of Yunnan's Mines and Muslim Communities

IN THE LATE NINETEENTH CENTURY, French policy toward China was based on considerations of an international power balance and colonial economic interests. Situated at the intersection of these two incompatible policy fronts, the French Ministry of Foreign Affairs and the Ministry of Colonies developed different views about France's colonial possessions. On one hand, French expansionism, represented by Paul Doumer in Southeast Asia, aimed to create a French sphere of influence in Yunnan, through military means if necessary. On the other hand, the presence of Britain in neighboring Burma and local resistance to increasing foreign activities in Yunnan motivated French metropolitan bureaucrats to refrain from direct military action.

If the constraints of realpolitik were one reason behind the French policy of "peaceful penetration," another reason can be attributed to the change in French colonial theory at the turn of the twentieth century. While colonial conquest and expansion were once seen as ends in and of themselves in the Napoleonic era, the emphasis shifted toward the exploitation of existing colonial lands for further economic profits and cultural hegemony as colonial competition intensified with the entry of new global actors. During the nineteenth century, France tended toward building a "velvet empire," as David Todd describes it, by using informal empire tools such as collaboration with indigenous elites, creating markets for French luxuries, providing loans to infrastructure projects outside France, and utilizing extraterritorial rights for the interests of French capitalism.[1] These strategies were as profitable as territorial expansion.

In this context, French operations in Yunnan focused on intensifying colonial *mise en valeur,* or economic development, rather than territorial expansion. Within this new iteration of French colonial policy, the French role in Yunnan was defined to transform the province's social and economic life according to the needs of French capitalism without dealing with the complexities of colony building. Even so, the realization of this soft power strategy required a strong military backing, which was provided by the memory of the Sino-French War and implicit threats of military intervention from the Indochinese side of the border.

The present chapter focuses on the French attempt to create an alternative site of power in Yunnan to the Qing territorial sovereignty where France could exert control over the common people, including city dwellers, ethnic tribes, miners, and railway workers. In the absence of a foreign concession in Yunnan, the railway provided the spatial parameters of this new sphere and served as a conduit for transmitting European notions of race and modernity to local populations. Therefore, the chapter argues, French colonialism in Yunnan evolved from the desire to expand French colonial territories to building French supremacy over local populations through informal empire strategies such as modernizing the province's mining industry and manipulating its ethnic tensions. These strategies were predicated on the assumed grandiosity of France as a modern industrial power and a cosmopolitan empire with control over world Muslims from Africa to China.

Anglo-French Mining Concessions and Local Rebellions

Yunnan played a significant role in the mining industry of the Qing dynasty, providing 80–90 percent of the empire's annual copper supply required for minting coins used in people's daily transactions and producing household utensils. Tin was similarly used for coin production and supplied in significant amounts by Yunnan's Gejiu mines. In addition to these two minerals, Yunnan also produced gold, silver, zinc, lead, and coal on free market terms, making an attractive destination for investors from the provinces of Sichuan, Henan, Hubei, and Guangdong. While the government exercised a monopoly on the sale of copper, its role in mineral production was limited to monitoring and supporting its growth.

Yunnan's mining industry had lost its dynamism by the nineteenth century, but proponents of the Yunnan railway found in Yunnan's mines a great potential for European heavy industry. The Mengzi Customs were opened on August 24, 1889, to facilitate the transportation of minerals extracted from Gejiu mines to Hong Kong via Vietnam. The Ministry of Foreign Affairs also supported the creation of Société d'études industrielles en Chine in 1897, with the expectation that the building of the Yunnan railway would overcome the reportedly main impediment to the growth of Yunnan's mining industry, transportation.[2]

Despite the enthusiasm for the prospects of mining and export trade in precious metals, French entrepreneurs were ultimately disappointed by French diplomats' reluctance to confront the Chinese officialdom's obstruction tactics. In 1898, all inspection teams were withdrawn from the province apart from Marcel Bélard, who carried out inspections until 1899 at the request of Société d'études industrielles en Chine.[3] In the meantime, Foreign Affairs sent another expert, André Leclère (1858–1915), to the area to survey the region's mineral sources to justify the Yunnan railway project.

Leclère shared the optimism of his predecessors regarding the potential of modern mining in southern China for the Tonkin industries. Despite finding local production methods primitive, he believed that the ongoing production was compatible with the region's limited transportation infrastructure. He understood through his communication with Qing officials that the French were seen as future partners who could assist China in modernizing the local mining and smelting industry. That said, he was aware that taking over the entire business at the expense of local producers was not option. Instead, he suggested a pragmatic strategy based on manipulating Chinese authorities to gain public sympathy; coercive methods would never prevail over the "irresistible power of the Chinese people."[4] He cautioned that the power of officials should be applied carefully because the officially regulated system, characterized by privilege and monopoly, not only impeded the modernization of mining but also agitated miners against the Qing government. The basis of local hostility toward foreigners was due to their anticipation that the association of modern industry with the "tyranny of mandarins" would lead to the people's enslavement. Thus, Leclère recommended a deliberate and gradual infiltration of European practices to eliminate impediments to efficiency, such as rebellions, banditry, and lack of capital caused by a "purely Chinese regime."[5]

Efficient exploitation of Yunnan mines by French businesses depended on the completion of the railway, modernization of mining, and persuasion of the officials, according to Leclère's firsthand observations. None of these were achievable in the short term. Moreover, the Qing government's negligible role in the Gejiu mining industry limited the scope of any concession to be attained from the government. Lacking support from French diplomats in China, French industrialists led by Emile Cellérier, the vice-president of Syndicat minier du Yunnan and a former employee in the Indochinese government, began to look for British capital and cooperation to strengthen the company's standing. Without notifying French authorities, they formed the Anglo-French Mining Syndicate in London as a company operating under British law.[6] The initiators and contractors of the Yunnan railway, including Pila, Gouin, and Vitali, contributed to the company's capital as investors. The syndicate's shareholders, with the confidence of knowing that there would soon be an opportunity to acquire the mining rights, expected enormous profits, primarily owing to the Yunnan railway project and abundance of inexpensive Chinese labor.[7]

After a prolonged period of inspections and diplomatic/business maneuvers, the planned mining concessions finally materialized with the compensation requested in 1901 as remuneration for the damage caused by the Boxer Rebellion in the north. The Seven-Prefecture Mining Agreement, signed between the Qing government and the Anglo-French partnership in 1902, granted the syndicate exclusive rights to exploit Yunnan's mines for sixty years. If mineral resources were insufficient in one location, the syndicate had the right to move to another site. Once the operations started, the syndicate's inspection teams, supervised by Emile Rocher (1840–1910), a mining engineer who surveyed the Gejiu mines in the 1870s and a long-time resident of China during his employment at the Mengzi customs, reserved twenty-seven silver mines, twenty-five copper mines, six gold mines, and one stone mine in the most critical locations of the province. Worried about the syndicate's uncontrolled expansion, Viceroy Wei Guangtao (1837–1916) sent a memorial to the foreign relations office, expressing his concerns that the syndicate was poised to turn the entire province into a mining zone. The agreement's vagueness regarding the types of minerals to be extracted motivated the company's discretionary activities, the viceroy claimed.[8]

In another telegram, Wei informed the Qing foreign relations office that many miner households in Gejiu had legal disputes with foreigners because Rocher prevented the locals from doing business in the area. Hence, Viceroy Wei asked the office to send an official warning to the French consulate and instruct Rocher to remove the ban on Chinese businesses in Lin'an and Gejiu to prevent further disturbances.[9] The following day, the Qing foreign relations office replied that the agreement was final, and they were not able to revise it. Instead, they suggested that Wei discuss the mining activities in Gejiu directly with Rocher.[10]

Indeed, the mining agreement was not entirely detrimental to the Qing government's economic interests. Putting foreigners in charge of crucial industries for technology transfer and rapid modernization was a common practice in the late Qing period. In the 1870s, the province's foresighted viceroys proposed mechanizing Yunnan's workings with government-backed loans lest Britain and France exploit the mining profits. Despite their purchase of Western machinery and employment of German and Japanese technicians, mechanization efforts failed due to insufficient capital and the challenging climate.[11] After several abortive attempts, the Qing government found it rational to enter into an agreement with a foreign partnership without compromising its sovereignty.

With the agreement, the local administration was assigned to represent the syndicate for leasing lands and finding workers to facilitate its operations. The syndicate controlled 65 percent of the profits; the central and provincial governments shared the remaining part as 25 percent and 10 percent, respectively. As stated in Article 16, the agreement was to benefit all parties; hence, the imperial and provincial governments were expected to safeguard the syndicate's interests "by all means in their power."[12] In other words, by combining a foreign company's profits with the state's fiscal interests, the government sacrificed local mining businesses but increased its tax revenues with a no-cost investment in mechanization. In the eyes of the local community, officials betrayed the people and sided with foreigners for their own interests.

Even in the face of apparent stability for the Anglo-French mining company, the lack of understanding among French and British entrepreneurs of the unique characteristics of mining in the region led to the failure of the European enterprise. Yunnan's mining industry operated under various business models, with most of the mineral production being controlled by small- and medium-scale ventures. Government-controlled deposits were limited in number. While some medium-sized businesses run by investors from other provinces paid salaries, most of the workings functioned according to the principles of traditional mining. In this system, starting a new exploitation shaft began with the individual initiative of a few dozen men coming together under an experienced and skilled miner who provided food and fuel. The workers were mostly paid on a share-profit basis and did not receive regular salaries until they discovered a vein. Hired workers arrived only after this initial stage of setup. Once a mine proved productive and needed additional laborers, it became subject to managerial and bureaucratic regulation.

Toward the end of the dynasty, contract labor became increasingly prevalent, providing contractors with the opportunity to levy extra fees on worker wages. In certain instances, employers or contractors tricked workers into debt to extend their terms of service, in contrast to the initial freedom to work as desired.[13] These characteristics rendered mining an inferior job with low status and low income, compared to farming. Hence, miners were mostly landless and transient individuals with no local family ties. A smaller percentage consisted of settled men, who were originally farmers working off-season for extra income. It was this latter group who guaranteed a peaceful work environment. Skilled miners preferred to work for reliable foremen, although some individuals were forced or even duped into mining due to scarcity of labor.

Traditional mining in Yunnan was also characterized by its reliance on kinship or hometown networks. According to David Atwill, "Yunnan's mines were a microcosm of broader Yunnan society, in that the miners tended to be divided into groups based on ethnicity or (if Han) province of origin."[14] Thanks to either ethnic/hometown connections or shared economic interests, miners usually worked as brothers, living together around the mining area as a closely knit community. This sense of camaraderie was seen as more important than mechanization to achieve efficiency.[15] However, this also meant that many of the province's ethnic rebellions, including the Muslim uprisings that culminated in the creation of an independent kingdom between 1856 and 1873, had their roots in miner conflicts with the government or competition among miner populations of diverse origins.

The miners' tendency for collective action accounts for the militant resistance against European attempts to gain control of the mining industry. The uprising after Doumer's visit in 1899 was instigated by Gejiu miners who were afraid of being dispossessed by the French, a concern explicitly conveyed to the French consul by the Mengzi *daotai* (circuit intendant).[16] The signing of the Seven-Prefecture Mining Agreement in 1902 only intensified tensions in the province's mining center. In May 1903, the mineworkers of Gejiu, led by Zhou Yunxiang (1872–1903), occupied the city and reached the eastern gate of Mengzi, the city with the customs office and the largest foreign population in the province. The rebellion quickly spread to ten prefectures in southern Yunnan, forcing the city's two hundred foreign residents, including twelve railroad employees, to take refuge in the hall of the Mengzi Customs Office, which was barricaded to protect civilians. Although the Qing government dispatched soldiers to safeguard the foreign nationals, these soldiers were reportedly "undisciplined opium addicts."[17] Eventually, the Qing provincial army, strengthened with additional troops from other provinces, suppressed the rebellion. French and Chinese records indicate that the local government executed Zhou on June 28, 1903, despite his conditional surrender. Still, there were rumors that Zhou was alive and gathering men under the pretext of recruiting workers for the railway or that he participated in the Hekou rebellion of 1908, but there is no definitive evidence.[18]

At the time, French officials contended that Zhou's rebellion was the resurgence of popular antiforeign sentiments provoked by the Boxer uprising. Conversely, Chinese nationalist historiography interpreted the rebellion as an initial phase of anti-imperialism in Yunnan for bringing the workers and peasants together for a nationalist cause. These scholars go so far as to suggest that Zhou Yunxiang was a member of Sun Yatsen's Revolutionary Party and that the revolutionary groups, then headquartered in Tokyo and Hong Kong, championed the rebellion.[19]

Despite the rebels' alleged use of slogans such as "Stop foreign railways" and "Protect mines and resist foreigners," Zhou wrote an apologetic letter to the French consul in Mengzi a few weeks before the rebellion was suppressed, seeking his support. According to Zhou's narrative, the rebellion broke out due to a previous feud between Zhou and local officials following a dispute between the residents of Gejiu and Lin'an.[20] He stated that the rebellion began only after the officials came to the mine to look for him and killed hundreds of miners. Vengeful miners attacked foreigners because they believed that the emperor was on good terms with foreign governments. From the very beginning, Zhou's sole intention, he claimed, was to convey to the authorities the injustices he had suffered, and it was the other angry miners who offended the emperor and the "honorable [French] country."[21]

Attaining exterritorial rights through foreign citizenship was a common way of evading the Qing judiciary in the late imperial period. Upon realizing that he would not win his battle against Qing troops, Zhou must have concluded that only French protection could save his life. To François's dismay, Mengzi Consul C. A. J. Sainson (1868–1954) appreciated Zhou's acceptance of his wrongdoings and extended him protection at the French consulate. Sainson promised to convey Zhou's letter to the viceroy and assured him that the French consulate would issue him a passport to facilitate his travel to Hong Kong and Tonkin. However, before the French consul could take any of these actions, Zhou was captured by Qing troops. The motives behind Sainson's desire to assist Zhou remain unclear. Nevertheless, regardless of his intentions, Zhou's rebellion presented new opportunities for French social engineering projects while impeding the expansion of French involvement in Yunnan's mining industry. These will be discussed in the next section.

Amid rebellions and official interference, Yunnan's tin production continued to grow consistently thanks to international demand, rich mineral reserves, inexpensive labor, and the partial opening of the

Yunnan railway. Tin output increased from 2,740 tons in 1898 to 6,347 tons in 1911, constituting at least 90 percent of national tin exports with the labor of more than 100,000 workers.[22] Increasing international demand for tin and rising nationalism motivated Qing officials and elites to conceive Yunnan's mining industry as keys to national sovereignty and economic prosperity. The state's drive for greater Chinese participation in local mining gained momentum with the arrival of a new viceroy, Xiliang, and the propaganda work of Chinese nationalists.[23] Xiliang personally supervised the creation of joint state-merchant companies to operate Gejiu tin mines in competition with foreigners. During his governorship, the foreign syndicate faced numerous administrative obstacles, ranging from delayed paperwork to intimidation of property owners who entered into agreements with the syndicate.

Concurrently, Chinese nationalists idealized traditional mining as a paragon for Yunnan's entrepreneurial development. Author Yi Ming recounted the life story of a mine owner named Mr. Zhao in a semifictional article featured in the second volume of the nationalist *Yunnan Journal*.[24] In the text, Mr. Zhao was portrayed as an "ambitious" man who spent his family fortune to establish a mine in Gejiu. Mr. Zhao's adventurous character was comparable only to people like Christopher Columbus, the discoverer of the New World. Despite numerous setbacks, Mr. Zhao persevered in his quest for success and earned the loyalty of his workers by living frugally alongside them. His workers' intensive work exposed a rich reserve of ore just as Mr. Zhao decided to abandon his pursuit to become a monk. This decision, which proved his open-mindedness and discontent with mediocrity, solidified his reputation as a pioneering figure in the transition to a modern economy. In the same article, Yi Ming also praised Weng Anzi, another mine owner in Gejiu, for his efforts to expand his mine by implementing modern managerial and production techniques. The author suggested that more people of this sort would have enabled Yunnan to connect with Tibet, Sichuan, Burma, and Annam through a developed railroad network funded by mining. In other words, as much as railways promoted the development of mining, increased mining activity was also expected to fund further expansion of railway networks.

This biographical account combines the contradictory principles of liberal and socialist economic theories by portraying Mr. Zhao as a representative of both. Thanks to its rich mineral reserves, Yunnan had the potential to compete with the most industrialized countries globally, but it lacked qualified human resources. Ideal figures like Mr. Zhao embodied the desired entrepreneurialism with their eagerness to explore new sources of revenue and learn modern technologies. On one hand, the author expresses a Smithian view on the naturalness of private property, a natural tendency to improve, and a conviction that individual profit could correlate with the common good. By promoting mining and increasing their income (within a system that recognized their property rights), Mr. Zhao and Mr. Weng improved people's livelihood through wages and expanded the national economy. On the other hand, Mr. Zhao's refusal of further gain and property was a moral lesson, emphasizing the mundaneness of private property. The author implies that even if private property may be in the interests of individuals, voluntary renunciation of such property can also bring about social gratification, which is a natural and desirable outcome of nationalist consciousness. This same moral conviction is evident in the author's argument against class antagonism. In depicting workplace relations in terms of harmony, companionship, and generosity, the author rejects the historical dominance of work hierarchies and antagonistic class stratifications even in modernized work settings.

The Chinese nationalist propaganda for the exclusion of foreigners from mining proved effective, as evidenced by the formation of the Association for the Protection of Yunnan's Mining and the subsequent rallies, demonstrations, and petitions organized by the locals. One particularly memorable demonstration saw two military students cutting their flesh and using their blood to write their demands for the termination of the Seven-Prefecture Agreement.[25] Facing widespread public resentment and official obstruction, the managers of the Anglo-French syndicate realized the impracticality of controlling the unruly miners through diplomatic channels. As a result, the mining concessions covering a vast area and plenty of minerals remained largely unused, except for a few tin mines in the Gejiu area.[26] When the Yunnan railway became fully active in 1910, foreign interest in Yunnan's mines revived briefly, but in 1911, following a popular campaign for the nationalization of mining rights, the Qing government paid 1,500,000 taels to the company to cancel the Seven-Prefecture Mining Agreement.[27]

Manipulating Yunnan's Ethnic Tensions

On the diplomatic front, the miner rebellion led by Zhou Yunxiang prompted French officials to adopt a more assertive stance in safeguarding their railway interests. A year before the rebellion, the French Ministry of War had sent Lieutenant Georges Grillières (1868–1905) to Yunnan to formulate a contingency plan. Grillières expressed caution toward the possibility of a military intervention, citing a pervasive hostility toward foreigners behind the "misleading courtesy of the Chinese."[28] He contended that Chinese subjects harbored a deep-seated disdain for the French, which transcended mere political considerations and instead stemmed from the cultural conduct of Asians:

> It is impossible to deal with Asians, who are so different from us. On the day their hatred is manifested, the same Chinese, who are considerate and kind, will turn against those [the French] who have the best traits. It is not only the mandarins who are full of hatred, but everyone would be happy to follow the secret instructions of their chiefs.[29]

Grillières's line of reasoning was typical in translating a political issue into a cultural one. In a manner whitewashing the colonial presence of Europeans in Yunnan, he pointed out the allegedly Janus-faced nature of Chinese people as the source of local hostility, echoing common colonial racial tropes that characterized the Chinese as irrational and backward. Despite such biases, Grillières acknowledged that Chinese people were capable of self-defense and self-aggrandizement.

From a military perspective, Grillières noted that the Qing government had taken steps to modernize its military organization and weaponry in the aftermath of the Boxer Rebellion. François observed similar modernization initiatives in military education. The Qing government had opened new schools and invited Japanese instructors to train a modern army.[30] French diplomats had proposed to the Qing administration providing French military instructors for this purpose. However, the central and local governments rejected their proposals on the grounds that the local administration did not have enough resources to finance such a project and that French was an unknown language to the locals. The response revealed a lack of trust in the French empire among Chinese officials.

Grillières predicted that China's modernization efforts needed time to bear fruit. Nevertheless, the rugged terrain in Yunnan made a French expedition via Tonkin challenging. Due to the lack of transportation infrastructure, troops would have to march through the Nanxi region, where Qing troops, accustomed to moving through mountains, would have ample time to unite their forces before French soldiers could arrive. Moreover, any inadvertent border violations would trigger local agitation, revive the Boxer spirit, and undermine the French policy of "peaceful penetration." Instead of a comprehensive attack aimed at territorial occupation, Grillières recommended the secret deployment of two battalions comprising eight hundred men to Mengzi.

Despite Grillières's reservations, François derived a baffling confidence from Grillières's report. He noted that the recently appointed Qing officials, having spent generously for their posts, had reduced the number of troops for budgetary reasons. He recorded in his journal that local officials, including Viceroy Ding Zhenduo (1842–1914), Governor Lin, and Manchu official "Hing," whom François identified as "the triangle of 1900" for their ostensible agitations against foreigners, asked François to relay a plea for dispatching auxiliary forces from Tonkin to suppress Zhou's rebellion.[31] Before military modernization emboldened the locals against Europeans, François intended to exploit this vulnerability to seek French protection of the railway.[32] His letters were more than enough to galvanize the hawkish Indochina administration to deploy three thousand men to the Yunnan border, demonstrating to the Qing government France's readiness to protect the railway by any means necessary.[33]

The protection of the railway was crucial to the French for several reasons. Beyond its symbolic value as a testament to French colonial grandeur, the 1901 convention signed with the railway company held the French government responsible for ensuring security along the railway. Following the miner rebellion in 1903, the railway company used the convention to their advantage and sought compensation for work disruptions and the safety of their employees. In addition, they demanded the establishment of a police force and allocation of powers to the French consulate for the protection of Italian employees who lacked a legation in Yunnan.[34]

Although French diplomats regarded the company's claims as excessive, they recognized the long-term benefits of establishing police forces. The legal basis for such an undertaking was already provided by the railway treaty. According to Article 15, France was authorized to create security forces to protect the construction sites as long as the guards were recruited from the local population. Despite the favorable conditions, Paul Beau, the newly appointed governor of Indochina, believed that the Chinese population was either excessively loyal to the officials or under the influence of secret societies. Under the circumstances, Yunnan's Muslims were the only group deemed trustworthy by French officials, given their significant role in suppressing the miners' rebellion in 1903.

Here it is important to highlight that the French focus on Yunnan's Muslim population was not coincidental. Rather, it was a deliberate extension of the French policy of pan-Islam, which aimed to strengthen French colonial power by gaining the confidence and support of Muslims worldwide.[35] Since the late nineteenth century, pan-Islamist groups in the Middle East and Africa had been advocating for global Muslim unity against colonial expansionism.[36] France had encountered pan-Islam as a political movement among the Muslim elites of North Africa during its invasions of Morocco, Tunisia, and Algeria.[37] While European colonizers generally viewed the pan-Islamist movement with suspicion, some French officials believed in the potential of co-opting Muslim elites in their colonial rivalry with other powers. Against this backdrop of pan-Islamist activism, French missionaries and explorers in China observed a resurgence of Islam among Chinese Muslims, both of Han and non-Han origins, who sought to forge a transnational identity in dialogue with their coreligionists in the Ottoman Empire. This revival of Islam, coupled with Russian and British activities in China's ethnic frontiers, brought Muslims into the focus of French attention as a distinct and influential group.

Paul Beau stood out among the French diplomats as one of the few who recognized the strategic significance of Chinese Muslims as a potential ally against the Qing government and other colonial powers. In 1901, when Ottoman Sultan Abdulhamid dispatched a mission to China with the encouragement of the German king, aimed at advising Chinese Muslims not to participate in the Boxer Rebellion, Beau served as the head of the French delegation in Beijing. Upon learning about the German-supported mission, he promptly issued a circular to French agents in China, urging them to provide detailed information on Chinese Muslims, including their chiefs, religious leaders with connections beyond China, their interactions with Europeans, and their involvement in secret societies and rebellions.[38]

Through this call for information, Beau came to realize the significant presence of approximately 20 million Muslim Chinese, which he considered an undeniable factor in China's future trajectory. Thus, he assigned the French consul Charles-Eudes Bonin (1865–1929) the task of establishing relations with the Muslim community in the Beijing area. Trained as an archivist-paleographer, Bonin was previously an explorer and semiofficial diplomatic agent who traveled extensively in Southeast Asia and China in the 1890s. He participated in the survey of the Yunnan railway and provided valuable on-the-ground information about Chinese Muslims and their rebellions, subsequently influencing the French perception of this community.[39] In 1902, Beau facilitated a meeting between Bonin and Muhammed Ali, an agent of the Ottoman Sultan dispatched to East Asia for pan-Islamist propaganda. During this encounter, Bonin learned that the Ottoman sultan was already familiar with Muslims in Yunnan and Kashgar, although his knowledge of Muslims in other parts of China was limited. The French delegation anticipated increased Ottoman intervention in Muslim affairs in the coming years.[40]

Around the same time, Jules Gervais-Courtellemont (1863–1931), a French photographer and explorer, approached Paul Doumer to secure funding for his travel to Southeast Asia and China. In 1898, Courtellemont had received funds from the Ministry of Colonies for a planned book focused on "the colonial empire of France at the end of the 19th century," in preparation for the upcoming exposition in 1900. A Muslim convert, Courtellemont had previously published works on Algeria and Tunisia, aiming to leverage his unique position and extensive knowledge of various regions within the French empire to facilitate political and commercial exchanges across French colonies.[41] Unlike the metropolitan elites who were critical of Doumer's expansionist policies, Courtellemont viewed Doumer's work in Indochina as a valuable substitute for the lost prospects in India, which had been acquired by Britain.

Accompanied by his wife, Courtellemont introduced himself as a pilgrim to Mecca (*haji*) and instructed the Yunnanese Muslims in the mosques of Kunming. Some French military men, such as Colonel Boutrois and Lieutenant Poppe, interpreted his arrival as a sign of an impending expedition to Yunnan, assisted by the Muslims of the province. Although the Indochina administration refused the claims that Courtellemont was in China on an official mission, François believed that financial support from Paul Doumer and Courtellemont's warm reception by the military authorities at the Tonkin–Yunnan border were evidence of his direct link to the Indochina administration.[42] He was convinced that Courtellemont's equipment was ill suited for a scientific mission, and he expressed concerns that his protection by French officials would close the doors of China to ordinary French travelers. As suspicions grew among Chinese authorities after the warnings of the British consul, the Indochina government not only severed ties with Courtellemont but also instructed François to eliminate him with proper measures.[43] In a letter to Viceroy Wei, François disclaimed any responsibility to be born out of Courtellemont's contacts with Yunnan's Muslims.

During his visit, Courtellemont made important observations about the social life of local Muslims, noting their interest in Middle Eastern Muslims.[44] Nevertheless, their religious practices diverged notably from the practices of Muslims elsewhere. For instance, Chinese Muslim women did not cover their faces, and they practiced foot binding as did Chinese women. While praising Chinese Muslims' peaceful demeanor and orderly life, Courtellemont used explicitly biased language for Chinese peasants, describing them as "deceitful" and their villages as "repulsive." Having visited numerous Muslim villages, Courtellemont concluded that the enduring trauma caused by the violent suppression of the Panthay Rebellion served as the main unifying force among Yunnan's Muslim communities. Their antipathy toward the Qing government and the economic potential of the Yunnan railway rendered them, in the eyes of Courtellemont, France's natural allies in Yunnan.

Courtellemont's observations were largely substantiated during the miner rebellion in 1903. Muslim communities in the Gejiu and Mengzi areas became involved in the events when the rebel miners raided their villages in mid-May that year. Faced with famine in their encircled strongholds, the rebels attacked the nearby Muslim villages that refused to align with their cause. As the rebellion began to wane, the Muslim forces joined with the imperial troops to deal a death blow to the uprising. However, despite their assistance, the Muslims were forbidden from entering the city of Lin'an after the incidents due to official suspicion stemming from their riotous record from the nineteenth century. Sainson, the French consul in Mengzi, reported that the Muslims, disheartened by the lack of trust from the authorities, approached French subjects in Yunnan and offered them protection during and after the incidents, should another rebellion erupt against corrupt officials.[45] François even claimed that the Muslims asked him to store weapons at the consulate for their potential use in the future.[46]

François interpreted the Muslim communities' efforts to engage with French diplomats as a radical change in the disposition of the Yunnanese Muslims toward Europeans, especially after the miner rebellion. The Muslims approached François to facilitate their travel to Mecca through Tonkin, and an influential Muslim leader visited him to establish connections with Algerian Muslims and request Arabic books and periodicals. François planned to maintain good relations with the Muslims, "without encouraging a rebellion or organizing a propaganda campaign," so that France could leverage their sympathy when necessary. Facilitating their passage to Mecca with the help of French navigation companies in Haiphong and providing them with French-published Muslim newspapers would be promising initial steps to strengthen their alliance. In concluding his letter, François emphasized the need for utmost caution to avoid arousing suspicion among Chinese officials, stating that he would "proceed with great prudence so that the mandarins will not doubt us [the French]."[47]

Governor Beau, thanks to his collaboration with Consul Bonin during his tenure in Beijing, had some insight into the distinctive characteristics of Chinese Muslim communities. As a result, when Francois sent these encouraging letters, he became fully convinced of the reliability of Yunnanese Muslims in safeguarding the railway and expanding French influence in the region. Among the province's population of six to ten million Muslims, it was not difficult to find individuals for the police forces "whose religious affiliation would act as a shield against secret societies and troublemakers."[48] Governor Beau's plan for the formation of a Muslim police force is worth examining in detail.

The governor acknowledged the potential risk of recruiting Muslim guards, as Chinese authorities were always suspicious of Muslim communities. Previous massacres and uprisings had revealed the cruelty and injustice of the officials but had failed to eradicate the Muslims' communal spirit. The Panthays, or Yunnanese Muslims, had remained peaceful since the suppression of Dali in 1873 and the death of Sultan Du Wenxiu, with his sons fleeing to Rangoon, Burma. However, there were still dissident groups, many of whom were descendants of military men brought during the Mongol conquest of Kublai Khan. These dissidents were present in three or four cities and were in good terms with French officials. As François claimed, during the troubles in May 1903, Muslims in Mengzi had provided protection to French nationals and offered a force of three hundred men to combat the rebels. It was among these Muslims that the governor proposed recruiting the first railway guards.

To avoid drawing attention from the Qing authorities, the governor suggested issuing recruitment calls without religious or racial distinctions and hiring whoever responded. The number of recruits would be limited due to the general distrust of the Chinese toward the French company. A mandatory medical examination would help eliminate undesirable candidates. The Muslim population would naturally contribute a significant number of recruits, and their admission could be justified by highlighting their martial reputation in China. Initially, a small number of Yunnanese individuals from other religions and ethnicities could be enlisted, with the intention of eventually phasing them out.[49]

Governor Beau's familiarity with Yunnan's local history, along with the superior military capabilities of the local Muslims, and the historical animosity between Yunnan's Muslims and the Qing administration, led him to perceive them as potential allies in creating an alternative power center against the ruling dynasty. To strengthen the police organization, the governor also proposed recruiting police chiefs from Algeria. According to the governor, employing Algerian guards would help reduce staffing costs, as they were accustomed to a more frugal lifestyle compared to French nationals. He stated, "These Algerian officers, accustomed to a more sober diet and a more modest way of life than our nationals, will find all of their necessities in Yunnan and be content with reduced renumeration."[50] Furthermore, since they would be able to communicate in Arabic with Chinese Muslims, France could avoid interpretation expenses.

Beyond the financial advantages, Beau considered the hierarchical dynamics within the police force. He believed that lower-ranking Chinese-Muslim officers would exhibit greater respect and obedience toward their fellow Muslims in positions of authority. The presence of Algerian foot soldiers in Tonkin, brought by the Indochina administration, served as evidence of the French empire's harmonious relations with diverse religious communities. The governor stated:

> One must witness the reverence shown by Chinese Muslims toward their religious brethren from abroad to fully comprehend all the benefits that can be gained by appealing to this sentiment. Moreover, we should show the locals that a significant number of their co-religionists serve France and take pride in being part of the French empire. Arab chiefs, who can communicate with the literate Muslims of Yunnan in Arabic, will be the best propagators of our influence within this segment of the population.[51]

With these considerations, Governor Beau appointed three Algerian police officers in August 1904 to monitor the railway construction sites.[52] However, French agents in the region held differing views on the employment of Algerians. Leduc, the successor to François, recommended sending these officers to the Nanxi area, where tensions between contractors and workers were most pronounced. After the failure of the Syrian doctor sent to Yunnan by the governor in the previous year for propaganda, Leduc believed that employing Algerians as police forces carried the risk of antagonizing officials and disrupting railway construction. Chinese authorities paid utmost attention to the local Muslims, whom they thought to be the most restive section of the population. Leduc was convinced that increasing the number of Christians would yield better results than provoking the Muslims, as expecting sympathy from Chinese Muslims was unrealistic.[53]

Sainson, the French consul in Hekou, found the presence of Algerian Muslim officers unnecessary in southern Yunnan. There were no Muslims between Mengzi and Hekou and only a few Muslim villages between Mengzi and Kunming.[54] Besides, Sainson expressed concern that the company's French employees would disregard the Algerians due to the prevailing French contempt toward their colonial subjects. If these men were sent to the isolated Nanxi area, they would be either plagued by nostalgia or succumb to malaria, since no provisions had been made for their accommodation. Sainson suggested employing two officers for justice and police services in Mengzi and assigning the third to Hekou or Kunming. In his view, there was no need for these men since Vietnamese and Chinese auxiliaries would suffice to staff the security forces. He thought that maintaining tranquility in Yunnan was beyond the jurisdiction of French consuls and the Indochina government, whose responsibility was limited to upholding order among French citizens and foreigners under French protection. As long as the French consulate could enforce their laws and protect their nationals in times of trouble, there was no need for the costly investment of creating police forces.

Even if the Indochina administration initially entertained the idea of maintaining security by manipulating local ethnoreligious tensions, it soon became apparent that employing Algerian Muslims to gain the loyalty of Yunnan's Muslims was unrealistic. Many French agents in China, including Georges Dubail (1845–1932), the minister in Beijing, concluded that such a feat could not be accomplished with just three Muslims, who were deemed "poorly educated and lacking moral authority over their co-religionists."[55] As a result, these Algerians were sent back to Hanoi and then made available to the governor of Algeria in April 1905. In their stead, the Ministry of Foreign Affairs hired nine Chinese auxiliaries to provide police services in Mengzi. The French strategy of manipulating local ethnoreligious tensions for their advantage was abandoned.

Conclusion

At the turn of the twentieth century, France's expansionist ambitions in East Asia faced constrains due to the intense interimperialist rivalry prevailing at the time. The presence of Britain as a rival colonial power in Burma and the limited financial and human resources available to the French colonial administration in Indochina compelled French diplomats to adopt a strategy focused on bringing Yunnan's mining industry under European domination through government-backed private investment and modernization. In like manner, the Indochina administration sought to integrate Yunnan into the governance mechanisms of the Indochinese colony by exploiting ethnic tensions within the province. However, their ambitious plan, which relied on merchant-state collaboration, ultimately failed due to the lack of a unified political perspective among French officials and business figures, as well as their limited understanding of local conditions.

The simple-minded French officials expected their colonial grandeur to be carried from Africa to Yunnan through the intermediary of Algerian Muslims. Instead, it was chronic malaria that was conveyed through these colonial exchanges. Where they aspired to generate a free labor force by implementing a European mining regime, they found ubiquitous resistance from local miners. To the extent that France adjusted its colonial policy in response to evolving global political dynamics, the local populations were similarly astute in developing their own forms of resistance. Although the Yunnan railway created a French zone of circulation for people and manufactures, the sterilization of this zone from local resistance was unachievable with the limited powers of French colonial agents in Yunnan. In the absence of repressive colonial institutions, the French resorted to indirect methods of governance, which inadvertently carried the resistance from intergovernmental negotiations to the broader population, to the sites of everyday encounters and interactions, instead of eradicating them.

CHAPTER 3

Navigating the Chinese Labor Market for Coolies, 1903–1907

Chemin de fer c'est chemin d'enfer.[1]

WHEN FRENCH MERCHANTS AND OFFICIALS planned the Yunnan railway project, they never anticipated difficulties in procuring laborers in China. Since the mid-nineteenth century, Western plantations all over the world had abounded with Chinese workers recruited through an overseas coolie trade. The sheer volume of Chinese migrant workers in colonial lands and their dismal recruitment conditions even compelled the American and British governments to implement stringent measures to curb further Chinese migration, following the backlash from their working classes and antislavery politicians.

Opposition was not solely directed at the influx of workers or their slave-like treatment. In 1873, Édouard Madier de Montjau (1816–98), the president of the French American Society, asserted that numerous migrant Chinese, upon the completion of their contract periods, established businesses and thriving communities in their new countries without changing their cultural habits. Beneath the ostensibly superior demeanor of Chinese coolies, he contended, resided an immense, unassimilable, and cunning community.[2]

Despite apprehensions, French planters in colonies found themselves compelled to engage in Chinese coolie recruitment and reassess their anti-Chinese stance in order to meet their labor requirements. Britain had restricted the deployment of Indian workers in French Réunion due to complaints that French planters frequently violated the terms of labor contracts.[3] As a result, the number of Indian coolies employed in French sugar plantations in the Indian Ocean fell from 60,000 to 25,000 in

1890.[4] French recruiters attempted to find workers from the African coast, but Africans lacked the "soft character" of Indians.[5] The resistance on the African coast increased the cost of recruitment up to 800 francs per worker. To circumvent the recruitment of Chinese coolies, who were presumed to bring "diseases and immorality," French officials considered recruiting coolies from Indochina, but the colony had a sparse population.[6] Consequently, despite persistent skepticism, the introduction of Chinese coolies in Réunion and Madagascar seemed inevitable.[7] France joined the British and Dutch colonizers in the region to recruit Chinese coolies, aiming to sustain its plantation economy. It was within this highly racialized and competitive context that France planned to build the Yunnan railway.

This chapter scrutinizes the initial interactions between Chinese workers and European staff during the recruitment process and the journey to the railway worksites. The purpose is to elucidate the mechanisms that facilitated the racialization of Chinese workers and their subsequent deployment in a challenging railway project, which operated under the principles similar to those of the overseas coolie trade. Drawing upon Cedric Robinson's concept of racial capitalism, the chapter substantiates the argument that the French management of the railway company, along with Italian contractors, predominantly perceived Chinese workers as a resource to be exploited for economic gain, with little regard for their well-being and dignity. Similarly, nationals of other colonial powers, even while criticizing French operation in Yunnan, aligned with the view that Chinese coolies were objects of a colonial business operation rather than subjects with agency. Yet, the experiences of Chinese workers, accumulated through years of participation in regional and overseas labor networks, ensured they had strategies to assert their rights. They skillfully navigated the competitive landscape of colonial powers vying for inexpensive Chinese labor, thereby leveraging Qing officials as their legal representatives to collectively negotiate their rights. These struggles engendered more favorable contract terms and higher salaries, although they were insufficient to prevent worker mortality due to Yunnan's lethal climate.

The Failure of Recruitment

The official report on the progress of railway construction, submitted to the French parliament in 1907, conceded that the initial foreign explorers and technical surveyors, including Indochina employees Guillemoto, Wiart, and Guibert, whose accounts formed the basis of the Yunnan railway project, had delivered a distorted image of Yunnan, particularly in terms of labor supply. Consequently, the railway company "did not assign the question of labor recruitment the importance it deserved." It was only after the signing of a more detailed version of the original railway agreement and the initiation of construction in late 1903 that the harsh reality was confronted: unlike southeastern or northern provinces of China, Yunnan did not offer an abundant labor force.

Historically, Yunnan was inhabited by a considerable population of miners, but the mining concessions granted by the Qing government to the Anglo-French Mining Syndicate had already antagonized them, as discussed in the previous chapter. The antiforeign winds of the Boxers in the northeast were still blowing over the southwest. Ethnic tribes residing near the railway route were reluctant to work for the railway, given their familiarity with the region's malarial climate and inhospitable geography. As if the local shortage was not enough, workers recruited from other provinces deserted the worksites or perished shortly after arriving at the railway construction sites, exacerbating the recruitment challenges. The flawed initial assessments and the lack of an accurate understanding of the local conditions thus played a crucial role in the labor shortage that the project experienced during its initial years.

In the winter of 1903, Engineer Guibert lamented to French diplomats that well-compensated European supervisors, lacking workers to oversee, spent their days unproductively. Contractors were able to attract a modest number of local workers with elevated salary offers in the vicinity of Mengzi and Amizhou, yet no local workforce was to be found near Kunming and Yiliang. Both the management's efforts to liaise with local officials and the contractors' individual attempts to secure labor proved unsuccessful in 1903. The officials demanded comprehensive details about work organization and recruitment conditions, which the company was unprepared to provide. Furthermore, the officials showed a preference for a more measured pace of progress out of concern for the potential difficulties that could arise from assembling an uncontrollable army of coolies. As a result, official involvement in recruitment did not commence until October 1904. Even then, the number of local workers fell significantly short of expectations, remaining at a meager 450 out of the promised 1,000.

French diplomats and company agents held differing views on the labor issue: diplomats attributed the failure in labor recruitment to the company's mistreatment of the workers while agents blamed Chinese officials' reluctance to assist with recruitment and the insufficiency of transportation infrastructure for the transfer of coolies from other provinces. Diplomats considered coolie recruitment and work management within the broader context of French colonial prestige, whereas company agents, focusing squarely on their profits, regarded coolies as expendable commodities.

For example, Auguste François, the French consul in Kunming, identified numerous contributing factors to the company's failure in procuring laborers. Initially, the company miscalculated the worker wages. Despite the management's decision to increase the initial salary offer from 15 piastres to 30, officials continued to demand 40, arguing that workers from other provinces could not sustain themselves on such a base amount.[8] Moreover, the Italian contractors employed by the company utilized excessively harsh methods with the workers, resulting in a higher number of laborers leaving the job than new ones arriving. This led to deserted worksites and contractors on the brink of reneging on their agreements due to managing an idle workforce.[9]

Sanitation conditions at the worksites were also a considerable concern. Almost 40 percent of the workforce was sick, over twenty-five European employees succumbed to their ailments, and the mortality rate was significantly higher among the Chinese workers. The company's employees could only receive medical attention at hospitals in Mengzi and Laocai operated by the French consulate. Local officials refused to facilitate this type of recruitment due to apprehension about inciting social unrest. To mitigate these issues, François proposed enhancing the planning of worker accommodations, sustenance, wages, and hygiene, and adopting a more prudent approach to the number of workers to be recruited. Meeting the company's demand for 40,000 men was not a straightforward task.

Raphaël Réau (1872–1928), the Mengzi consul, also held the company accountable for the recruitment problems, pointing out that frequent disputes at the worksites arose due to the "dubious morality" of the railway employees, which included Italians, French, and individuals of unknown nationalities.[10] These employees were behaving in brutal and ignorant ways, "as if they were trying to revive the old customs of American Far West," and "as if the life of a poor coolie is not worth a pipe of tobacco."[11] Réau noticed that many Italian contractors and French engineers demonstrated a superiority complex over the Chinese, oblivious to their guest status in China, and to the fact that the success of the railway project relied on maintaining positive relations with Chinese authorities. He suggested that the prevalent crimes were justifiable because the wronged or mistreated workers "did not hesitate to reclaim their dues from the property of their employers, either in cash or in-kind."[12]

Not all French diplomats echoed Consul Réau's empathetic disposition toward the workers. On the contrary, a significant number deployed racially charged discourse when discussing deserting or defiant workers, mirroring the rhetoric of French colonial agents in other contexts.[13] For example, Hekou Consul Sainson characterized the inhabitants as "miserable, opium-addicted, feeble, indolent, and lacking intelligence."[14] Contractor Waligorski, having failed to recruit workers in Yunnan, managed to secure 1,100 coolies from neighboring Guangxi in 1904, but he arrived at the worksite with only one-third that number. According to French diplomats and Italian contractors, the southern Chinese refrained from work because strenuous labor was antithetical to their culture, lifestyle, or potentially, even their genetic predispositions. To attract such a "lethargic population," the management had to offer seventy-five cents per day as opposed to fifty cents, which was deemed too costly at the project's inception.

The racialization of the labor question by French diplomats and the company implied a distinction in the French imagination between a Chinese coolie and a worker in the European sense. This distinction primarily stemmed from the image crafted by European recruiting agents, among whom Francis Vetch (1862–1944) was the most prominent. Vetch, a Réunion-born French businessman, was active in mining, rice, and coolie trade in the east coast city of Fuzhou, enjoying the support of French consul Paul Claudel (1868–1955).[15] When Britain ceased sending Indian coolies to French islands in South Asia, Vetch seized the opportunity to transfer Chinese coolies to Madagascar and Réunion in 1901. His first shipment to Madagascar failed, as 550 of the 750 coolies opted in less than a year to return to China following diseases and numerous conflicts with their employers. Vetch concluded that the workers in Chinese port cities were "mediocre, undisciplined and of detestable morality," so for his next shipment to Réunion, he ventured into rural interiors to find Christian converts who would better adapt to working on these tropical islands.[16] He also provided French plantation managers with strict instructions on how to best utilize coolies by exploiting traditional Chinese customs.

Vetch's strategy involved shipping coolies in groups of fifty under the supervision of a Chinese foreman who would serve as the primary point of contact between workers and employers. Foremen required a balanced approach: if granted excessive power, they could act like "little mandarins" and take advantage of their position against both workers and employers. By the same token, Chinese workers should neither be asked nor permitted to cut their queues, as doing so symbolized "emancipation" and typically indicated alignment with rebels or outcasts. Another characteristic of the Chinese work culture, Vetch claimed, was the normalcy of corporeal punishment. As in Persia and Turkey, beating was the best way to set a rebel or culprit right as long as it was done according to Chinese customs, with a bamboo stick on which the culprit's name was engraved. Vetch claimed that even the British, who initially treated the Chinese as their own subjects by imposing prison or forced labor sentences, eventually abandoned their "misplaced philanthropy" and resorted to bamboo sticks for discipline.

Vetch discerned parallels between China and Muslim nations in their implementation of forced labor. According to his understanding, slave prices in these countries were regulated by the central governments, which underscored the normalization of this institution. Vetch described the Chinese in a condescending manner, likening them to "big children," much like "the Negro," living under the perpetual "intimidation of the mandarins." Intriguingly, he attributed the rebelliousness of Chinese laborers in Réunion to the unanticipated benevolence of French settlers and officials. He contended, for instance, that paying coolie salaries in full would merely encourage workers to engage in gambling or independent business endeavors. Instead, they ought to be forced to send their remittances back to their families in China.

Reflecting on his decisions, Vetch criticized his choice of sending Christian converts to French plantations. These converts seemed to cherish their independence more than the non-Christian or "pagan" Chinese laborers. This preference for independence led Vetch to speculate that this was the reason many Europeans in China favored more subservient "pagan" Chinese as their servants. Still, he reasoned that French settlers could have maintained better control over Christian laborers by keeping the head Chinese (Catholic) priest close to them. Converted laborers also presented another advantage, in that they were more receptive to the idea of being buried outside China. A non-Christian Chinese laborer would require repatriation to China if they died while working in French territories, which would mean a major cost increase.

The perspectives of a significant French coolie trader reveal how European colonizers racialized Chinese workers, pigeonholing them rather than viewing them as free wage laborers. Their marginalization and infantilization, classified alongside other "Oriental" groups, served to justify their slave-like treatment and encapsulation into a distinctively "Chinese" labor system. Modernizing the working conditions of these laborers or acknowledging them as workers in a European sense by giving them more autonomy would have threatened the profitability of colonial plantations. Instead, capitalizing on Chinese customs to boost production in colonies emerged as the key to realizing financial gains in the highly competitive circumstances of the colonial age.

That said, the distance provided by overseas employment endowed migrant workers with a position of relative advantage in comparison to their compatriots back home. Their engagement with foreign colonists allowed them to confront workplace injustices outside their accustomed social hierarchies. This is not to suggest that they completely abandoned their cultural traditions or familial relationships. On the contrary, the letters they sent home along with their remittances served as conduits to preserve those ties and facilitate moral counsel. Nevertheless, these letters also served to perpetuate and broaden chain migration within families. They included meticulous accounts of overseas journey, recruitment logistics, reception at their destinations, procedural requirements at ports of entry, job availability, costs and wages, and strategies to overcome potential impediments.[17] This knowledge, disseminated through migrant letters, remittance bulletins, and public press, afforded coolie recruits a comparative vantage to determine their own position in the labor market and was integral to the emergence of a modern worker identity within China.

Although Yunnan was located within China's sovereign territory, labor recruitment for the Yunnan railway essentially mirrored the principles of the overseas coolie trade. Over time, the terms of contracts for the Yunnan railway began to shift as a result of worker mobilization and negotiation through officials across various Chinese regions. For example, Beihai (Pakhoi), a port city in the Gulf of Tonkin in the southern part of neighboring Guangxi province, had been a major labor supplier for the French and British colonial projects in Tonkin, the Malay Peninsula, and Singapore. For the railway company, transferring workers from Beihai to Yunnan via the Haiphong route was a simple task. The company's chief engineer, Albert Dufour (1858–1947), planned to recruit twenty thousand men from Beihai, two thousand of whom he expected would be skilled workers, including stonecutters, blacksmiths, and masons.[18] He sought information from the French vice-consul in Beihai, Léonce Flayelle (1863–1927), regarding any reliable recruitment companies operating locally, as well as details pertaining to travel expenses, intermediary commissions, labor contracts, and other conditions. Dufour's plan was to have at least eighteen-month contracts, requiring laborers to work for nine hours a day from September to May, and ten hours from April to August. He proposed no payment for days the workers were absent, and quarter pay on rainy days. The workers were supposed to have three days to build their own shelters out of the materials designated for railway construction. The company preferred the contracts to be individually made by the contractors rather than directly by the company, although they expressed commitment to the contract's full execution.

These unrealistic expectations of the company engineer indicate that the French colonial agents in the Far East were trying to operate a peculiar contract system that disregarded labor sustainability and reproduction. By way of a privately regulated coolie trade, they sought to purchase the Chinese labor power on free market terms, even leaving the individual contracts to the contractor companies to evade responsibility. This system offered no guarantees for workers, who would lose contact with their recruiters once they departed from their hometowns. Indifferent to the workers' well-being, the company even intended to withhold pay for hours the workers could not work due to sickness or rain, despite the subtropical climate.

Recognizing the impracticality of Dufour's plan, Flayelle, after a brief consultation with Mr. Schomburg, a German businessman recruiting coolies for colonial projects, advised Dufour to reassess his expectations and offers.[19] French plantations elsewhere were offering better wages and conditions. In British and Dutch colonies, medical care and additional benefits were mandatory. Given that the local population in Guangxi knew the harsh conditions in Yunnan, the company would have to offer more attractive terms to entice workers to this region.

As for the costs in Beihai, recruiters were charging $18–$25 per coolie, including all travel expenses and food.[20] This amount was paid by the main companies and subsequently deducted from the workers' salaries at a rate of $1 per month. That is, coolies were expected to finance their own recruitment and travel expenses. A Chinese recruiter employed by a Tonkinese industrialist was offering $9 per month to coolies, a sum lower than the $15 they could earn in Annam, and the $10–$14 in Sumatra. In all contracts, laborers were assured of full payment in the event of work disruption due to rain, floods, and typhoons. Without such provisions, it was almost impossible to find workers.

Considering the company's intent to recruit Chinese workers for employment within China, the help of local authorities both in recruitment areas and destinations was crucial. Without official endorsement, workers would lack confidence in the execution and fulfillment of their contracts. In the end, both Flayelle and Schomburg advised Dufour to seek workers either along the Tonkin borders or in the northern parts of the country. Many companies recruiting Chinese workers from the southern regions expressed dissatisfaction with the efficiency of these workers. The local populace was primarily linked with banditry and secret societies, which could lead to complications at worksites.

Realizing its initial expectations were out of alignment with the supply-demand dynamics of the Chinese labor market, which was well integrated into a competitive global market, the railway company entrusted one of its contractors, de Boyer d'Eguilles (1859–1929), with the task of revising the preliminary recruitment conditions. During his visit to Beihai in late 1903, d'Eguilles offered monthly wages of $12 to regular workers, $14 to smiths and joiners, and $18 to guards, instead of daily wages. He also abolished the company's demand for compulsory medical examinations and guarantors. Following these revisions, Flayelle coordinated with local authorities and successfully recruited workers to be shipped in early 1904. In his letter to the Ministry of Foreign Affairs, the vice-consul reminded the metropolitan bureaucrats the importance of treating the first batch of recruits properly to sustain the labor flow into Yunnan.[21] Flayelle hoped that occasional directives from the metropolitan government would keep the company and the contractors in check.

The allocation of work to separate contractors rendered the fulfillment of Flayelle's expectations unattainable. As the route inspection drew to a close in 1902, the company—a consortium formed by la Régie Générale de Chemins de fer and la Société de Construction de Batignolles—dispatched representatives to Yunnan along with several Italian contractors who had previously collaborated on similar projects in Turkey, Syria, Greece, and Africa. French entrepreneurs were reticent to assume such risks. By the fall of 1903, Italians comprised more than half of the foreign population in Yunnan. Given that Italy had no established diplomatic agreement with the Qing government concerning its subjects in China, the Italian contractors, capitalizing on their nebulous legal status, frequently displayed abusive behavior toward their workers and other foreigners. In many instances, French consuls found themselves in the incongruous position of defending the Italians against their own nationals.

Complaints from Chinese workers were ubiquitous. In June 1904, the Chinese Foreign Relations Office penned a letter to the French minister in Beijing expressing their concern over the brutality of the Italian contractors, which had resulted in the murder of a Chinese worker on June 14.[22] On that fateful day, a group of workers demanded their salaries from their European employers, only to be met with severe beatings by sticks and iron bars. The following morning, two Italian contractors fatally shot the worker "Pan-hong-tchoun," who died from the ten bullets lodged in his back. The contractors took refuge in the company office in Mengzi. While the Mengzi *daotai* requested the French consul to punish the offenders, the consul was hesitant due to the absence of regulations pertaining to Italian subjects in Yunnan. Upon receiving an official reprimand from the highest Qing authorities over a local incident, Dubail, the French minister in Beijing, also voiced his disapproval of the maltreatment of Chinese workers. He maintained that Chinese workers performed well as long as they were appropriately paid and treated.[23] He was concerned that the worksites would be deserted if this ruthlessness continued.

Maurice Casenave (1860–1935), a French inspector who visited China's southwestern borders in mid-1904 as the first embassy secretary on mission, approached the issue from a broader perspective. He reported that the mistreatment of contracted labor was a systemic issue in the French empire.[24] According to Casenave, many Chinese workers employed in Indochina were poorly treated and inconsistently paid. Some companies, driven to bankruptcy, closed their businesses without paying their workers, who were then stranded and unable to return home. Similar issues were prevalent in other French overseas colonial ventures. Compared to British and Dutch colonies, where stringent and effective legislation protected Chinese workers, France lacked specific legislation regarding coolie emigration.[25] As a result, while emigrants to other colonies were often willing to relocate their families to the new country at their own expense, workers in French colonies advised their compatriots to steer clear of the French. Casenave noted that many of the workers employed in the Nanxi valley for the Yunnan railway project perished due to the unhealthy climate and lack of basic medical facilities. Company agents turned a blind eye to the brutality of contractors and foremen, fearful that any additional costs would be vetoed by the company headquarters.[26]

Casenave disagreed with the company's assertion about local officials' apathy, believing that local officials in Guangdong and Guangxi were well aware of the Yunnan railway's importance. Hence, he argued, it was not the local officials who impeded recruitment, but the inappropriate behavior of company agents and their associates. Finally, Casenave proposed the enactment of new legislation to regulate Asian labor migration to French colonial projects, drawing on models that successfully attracted emigrants.[27] In his words, "the Chinese coolie is a commodity which is, like all other commodities, subject to the general laws of supply and demand."[28] That is, the only solution to the problem of labor shortages was to follow the rules of the Chinese labor market, which was highly competitive due to the high demand from various colonial powers.[29] Institutional reform aimed at recuperating the terms of recruitment could provide the French with a competitive edge in the scramble for cheap Asian labor.

A year later, the French consul in Canton, Gaston Kahn (1864–1928), rebuked the company and its recruiters for prioritizing profit from recruitment over the outcome of the work. He noticed they made no distinctions in the physical fitness or professional skills of the recruits. This negligence resulted in losses for the employers, as they had to "feed these useless mouths" who could not adapt to Yunnan's circumstances.[30] Included in the same correspondence was another note from Casenave, claiming that it was primarily the recruitment agents who, in their rush to meet their quotas, boarded workers unfit for work in Yunnan.[31] He observed that in English and Dutch colonies, workers were subject to strict regulations from the moment of their recruitment. These rules, which left nothing to the employers' discretion, covered their travel and accommodations. On the contrary, French employers disregarded the needs and desires of indigenous workers, mistakenly believing that a high salary would suffice to satisfy the workers. Under these circumstances, France stood little chance of competing with its rivals in the pursuit of coolie labor.

Both Casenave and Kahn were ahead of their compatriots in understanding the recruitment issue within the broader context of the global coolie trade and the transition to free labor. While coolie labor was still regarded as a commodity, coolies had the freedom to choose which contract to sign, barring instances where recruitment agents deceived them.[32] In other words, the supply of "coolie-commodities" in the newly emerged labor market depended on the conditions offered by hiring agents in a competitive setting. Taking advantage of global competition, Chinese workers could raise the price of their labor power. In addition, the coolies' productive capacity was embedded in their physical being, namely, in their bodies. Once they died or disappeared, the "coolie-commodity" consumption cycle abruptly ended and caused a crisis, as their supply was not infinite. Thus, it was necessary to develop the means and mechanisms to maintain coolie labor by keeping them healthy and working.

During these years, France was revising labor law and introducing the first state welfare provisions in the mainland.[33] A new question arose regarding whether to implement these changes in French colonies, where the drive to turn colonies into economically independent units necessitated further reductions in labor costs. To the dismay of colonial investors, pressure from Britain, coupled with the anticolonial movement in France supported by missionaries decrying atrocities in the African colonies, forced the minister of colonies to enhance contractual terms and grant colonial government agencies more power to intervene in recruitment processes.[34] In China, Casenave and Kahn suggested similar solutions, whereas the railway company, even amid an acute labor shortage, remained committed to a free-functioning labor market.[35]

When Chinese authorities suggested recruiting local workers on a trial basis in 1905, the company engineer de Traz told the Kunming consul that he could not "admit that the authorities impose upon [the company] a mode of labor organization not compatible with the requirements of the work and the wage rates for the chiefs, which must be determined only by the laws of supply and demand."[36] The authorities wanted to recruit foremen who would oversee a hundred workers and would be paid 20–30 piastres per month for their supervision. Compared to the 18 piastres paid by the company, this amount was considered too high. It was clear that the authorities wanted to entrust the work to men in whom they had confidence.

De Traz had come to understand that locals, who were familiar with the region's challenges, would resist working for the railway even under government enforcement. In January 1905, Director Guibert reached an agreement with local officials to recruit 1,000 local workers. The workers would be recruited from Lufeng Village in Chuxiong County, home to primarily the Yi ethnicity.[37] The first group would consist of 300 men under the supervision of a chief recommended by local authorities, who would remain in charge until the work was complete.[38] As agreed, the group arrived at the end of February under the supervision of a chief named Ma, but it consisted of only 170 men. For the first three days, the coolies refused to work. By the fourth day, many had already vanished. Those who remained, led by Chief Su, used their construction tools to threaten the company employees who hired them. They even tore down the wooden bridges and set up ambushes on the service track to prevent work from proceeding. Following that, two more groups arrived under the supervision of two Chinese colonels, but instead of 600, they were able to bring only 260 men. According to company reports, these men did not work diligently and revolted at the first signal from their chiefs.[39] As a result, the contractor, with Leduc's assistance, convinced the authorities to pursue re-recruitment from Sichuan. They noticed that men from other provinces, who came to the company without any knowledge of the area, would likely remain, usually until their death. Similar to the overseas coolie trade, it was thought to be easier to control workers with no local ties than those with strong local communal networks.

While scholars often cite the following recruitment table as the authoritative count for the railway labor force, a careful comparison with narratives from French diplomats and company representatives reveals

TABLE 3.1 Recruitment by Province and Year, 1903–1910

Year	Worker origin	Number of workers
1903	Guangxi	2,000
	Vietnam	500
1904	Guangxi	2,300
	Eastern provinces	1,800
	Tianjin	5,500
	Guangdong	2,500
1905	Eastern provinces	4,000
	Fuzhou	1,000
	Ningbo	1,000
	Guangdong	800
	Tianjin	1,500
	Vietnam	3,800
1906	Guangxi	15,000
	Vietnam	7,000
After 1907	Guangxi	5,000
	Vietnam	5,000
	Eastern provinces	2,000
	TOTAL	60,700

discrepancies. These discrepancies can be attributed to several factors, including the fact that agreements with local officials for recruitment often did not materialize, and recruits who were initially enticed with higher salaries frequently left the worksites immediately due to deplorable working conditions. Recruitment in Yunnan was particularly problematic. For instance, in March 1904, a contractor managed to recruit 1,293 coolies and 128 skilled workers, only for them to escape immediately. In 1905, with official assistance, the company was able hire 1,000 local workers. The recruitment effort peaked in 1906, a year marked by famine and rice scarcity, leading many farmers to apply for railway work. This resulted in the employment of 40,000 workers all at once during that famine year, the highest number across all work seasons. Additionally, demand for railway work among locals increased just before the Chinese New Year, a time when money was needed to pay off debts or prepare for the celebrations.[40] Throughout the construction, the company employed a total of 929 European staff members, including 262 technicians, 133 administrative personnel, and 534 auxiliaries, surveyors, and others. This number is more reliable because the employment of Europeans had to go through consular paperwork, and their numbers were limited.

Beyond the Paradigm of the Middle Passage: Journey to the Railway

Scholars have examined the journeys of coolies to overseas worksites during the colonial era and made comparisons to the Middle Passage of the Atlantic slave trade.[41] While there are significant parallels between slavery and overseas contract labor, it is important to note the differences between domestic and overseas coolie trade. The fact that the railway construction fell within the boundaries of the Qing Empire meant that the workers had the advantages of official protection by Qing officials, a shared culture, and familiar geography. These advantages provided workers leverage to breach contracts through absenteeism, mass desertion, or even confronting their employers with acts of rebellion, theft, and homicide, tactics largely unavailable to their overseas counterparts. In stark contrast, workers overseas often resorted to suicide as a means of escaping their horrendous work conditions.[42] This contrast highlights the varying experiences and challenges faced by laborers within the broader coolie trade, influenced significantly by their geographic location and the nature of colonial power dynamics in these regions.

It is evident that mass desertion was a widespread reaction among workers to mistreatment and dreadful working conditions in Yunnan. In 1904, a group of workers recruited from Canton was transported by sea to Haiphong and then by rail to Yen Bay. From there, they had to undertake a strenuous journey on foot to reach Laocai, a border town between China and Vietnam. However, when the Chinese intermediaries overseeing the recruitment process declared bankruptcy, the workers, now without guarantors, abandoned the journey before even reaching the worksite. In another instance, only seven out of eight hundred men made it to Laocai. The French representatives of the railway company accused the workers of stirring up and inducing other coolies to desert the worksites. They were labelled as "the waste population of Canton, who were picked up from refugee shacks."[43]

Similarly, workers from Tianjin recruited in November 1904 also reacted to their dire conditions. Their recruiter and foreman were held in Tianjin due to a dispute with Qing authorities. The unescorted workers were lucky enough to reach Laocai without much trouble, traveling mostly by sea and along the Red River. After a difficult sixty-mile walk to the Nanxi valley, they discovered that the company directors, in their ignorance, had only stored rice to feed the northern workers, whose dietary habits were not rice centered. The workers had departed from the north in the early winter and passed through the hot climate of Hong Kong before arriving in the Nanxi area barely clothed at the onset of a cold, damp season. Although the workers from Tianjin were more robust and had gained experience during the construction of northern railways, approximately five hundred of them had fallen ill or died within a few days. Witnessing the disorganization and conflicts between the foremen and European employers, the surviving workers eventually dispersed into small groups. Seeking daily subsistence along the way, they continued moving northward with the hope of returning home. This resulted in the complete desertion of the worksites in the Nanxi area within a few weeks. In all these instances, the inadequacy of living and working conditions provided by the company was a recurring theme that led to dire consequences for the workers and labor shortages for the company.

The departure of new recruits from their hometowns was the beginning of a transformational process. The workers began to form a collective identity based on common experiences of wage earning, shared hardships, and the basic instinct to survive. During their trip to the worksites, the workers were headed by Chinese chiefs, who were employed by either the recruitment agents or the railway company. Because the workers in a convoy usually hailed from the same location, they could communicate with each other easily. Their communal bonds were strengthened during the trip and continued after the arrival at the worksites, turning them into a unified group that posed a threat to both Qing administrators and French officials.

In one of the incidents, a coolie convoy from Sichuan was dispersed after a confrontation with local troops. Following a recruitment agreement with the Chongqing-based Reynaud Company in November 1904, a group of 204 workers commenced their journey to Yunnan, headed by foremen who had been given funds to cover travel expenses.[44] However, the funds were limited, and there were no shelters along the way to protect the workers from the cold nights. In a short period of time, the convoy ran out of money. As part of the transfer plan, the company had negotiated with local prefecture officials. Upon these agreements, the officials would provide chiefs with necessary advances for the trip, on the condition that the company would later reimburse these advances to the local administrations. In an attempt to prevent any trouble, the workers were instructed to abide by local rules and regulations and were prohibited to stay in one location for more than one or two days.

Despite all precautions, the workers got into trouble in the city of Loufang, where a dispute with locals—likely over the payment for a horse—escalated into violence. The local prefect dispatched troops to intervene, but this intervention only exacerbated the workers' anger. In response, the workers broke into the residence of the prefect and were reported to have stoned and plundered houses in the area. The unrest was only quelled after the local troops used force, allegedly causing injury or even death to some of the workers. When the convoy, now reduced to just sixty men, reached Mengzi, Chinese authorities demanded the handover of the convoy chief, Cheng, and his men for interrogation and trial. Their claim was that Chief Cheng was a devious man who dismissed a good number of workers before their arrival in Loufang so that he could seize their travel allowance.[45] However, the company refused to surrender Cheng on two grounds: first, the company was under no obligation to help the authorities in arresting a Chinese subject, and second, they had already sent a petition directly to Beijing against the local authorities to claim an indemnity for the losses caused by the intervention of local troops. The company maintained that many of the workers, having been severely beaten by the soldiers, had abandoned the convoy with the advance money paid by the company.

The company, which was known to prioritize profit and had a strained relationship with French diplomats in Yunnan, appeared to seize any opportunity to request compensation for alleged losses. However, this approach irritated French officials, particularly because the company had contacted Beijing officials directly, bypassing diplomatic intermediaries. Article 14 of the railway treaty required French authorities not to intervene in the functioning of Chinese justice for crimes committed by Chinese employees. Not submitting Chief Cheng to police was a violation of the agreement, but the company showed little interest in adhering to diplomatic protocols. The Qing side demanded the formation of a commission to investigate the incident, but the company declined to send a delegate. Their claim was that the workers were not directly involved in the affair. Rather than focus on this incident, the company wanted to ensure that their future coolie convoys could operate without interference from the central government so that they conduct their business according to the principles of a free-market economy.[46]

The Loufang incident was only one among a series of disturbances that occurred during the passage of coolie convoys. The French consul in Kunming reported having a huge file of official complaints pertaining to theft, looting, and sexual assault perpetrated by coolies or their chiefs on the way to construction sites. Interestingly, some coolie chiefs claimed to be the "servants of the great French country," a declaration they believed endowed them with exceptional authority in the face of local officials. In an incident in "Nan-tchen" city, a coolie convoy, which had been waiting for the payment of their advances by the local administrator, had a conflict with locals after allegedly behaving atrociously during a funeral procession. The accusations against them included inappropriate laughter, harassment of women, and theft.[47] Although no legal precept delineated the status of the workers, the local prefect hesitated to intervene, presuming that the convoy was under French protection. The next day, he resolved the situation by paying the workers' travel expenses, which allowed them to proceed on their journey. In many similar cases, officials sought to avoid open confrontation with the workers, as the workers easily burst into anger and reacted collectively.

Not all instances of worker desertion occurred in response to an apparent disturbance. In some cases, recruits absconded from the convoy with their advance money soon after they departed their hometowns. Many of the workers recruited in Fuzhou in January 1906, for example, left the convoy before Francis Vetch's company boarded them on ship, allegedly because of the "rumors" about the mistreatment of workers in Yunnan by the railway company.[48] Similarly, skilled workers were often disheartened by the substandard living conditions provided, which were typically arranged based on the needs of an unskilled workforce.[49] Chinese workers generally possessed a clear understanding of what constituted an acceptable workplace and carefully evaluated their options even in the absence of modern trade unions. This knowledge was a product of the longstanding experience of Chinese workers signing contracts with foreigners for overseas work and allowed them to navigate labor market intricacies with an informed perspective.

Reactions to the Workers' Plight and the French Colonial Prestige

The deplorable conditions experienced by Chinese workers under French and Italian overseers were more than just a matter of humanitarian concern; they represented a fundamental challenge to Qing imperial sovereignty. The capacity of the Qing state to maintain power relied as much on the dignity of its subjects as it did on the territorial integrity. Since the mid-nineteenth century, the Qing government was aware of the humiliation of Chinese workers at the hands of foreign agents and their local collaborators. In the 1850s, as the overseas coolie trade began to emerge by way of forceful recruitment and kidnapping in southern China, the government initially chose to ignore this labor migration, in keeping with traditional Chinese laws that prohibited subjects from leaving the country.[50] Once labor migration reached conspicuous levels, officials became increasingly apprehensive about the potential for harming relations with militarily superior foreign governments. Still, by the early twentieth century, Chinese labor migration abroad had an established institutional structure, regulated by the central government and monitored by local officials. Given the extent of Chinese labor mobility, it was not surprising that several articles of the Yunnan Railway Treaty directly addressed worker welfare.

The escalating labor crisis in Yunnan compelled Chinese officials to act in defense of their subjects. In 1905, Cen Chunxuan (1861–1933), the viceroy of Guangdong and Guangxi provinces, responded to the "inhumane" working conditions on the railway by banning recruitment in the Canton area and calling back Cantonese workers already employed on the railway.[51] Hearing this decision, the French minister in Beijing, Dubail, lobbied officials in the central government to prevent Cen from proceeding with his radical move against the French company. Dubail complained in his report to the Ministry of Foreign Affairs that contractors were recruiting "workers with no guarantees and preliminary medical examinations," which resulted in the employment of "coolies who did not meet the requirements of age, strength, and health, necessary to resist the climate and diseases waiting in Yunnan."[52] Such was the company's tarnished reputation that recruitment became virtually impossible in certain districts even with the help of officials.

Three months after Viceroy Cen's ban, the French Minister of Colonies was still complaining about the company's laxity in implementing worker contracts. In particular, Chinese recruitment firms, hired in various provinces, did not execute the contracts at all. Many workers disappeared during their trip to the railway because recruiters did not provide them with the necessary instructions and roadmaps. As if the missing workers were not enough, the company asked officials to repay advances given to the families of the lost workers. Another point of contention was the disrespect shown to deceased workers. It was commonly reported in Canton that the dead were not properly buried, but haphazardly placed in coffins or buried in shallow graves. The minister of colonies blamed these disrespectful practices and the company's negligence for revolts at worksites, murders of foreigners, and failures in recruitment.[53]

When word of Viceroy Cen's ban spread both domestically and internationally, the Indochina governor called for an investigation into the conditions at the construction sites in May 1905. However, according to Leduc, the consul in Kunming, the company was resistant to an investigation. They believed it would be impossible to change Viceroy Cen's decision. Since the promulgation of the recruitment ban, mortality among Tianjin workers in the Nanxi area had increased due to a beriberi epidemic, which was caused by malnourishment and inadequate shelter against the continual rain. The situation was so severe that some people in Hanoi had started to take steps to transfer the work to the Indochina

Department of Public Works. Leduc was worried that this move could trigger further issues by reigniting the expansionist plans of former governor Doumer, who had been recalled to France in 1902.[54] Engaging in a colonial conflict on Chinese territory would disrupt France's delicate foreign policy. Furthermore, while the vice-consul in Hekou believed that the suffering coolies in Hekou required aid, he was concerned that news of an epidemic would soon spread to the neighboring Tonkin provinces that supplied the workforce for the Laocai–Yen Bay (Vietnam) section of the Indochinese railway.[55]

Viceroy Cen was known for his patriotic fervor, but the harsh working conditions on the railway prompted similar antirecruitment decisions in other provinces as well. As part of the recruitment campaign organized for 1905–1906, de Traz traveled to Hong Kong, Tianjin, Beijing, Shanghai, and Ningbo, where they located many willing workers, but needed official authorization from the Qing central government. Despite their personal and French consular efforts, they could not gain proper authorization for recruitment in Ningbo, Shanghai, and Hangzhou. The head of the Chinese Foreign Relations Office, Prince Qing, simply wrote that no workers were willing to work for the company due to the long distance between Ningbo and Yunnan.[56] Qing officials knew that the treaty signed in 1903 required them to help with recruitment, but they subtly maneuvered circumstances, thereby indirectly empowering the workers.

In December 1905, Viceroy Cen agreed to lift the recruitment ban in Guangxi and Guangdong on the condition that workers received fair treatment, regular payment, sufficient food, and proper medical care.[57] Because these provinces were the main sources of labor, the French consul in Kunming acknowledged the company's wrongdoings and assured the Viceroy of Yunnan that they would not repeat past mistakes.[58] Before lifting the ban, Viceroy Cen asked for new contracts that would be more favorable to workers and demanded the company deposit money into a Canton bank as assurance to the local populace.[59] However, the company sought ways to circumvent the ban, announcing that they did not need workers from Canton and arguing that any ban on recruitment or any official intervention preventing the transfer of coolies from other provinces was against Article 12 of the railway agreement that allowed out-of-province recruitment if the local labor force was insufficient.

Such interventions and Cen's demand for a new contract changed the recruitment playing field. After all these difficulties, the "price of a coolie" in Haiphong increased from 26 to 35 piastres. Just as the time for the interim payment approached, the company hoped to secure the promised remuneration, although they could not complete the planned work. By March 1906, the company had been disappointed by the outcome of clandestine recruitment in Guangxi. The available population was scant and weak. The native "T'ou" tribe was vigorous but refused to migrate.[60] Thus, the French consul in Canton recommended that the Indochina governor approve Cen's demands. The governor ordered the usage of the sum of 8 million francs deposited earlier in Credit Foncier de France for the recruitment of workers.[61]

These negotiations resulted in more favorable contract terms for the Yunnan railway workers compared to overseas employment. In Fuzhou, Francis Vetch handled the recruitment and contracts for El Boleo mining deposit in Mexico, Réunion Island, and the Yunnan–Indochina railway. Contracts for Yunnan required workers to work for nine hours a day for a specified season, while overseas workers were bound for five years with an expected ten-hour workday. Also, there was a clause prohibiting overseas workers from engaging in independent business at their destinations, while no such clause existed for Yunnan railway workers. Overall, the conditions for domestic coolies seemed better with a higher salary depending on the work category. Other than these differences, the terms of both domestic and overseas contracts were similar in emphasizing the voluntary nature of agreements; guaranteed payments for nonworkdays due to holidays, sickness, or inclement weather; and fines in the event of workers' breaking the contracts. These improved conditions in 1905 can be credited to the interventions of Qing officials after worker complaints.

However, these formal safeguards were not sufficient to pacify public outrage in recruitment hubs. In March 1906, the French consul in Fuzhou reported the posting of placards by a group of Chinese citizens who opposed recruitment for the Yunnan railway. The placards read: "We recruit workers in Fuzhou—secretly and without the authorization

FIGURE 3.1 Work contracts prepared by Francis Vetch's company in Fuzhou. The contracts were drafted in both Chinese and French and endorsed by provincial Qing authorities. Courtesy of the Centre des Archives diplomatiques de La Courneuve, France.

of the Chinese government—to whom we promise work in Yunnan, but we ship them, in reality, to Laocai, where they are mistreated and where they die from hard work and unhealthy conditions."[62] Upon noticing the protest, the consul promptly asked local authorities to tear down the placards and punish "the perpetrators." Concurrently, he wrote a letter to the consul in Mengzi, urging him to inform the company that if they wished to continue recruitment in Fuzhou, they needed to improve their treatment of the workers.

Similar to Canton, Fuzhou was a port city that sent Chinese workers to overseas projects. Francis Vetch's company conducted recruitment for the Yunnan railway in tandem with the recruitment for French mining ventures in El Boleo, Mexico. The consul was more concerned about the overall reputation of French businesses in China than the completion of the Yunnan railway. A negative public image triggered by the Yunnan incidents would be highly detrimental to the interests of French companies, which had been making substantial profits from the coolie trade to the Panama Canal, especially during the Chinese anti-American boycott. The consul stated that the company's attempts to prolong the contracts and retain workers for more extended periods would serve as poor publicity for future recruitment efforts.[63]

Just as the French press widely reported on the Dreyfus Affair and the Panama Canal scandal, foreign press in China carried news of the railway workers' suffering and protests. Numerous English- and German-language newspapers eloquently recounted the tribulations of the railway workers, including instances where firearms were employed to force laborers into laboring in perilous, gas-leak-ridden tunnels.[64] These narratives served to ignite a debate regarding the French "civilizing mission" within an inter-imperialist discourse that was predicated on issues of morality and humanitarianism. As the consul predicted, the bad image of the Yunnan railway could be used as a propaganda tool by the British, German, and Dutch firms competing against the French companies in the coolie market. Therefore, maintaining the company's good reputation was not merely a local issue for French diplomacy; it was a matter of national interest.

The question of morality ascended to the forefront of public discussions in France after abuses by French colonial agents were brought to light by the Committee for the Protection and Defense of Indigenous People, founded in 1881.[65] French humanitarianism in this period was predominantly focused on justifying French expansionism vis-à-vis other colonial powers, as manifested in campaigns purporting to liberate enslaved individuals from their "uncivilized" oppressors, rather than problematizing the unequal relationship between French colonists and their subjects.[66] Despite these assertions, French labor practices in Yunnan starkly contravened the fundamental tenets of nineteenth-century French humanitarianism. Within the limits of a racialized discourse, the resistance exhibited by Chinese workers to unfair recruitment practices and workplace abuses, which often took the form of mass desertions, open revolts or negotiations through officials, were not recognized as legitimate worker struggles in the European sense. Instead, these actions were portrayed by all colonial actors as instances of victimization within an unethical business operation.

Conclusion

The period starting with the inception of the Yunnan railway construction in 1903 and continuing through its progress up to 1907 was characterized by a severe labor shortage. The primary factors contributing to this crisis were an alarming rate of worker mortality, rampant desertions, and persistent obstacles encountered during recruitment. Despite a prevalent assumption that casualties among workers were an inevitability dictated by the harsh climate and topography of Yunnan, accountability lies squarely with the French railway company and the Italian contractors. The former opted for a more challenging route to curtail construction costs and entrusted the work to separate contractors without a proper auditing system. The latter resorted to cruel and demeaning disciplinary practices to maximize profits. Ultimately, it is the shared perception of the coolie as a racialized commodity that spawned this tragedy.

In stark contrast, Qing officials conceptualized the worker as a symbol of imperial power and turned their interventions for labor control into exercises of national sovereignty. Their endeavors to enhance contract terms helped in augmenting the bargaining power of the workers. Amid the tides of colonial competition and capitalist avarice, the workers crafted their unique forms of labor politics to protect their interests. Even though these efforts were not centralized, their unruly protests led to delays in construction, drawing attention from both foreign and Chinese public to the devastation wrought by the march of modern development.

In the evolving landscape of the labor market, Chinese workers transformed their productive capacities into a foundation for collective identity. This phenomenon represents a potent illustration of how racial capitalism can spur the development of worker consciousness and resistance, even in conditions marked by severe exploitation and dehumanization. This chapter has aimed to illustrate this transformation, not just in terms of the oppressive systems and structures the workers faced, but also the strategies and methods they employed to assert their dignity and worth. Situated at the intersection of race, labor, and capitalism, these dynamics shaped the construction process of the Yunnan railway, a critical node in the broader history of colonialism and capitalism in Asia.

CHAPTER 4

Dominating the Laboring Body

French Medicine and Jurisdiction in Yunnan

THE FRENCH PURSUIT OF CONNECTING Indochina to Yunnan through a railway line between 1898 and 1910 was emblematic of a broader colonial project that sought to assert control over the region. The interactions with Yunnan's local population evolved through different phases, each marked by its unique challenges and strategies. The initial phase (1898 to 1903) was characterized by local rebellions that erupted in reaction to the bourgeoning foreign involvement in Yunnan's socioeconomic life. Although these rebellions could be seen as the tail end of nineteenth-century antiforeignism (*pai wai*), these uprisings, far from being mere xenophobic actions, were expressions of resistance to local repercussions of global and national politics. During this phase, insecure French officials chose to flee when violent rebellions broke out.

Once the railway treaty was instituted in October 1903, French officials adopted a more assertive approach in dealing with local unrest. This marked a phase of "imperial globalization," similar to what Pierre Singaravélou details for the post-Boxer restructuring of Tianjin's foreign concession area through modern policing, jurisdiction, and sanitation in the spirit of "civilizing mission."[1] Although Yunnan did not have a designated concession area, French officials used Article 13 of the railway agreement, which tasked the local government with maintaining peace and order, to create a disciplined and sanitized space along the railway. However, these machinations were complicated by financial constraints, intracolonial conflicts, and the intrinsic complexities of colony building, while simultaneously exposing the changing dynamics of social conflict in the "uneventful" life of a peripheral province.

This chapter delves into two specific domains where these complexities manifested: medicine and criminal justice. Both domains were shaped by France's need to govern the Asian laboring body, a precondition to produce colonial exploitation systems. This was not achievable in a setting where people already held intricate notions of justice, paid work, and physical well-being, particularly when France did not possess the unrestrained power of a forceful colonial regime. Thus, the chapter suggests placing labor at the center of the analysis of these domains, which were previously studied merely as cultural aspects of colonialism.

The proliferation of French medical theories and infrastructure during the colonial era has often been classified by scholars as "a vector for French cultural imperialism."[2] This viewpoint encapsulates the process of educating colonial subjects in French medical institutions and the global establishment of French medical infrastructure as mechanisms to vindicate French civilizing mission. Particularly in China, the augmentation of French medical practices, beginning with the initial efforts of Catholic missionaries, was perceived as a tool to bolster French sway in rivalry with other colonial powers. Florence Bretelle-Establet, having undertaken an in-depth investigation into the French medical dispensaries in Yunnan, Guangxi, and Guangdong, posits that the two primary impetuses driving the foundation of these medical outlets in southern China were, first, the intent to extend French influence, and second, the aspiration to create a sanitary zone to prevent potential epidemics from spreading southward from the Chinese borders into Indochina.[3]

While concurring with Bretelle-Establet's deductions, this chapter offers an additional perspective. In the immediate context of the Yunnan railway's construction, the labor shortages attributed to endemic malaria in the Nanxi region significantly spurred the enhancement of French medical facilities in Yunnan. To address the problem of worker mortality, hospitals operated by the French consulates in Yunnan's big cities were supplemented by smaller, company-operated clinics at different sections of the railway. This led to the involvement of Italian and Vietnamese personnel in the province's modern medical establishment, initiating a new rendition of race and ethnic difference.

This process of medical racialization was reinforced by judiciary processes that favored Europeans over local inhabitants and railway workers. Empowered by extraterritorial rights granted by unequal treaties signed since the mid-nineteenth century, European railway staff criminalized any act of workers' disobedience and subjugated them to an exploitative labor regime where worker salaries were unjustly withheld by contractors and defiant workers were punished without impunity. While viewing Chinese workers as rational, interest-seeking individuals (akin to European workers) was unfeasible for European business owners entrenched in nineteenth-century racist tropes, both Chinese and Vietnamese railway workers actively pursued their interests through both legitimate channels such as petitioning and court appeals, and more unconventional methods like absenteeism, theft, or even homicide. The following sections will unravel how these interactions contributed to a volatile setting that simultaneously fueled and hindered France's colonial ambitions in the region, with a specific focus on the experiences and predicaments of the laboring workforce.

French Medicine in the Service of Colonialism

The inception of medical services along the Tonkin borders of China was first mooted in 1897 by Sir Robert Hart, the (British) second inspector-general of the Chinese Maritime Customs Office.[4] Seeing Hart's proposal as a fortuitous means to expand French influence in southern China, the Indochina governor, Doumer, orchestrated the creation of French medical dispensaries attached to the consular services in the southern cities of Longzhou, Simao, and Mengzi.[5] Doumer believed that besides contributing to the amplification of French prestige in China, these dispensaries, through vigilant surveillance of public health along the Tonkin borders, would act as a safeguard against the spread of epidemics from China to Indochina.[6] In late 1898, a second-rank French naval doctor, Dr. E. Reygoudard, was appointed to the consular medical service in Mengzi, while Doctors Thoulon and Gaide were commissioned to Longzhou and Simao, respectively.[7]

Beyond the trepidation of a potential epidemic, Yunnan assumed a pivotal role in maintaining the health and efficacy of the colonial labor force in Indochina. Many French colonists encountered serious health complications upon their arrival in the Indochinese colony, particularly as a result of a malady called "tropical anemia," which rendered them physically enervated and cognitively impaired, thereby diminishing their efficiency.[8] A substantial number of French colonists traversing from Indochina to Yunnan perceived this Chinese border province as a sanctuary for the convalescence of their compatriots who were beleaguered by the exacting demands of the colonial project. In acute instances, colonial doctors had to repatriate patients who were incapable of physiological or psychological adaptation to the climate. This phenomenon manifested as an evident frailty in the operational mechanics of the colonial apparatus.

In comparison to Indochina, the middle and northern regions of Yunnan were characterized by a more temperate climate with its defined dry and rainy seasons. The first group of European doctors employed within the province lauded the fresh air and ventilation facilitated by Yunnan's altitude. Dr. Magunna, for instance, theorized that the air circulation in the area functioned as an antioxidant and purged the "colonial toxins" that had accumulated within the liver.[9] Although those journeying from Indochina to Kunming experienced an initial surge in nervous excitation due to heightened cellular activity, their metabolic function typically reverted to a baseline state within a matter of days. Given the scarcity of contagious diseases in Kunming, Dr. Magunna suggested Kunming as the optimal location for an Indochinese sanatorium. Concurrent with the inception of the Yunnan railway project, French colonialists had similarly conceptualized Yunnan as the sanatorium of Tonkin, where their colonial agents could recuperate without necessitating a return to France.[10] In his Indochinese report in 1902, Paul Doumer depicted Yunnan, with its European-like climate, as "a temperate and healthy province, receptive to the civilizing activity of France."[11]

While Doumer's enthusiasm was directed toward the introduction of what he considered "superior" French medicine to Yunnan, the local populace's initial motivation seemed inclined more toward forestalling foreign settlement within the province rather than assimilating their knowledge. During 1899 and 1900, a pair of significant uprisings forced all foreign nationals in Yunnan to retreat across the Tonkin borders. It was only subsequent to the restoration of tranquility in 1901 and the progress of the railway route inspection surveys that the Indochina government appointed another medical supervisor, Georges Barbezieux, to oversee medical operations. Initially, Barbezieux gave consultations in the concession area used in Mengzi by the Indochinese Public Works Department. The dispensary relocated to a permanent facility in January 1903 and commenced operations as a consular hospital.[12] Another consular hospital in Kunming was inaugurated by Dr. Delay, a member of the railway route inspection teams of 1899. In 1904, Dr. Barbezieux, the erstwhile physician of the Mengzi hospital, was appointed as its chief physician.

Funded through financial endowments from the French Ministry of Colonies, Ministry of Foreign Affairs, and the General Government of Indochina, consular hospitals in Mengzi and Kunming were able to provide complimentary health services to the local population while simultaneously generating revenue from foreign patients, local dignitaries, and officials. For example, the provincial government disbursed a monthly allowance of 100 taels to the Kunming hospital for medical services provided to military personnel. Nevertheless, the principal patrons of the hospital remained the Indochina government and the railway company until the culmination of the construction work around 1909.[13]

However, the endeavor to entice local patients to French consular hospitals in Mengzi and Kunming proved to be a gradual process. In the first seven months of 1904, the Kunming hospital admitted a mere fifty-seven local patients, the majority of whom were referred by local authorities.[14] In an effort to engender trust among the local populace, inpatients were offered a range of liberties, such as permission to leave the hospital premises to visit the town center. The doors to the inpatient rooms were deliberately left ajar during afternoons to allow outpatients the opportunity to observe the considerate care bestowed upon their compatriots. In like manner, the doctors refrained from taking measures to combat the common habit of opium smoking, so as to avert popular resentment.[15]

Despite these accommodations, resistance to French medical practices persisted among the local populace. Initial attempts by French doctors to administer vaccinations, such as those for smallpox, were met with considerable opposition. The inaugural vaccinations were only successfully performed within the Kunming hospital in 1907. Even within that year, some Chinese patients exhibited such a profound "prejudice" against European medical methods that they opted to succumb to their ailments rather than consent to surgical intervention, as reported by Dr. Magunna.[16] This cultural apprehension led the locals seek medical assistance in "medical pagodas," where Chinese healers employed an array of traditional techniques, encompassing practices such as herbal treatments, acupuncture, and even spiritual communication, all of which were deemed either septic or ineffective by European physicians. The divergence in medical philosophies revealed not only a clash of methodologies but also a profound mistrust informed by the political context of the encounter.

As the Mengzi and Kunming hospitals continued their efforts to challenge the deep-seated reliance on native healing traditions, the railway company was compelled to develop its own health services. This necessity arose particularly in regions where worker fatalities, due to endemic malaria, were most acute, and the consular hospitals were inconveniently remote. While certain cases of malaria were susceptible to known treatment methods, such as quinine and ipecac, others proved more recalcitrant. For example, two railway employees, who arrived in Yunnan in 1902 and 1903 after extended stays in Algeria, manifested symptoms of malaria and were subsequently conveyed to the consular hospitals in Yunnan.[17] Even with consistent quinine administration, these patients suffered from recurrent and erratic bouts of fever, which could only be alleviated by the medicine Calliandra. This persistent form of malaria, often transmitted between French colonies, constituted an insurmountable obstacle for modern French medicine. Faced with limited resources and an urgent need to prevent potential epidemics that might hinder construction progress, the company's directors petitioned the Ministry of Foreign Affairs for the creation of a sanitary department tailored to the needs of the railway personnel.[18] Heeding the counsel of the Pasteur Institute in Paris, the company resolved to organize a specialized unit in bacteriology and extended an invitation to Dr. Jules Regnault, then the chief of the surgical clinic at the Toulon Naval Hospital, to assume its directorship.

Jules Regnault was a twenty-eight-year-old multilingual physician fluent in English, German, and the vernacular of Tonkin, capable of attending to Chinese patients from southern China without an interpreter. His experience included serving as the chief physician of a dispensary in Tonkin during 1898–99, where he treated patients along the Guangxi borders twelve days a month. Before returning to France in 1900, he worked in Mong Cai, a border city in Tonkin with a considerable Chinese population.[19] Dr. Regnault was a distinct personality with particular interest in sorcery, folk beliefs, and traditional folk medicine.[20] His interest in Far Eastern medicine possibly incentivized him to accept the position, which required him to take a three-month training in bacteriology at the Pasteur Institute. Akin to his political superiors, Dr. Regnault viewed medicine and doctors as heralds of modern civilization—lamenting the scarcity of French doctors in the Far East compared to British and American peers—though he appreciated the necessity of understanding diverse cultural practices before rendering judgements. He exhibited profound respect and admiration for traditional Chinese medicine and local medical practices in northern Vietnam.

During the railway construction, the company engaged similarly experienced doctors, previously serving either in the French military or various roles in Indochina. In conjunction with individual initiatives by Italian contractors to employ Italian doctors, labor recruiter Francis Vetch also supplied Chinese physicians to accompany the coolies hired from eastern provinces. Under the aegis of these European, Vietnamese, and Chinese physicians, localized medical clinics, overseen by Vietnamese nurses and Chinese physicians, were instituted at each major construction site. For every 30 km section of the railway, a European doctor supervised medical care, assisted by an auxiliary physician.[21] This doctor conducted weekly visits and consultations with both European staff and Chinese workers.[22]

The Nanxi region, with its extreme conditions, required exceptional measures: seven European doctors were allocated to the seven medical clinics in a 144 km stretch, and in lower Nanxi, eight medical posts covered 88 km.[23] Nevertheless, French agents' reports consistently highlighted that these facilities were inadequate. In 1903, Dr. Barbeziux detailed the "medical population" of the railway company at the Mengzi hospital as 236 Europeans and 56 Vietnamese, with 193 of these patients hospitalized.[24] This suggests that only European and Vietnamese employees were transported to consular hospitals, probably because the number of ailing Chinese workers, especially during the epidemic season, was too high for the limited capacities and resources of the consular hospitals.

Interestingly, company inspectors' reports from 1904 to 1908 consistently portrayed positive sanitary conditions, with the sole exception of the lower Nanxi region, and asserted that the section clinics were functioning appropriately. These reports raise a troubling question: if sanitary conditions were satisfactory, who were the thousands of deceased workers that Swiss engineer Otto Meister described as "dying like flies"? An April 1906 report alleged that nearly one quarter of Chinese workers were staying in their huts instead of laboring on the railway during work hours.[25] What the reporter disparagingly labeled as "the laziness of the Chinese" was likely symptomatic of the adverse effects of the malarial climate and its accompanying maladies. Yet, the company's supervisors chose to turn a blind to the workers' plight, allegedly due to underlying corruption.

Contrary to these optimistic inspector reports, the Mengzi consul contended that the company, hampered by insufficient staff and facilities, would have neglected to provide any medical treatment to its employees were it not for the Mengzi hospital.[26] Supporting this assertion, ninety-nine Vietnamese coolies at Laocai sought the French resident to voice their complaints regarding the lack of quinine distribution and hospital services. These workers were burdened not only by extremely low wages but also the deprivation of essential items like salt, rice, and quinine, as promised by the company. Worse still, many were ill for weeks without receiving any medical attention.[27] At the intersection of cultural disparities, capitalist self-interest, and the harsh realities of a subtropical disease environment, workers were cognizant of their rights and determined to advocate for them, even in the face of considerable adversity.

The high mortality rates among railway workers and the unsettling presence of abandoned corpses confirm the inadequacy of medical services at the worksites. Nonetheless, the primary duty of the railway doctors was to maintain the labor force's vitality. In 1904, Indochinese doctor-inspector Charles Grall (1851–1924) pioneered the first prophylactic program against malaria during the Yunnan railway construction. This multifaceted strategy went beyond quinine administration and included cleaning and reorganizing encampments and barracks, limiting work hours, improving nourishment, supplying warmer clothes in winter, mandating prompt evacuation of the sick, and rotating the workforce every three months.[28] Within the Nanxi region, workers were administered 50 centigrams of quinine every two days.[29] European staff had to diligently monitor the workers' quinine intake, fearing that native workers, suspicious of this "foreign drug," might dispose of it into the Nanxi valley.[30] In several instances, injured workers were seen fleeing the clinic to substitute their bandages with chewed tobacco leaves, a practice considered unhygienic by Western medical standards.

The enforcement of Dr. Grall's program marked a substantial advancement in the battle against malaria during the railway construction. Between October 1904 and April 1905, morbidity rates at the worksites decreased by 28.77 percent, while the mortality rate declined by 31.77 percent. Buoyed by the success in Yunnan, the same measures were adopted at other railway construction sites across Indochina, with regular distribution of quinine to locals as a preventive measure. However, the progress was not unmitigated, nor were the results consistent across regions. The doctor responsible for the Vietnam section of the railway found that, despite an increase in the quantity of quinine administered, the measures failed to halt a spike in malaria cases by mid-1905.[31] By August, a startling 57 percent of the workers were ill. This troubling trend echoed the observations of Dr. Barbezieux, the physician at the Mengzi hospital, who noted a significant surge in cases during the middle of the year, coinciding with the onset of the hot and rainy season.

These medical challenges in Yunnan were not confined solely to the realm of disease control and prevention; rather, they prompted Europeans to extend their observational purview to encompass broader cultural aspects of the region. The French physicians stationed at the two consular hospitals produced immense knowledge on the local population, discerning and documenting various facets of their daily existence, from physical environment to customs and behavioral norms. From the prevalence and nature of venereal diseases, Dr. Magunna was able to posit, with apparent authority, that "all the poor households with daughters functioned as prostitution houses" in Kunming, further noting that pederasty was an endemic practice.[32] Every minutia of Chinese domestic life was interpreted as evidence of a deficiency in sanitary consciousness and understanding. The state of public health was no better, notwithstanding the efforts of Viceroy Xiliang. Canines and swine roamed freely on the streets of Kunming, where prisoners collected refuse on rudimentary ox carts. Public toilets, similarly primitive and composed merely of a cabinet and a diminutive receptacle, suffused the thoroughfares with an unbearable stench.[33] As in other colonial domains, the French doctors' critical appraisals of these local practices were instrumental in accentuating racial demarcations between Europeans and indigenous communities. Such judgements did not contribute to enhancing the quality of life for the local populace, nor did they augment French colonial prestige, despite being ostensibly justified by the purported superiority of modern Western notions of hygiene and wellness.

The aspiration to transform Yunnan into a sanatorium for the Indochina colony met with stark challenges, illuminated by similar observations that were as dim as they were disheartening. When consulted about the feasibility of establishing a sanatorium in Mengzi—a city romanticized by numerous French travelers as "a paradise on earth, where malaria was unknown"—Dr. Barbezieux voiced strong objections. He pointed to the unburied cadavers lying on the surface of the ground, open cemeteries, a general lack of hygiene, contaminated water sources and the ubiquity of infectious mosquitos in desiccated watercourses and rice fields as formidable obstacles to such an initiative.[34] Although the Mengzi consul did not wholly concur with Dr. Barbezieux's contention that Mengzi was within the malarial zone, he found himself ill equipped to advocate for the creation of a sanatorium in the city.[35] Thus, another battle was lost in the ongoing struggle to tap into China's seemingly inexhaustible resources and opportunities through the strategic gateway of Yunnan.

The struggle for cultural hegemony within Yunnan extended into the field of medical education, where it found a complex battleground marked by individual ambitions, diplomatic restraint, and shifting allegiances. Dr. Barbezieux, ever zealous in his pursuit of expending French medical institutions, took the initiative to organize medical courses in response to the requests of Yunnan and Guizhou authorities. Though hindered by a language barrier, he offered supplementary language classes, forging ahead with his personal mission to extend French influence in the region.[36] However, Barbezieux's personal efforts were met with disapproval from French diplomats who found his actions impulsive and beyond the limits of his powers. The exception was Kunming consul Leduc, who attempted to bolster Dr. Barbezieux's work by seeking additional support. Yet, budgetary constraints led the Indochina government to reject the request. The courses were terminated, and five of the thirteen students were sent to Hanoi to complete their education.

The significance of these early efforts was understood five years later when a local Chinese commander struck an agreement with the Italian physician of the railway company, Dr. Mazzaloni, for the treatment of soldiers in the Nanxi area during clashes with Chinese revolutionaries. This maneuver posed a potential threat to French influence, according to the French consul. Upon reminding Viceroy Xiliang of French sacrifices in providing free health services to the locals for many years, the consul was met with sympathy and assurances, as well as official recognition of the French hospitals with wooden tablets.[37] Yet, Xiliang's simultaneous endorsement of the Chinese commander's autonomy—permitting a contract with an Italian doctor—highlighted the multifaceted and pragmatic nature of provincial diplomacy. It also underscored France's inability to impose its will within a relatively marginalized peripheral border province.

Faced with competition from the Italians, who seemed more eager to serve in Yunnan than many of the French colonial agents, the French diplomats viewed the assignment of a second doctor and the establishment of a French medical school as critical necessities. Dr. Feray, then the chief physician of the Kunming hospital, lauded Dr. Barbezieux for his foresight in understanding China's shifting paradigms despite his eventual failure.[38] According to Feray, the absence of a French medical school in Yunnan had driven local authorities to seek assistance from other foreigners. Despite failing to secure the immediate appointment of a second doctor from Indochina, Consul Bourgeois and Dr. Feray, relying on Dr. Feray's language skills, reopened a medical school on July 1, 1909, with nine students. This school later closed in June 1911 due to conflicts between Dr. Feray and the new French consul in Kunming, Henry Auguste Wilden (1879–1935).[39]

Ironically, when Dr. Feray requested a second doctor to aid his medical education initiatives in Yunnan, the Indochina governor proposed appointing an indigenous Vietnamese doctor trained in Indochina, as it would be more cost effective. Consul Bourgeois countered that an Annamite from Vietnam would not be recognized in a foreign country like China, especially where "no one is more antipathetic to the Chinese than the Annamite."[40] In his view, an indigenous (Vietnamese) doctor would be unacceptable to Europeans, mandarins, or the common Chinese and would diminish French prestige. In other words, only a white European man could adequately represent and apply the superior medical knowledge of France. Furthermore, the medical schools in Kunming and other French colonial territories were designed to train practitioners, aides, or nurses, but not top-tier physicians. Thus, irrespective of the personal intentions of instructor-physicians, French colonial administrators intended to run these schools to emphasize both the primacy of modern French medicine over indigenous practices and peoples, and the racial superiority of Europeans.

By the time railway construction approached its final stages after 1908, the number of Europeans, who had been the primary sources of revenue for consular hospitals, diminished significantly. Coupled with significant revenue declines from the railway company, the Indochinese government struggled to sustain the consular hospitals in Yunnan. Amid growing influence from Chinese nationalists and negative reports from French medical experts, the idea of building a sanatorium was already discarded.[41] In early 1909, the French consul in Kunming engaged in negotiations with local officials to transfer the consular hospital's management to the local government, insisting that neither a Japanese nor Italian doctor be appointed as its chief physician.[42] Surrendering the hospital's outdated medical equipment, which was deemed inadequate for Europeans but sufficient for locals, was perceived as a valuable investment to secure future concessions for a European-exclusive hospital. After months of negotiations, the Chinese director of international affairs in Yunnan informed the French consul that the consular hospital was inadequate for the planned military hospital.[43] Hence, they resolved to continue receiving medical services from the French consular hospital until a new facility for military personnel could be established. Despite their concerted efforts and strategic maneuvering, French doctors and diplomats ultimately failed to gain the upper hand in the creation of Yunnan's medical establishment. This failure stemmed largely from their incapacity to mobilize a qualified labor force, a problem exacerbated by budgetary constraints and racial prejudice against indigenous medical practitioners.

Legal Pluralism as a Method of Producing Racial Hierarchies

Although Yunnan never succumbed to formal French colonization, its social landscape had been indelibly marked with the features of a racially segregated colonial milieu by 1904. Europeans lured to Yunnan by the prospect of luminous career opportunities on the periphery of the French empire crafted a distinctive quotidian existence, particularly in the urban centers of Kunming, Yiliang, Amizhou, and Mengzi, where foreign populations congregated in significant numbers.[44] The daily interactions of domestic servitude, sporadic social convocations, communal dining, and annual celebrations such as Bastille Day epitomized the insulated and fortified expatriate existence of the railway agents.

The contrast between European and local ways of life manifested itself starkly on the "dirty and hilly" avenues where the "coolies" accorded foreign employees with military salutes.[45] Despite the railway agents' incessant grievances concerning their security, it was the indigenous inhabitants who found themselves overawed by the alien presence in Yunnan. French engineer Albert Marie's (1875–1940) encounter with a local woman illustrates poignantly the racialization of the Yunnanese by French citizens and the attendant trepidation with which the natives regarded outsiders:

> Despite my low interest in this dirty and filthy race, I can't help fighting off sentiments of pity when I see, on rough tracks, a poor Chinese mother, jigging on her poor legs, on her way to the market, holding with her right hand some kind of brolly, and with her left hand a huge basket full of turnips . . . or other things, and on her back, a little dirty one that screams diligently. As soon as she sees a European person, she goes down in the verges of the road and turns her back...because they are deeply frightened by us. . . . (Yiliang, December 29, 1904)[46]

The legal underpinning for this segregation was encapsulated in the doctrine of exterritoriality. Operating within a pluralistic legal framework parallel to the Qing code, extraterritoriality served as a defensive bulwark for foreigners in China, subjecting them to the legal edicts of their home countries via consular jurisdiction. Far from being antithetical to Qing legal pluralism, which itself accorded disparate treatment to various ethnic constituencies within the empire, extraterritoriality enabled nationals of treaty countries to circumvent retribution for transgressions against the Chinese populace.[47] In Yunnan, European malefactors frequently took refuge across the Tonkin border or commodified the lives of their victims through pecuniary compensations.

In September 1904, a grim tableau unfolded when an Italian individual by the name of Cagnotti assaulted a Chinese merchant from Guangxi who came to Yunnan to purchase opium, for reasons that remained enigmatic.[48] Concurrently, another Italian named Tognetti discharged his firearm at two Chinese workers who had demurred from work on account of illness. The ensuing reports indicated that these two Italians were dismissed by their employers, leading the Yiliang subprefecture to level charges of attempted murder against them, and subsequently petitioning the French consulate to pursue the apprehension of these culprits. French records reveal that Tognetti found continued employment in the vicinity of Mengzi, while Cagnotti's whereabouts remained obscure.[49]

In a parallel incident, two Italians identified as Scala and di Giorgi, both in the employ of the contracting firm Piviotti, shot at two of their workers. One of the workers sustained injuries and received medical treatment in the French hospital in Mengzi. While di Giorgi managed to evade capture, Scala's punishment was monetary, amounting to 350 piastres. This fine encompassed not only a penalty for the violent transgression but also for the breach of the business contract through the employment of such violence.

Further escalating this pattern of brutality, three Italians were implicated in the murder of a Chinese individual on January 10, 1905, an act committed through the heinous method of casting the victim into a ravine. In a move that further highlights the lack of accountability, the contracting company associated with the assailants declined to divulge their identities and actively facilitated their flight. Later that month, on January 27, 1905, an Italian employee named Ghizio escalated a dispute with a group of workers into fatal violence, killing a Chinese worker at point-blank range. He too managed to abscond, aided financially by his employers. An anomalous instance in these grim narratives, preserved in archival records, pertains to the punishment meted out to an individual named Zanini, previously marked by a criminal record in Italy. Singular in nature, his case resulted in deportation, a consequence perhaps stemming from the distinction that his act of violence was directed not to the indigenous populace but against his fellow compatriots.

The exemption of Europeans from rigorous legal proceedings served to entrench the existing racial hierarchy between locals and foreigners, effectively immunizing the latter from the full extent of legal reprisal. A particularly telling instance of this dynamic was recorded in a Hanoi court on December 14, 1904. During this incident, a French employee named Bedel, while aboard an empty ballast train accompanied by two mechanics and one operator, encountered a Chinese worker sitting on the right lane rail.[50] Despite warning signals and the operator's attempts to drive the man away by throwing stones, the worker remained immobile, necessitating the train to stop. Enraged by this inaction, Bedel descended from the train to beat the worker, chasing him for 40 meters before seizing him by the hair. The subsequent assault involved slapping

FIGURE 4.1 Workers taking a break on a stone bridge in front of a tunnel at 232 km of the railway. They were supervised by Italian contractors. ©Archives Cité du Train–Patrimoine SNCF.

the man, throwing him to the ground, administering a kick that resulted in internal bleeding. Bedel then returned nonchalantly to the train and glanced at the worker who rose momentarily and fell again. Forty-five minutes after the incident, the fellow workers of the man found that he was dead. Bedel's trial in Hanoi culminated in a one-year suspended imprisonment sentence, a leniency afforded due to his lack of previous criminal convictions.[51]

The practice of extraterritoriality furnished the legal framework that facilitated such evasion of penalties, but the injustices were further exacerbated by an exaggerated sense of solidarity among Europeans in their opposition to the local populace. This led to situations where European individuals, if accused, would benefit from a collective effort to provide exculpatory testimonies, even when material evidence contradicted their accounts. The consular court often found itself compelled to exonerate the accused, despite discerning the falsehood of these testimonies, and the consequent need for perjury investigations.

The cumulative effect of these legal failings engendered profound disillusionment among Chinese authorities and the local populace. The perception emerged that such crimes were not isolated but part of a systematic pattern, where inflicting harm or even death upon a Chinese person was trivialized.[52] Such was the extent of European contempt toward locals that the consulate manager in Mengzi felt compelled to issue a circular, explicitly admonishing against violence toward indigenous people, and warning of the potential legal ramifications. This formal pronouncement, though reflective of official policy, was somewhat at odds with the underlying reality, where acts of brutality often went unpunished, reinforcing a stark racial dichotomy and further undermining trust in the prevailing system of justice.[53]

If extraterritoriality acted as a shield that emboldened French citizens in Yunnan in their actions against the locals, its absence (for Italians) was a contributing factor to even more frequent abuses by Italian contractors toward railway workers. This dichotomy between the legal standing of the French and other foreigners also provided a platform for the French to assert moral superiority over other Europeans, especially the Italians.

This complex legal landscape became particularly evident in January 1905, following an incident in which an Italian employee killed a Chinese worker. The situation left the Mengzi consul, du Halgouet, in a state of confusion regarding jurisdiction and responsibility. The consul found himself tangled in a question such as whether the pursuit of the offender was a matter for the Italian consul, who, in his words, had nationals "more likely to be involved in this kind of affairs than anyone else."[54] Under pressure from Chinese authorities and company agents to ensure security, the consul faced a dilemma: how to apprehend the culprits without sufficient police forces at his disposal. Moreover, the situation raised critical ethical and legal questions: Should the offender be handed over to Chinese authorities without any judicial process? Or was the consul supposed to "tolerate the acts that we [the French] find punishable even according to the most basic principles of justice?"[55] In this case, the claims of French moral superiority were compromised by the complexities of a legal landscape marked by racial bias and a lack of consistent principles.

The consul's detailed consideration of the situation revealed a legal quagmire under the provisions of extraterritoriality, as this system was rendered inactive when dealing with offenders from nations whose extraterritorial rights were not recognized in China. Distressed by the behavior of the Italians, the French consuls exerted pressure on the French Foreign Affairs to negotiate the establishment of an Italian consulate in Haiphong and Yunnan. Although the Italian Foreign Ministry consented to appoint a consul to Kunming in 1904, this measure did not alleviate the burdens faced by the French consuls in managing transgressions committed by the Italians.[56]

Since these Italians were employed on a project underwritten by the French government, Chinese authorities held both the company and the French consulate accountable for their disgraceful conduct. Until that point, the French consuls had made attempts to refer cases of theft and other offenses to the Chinese judicial system. Nevertheless, many of these inquiries remained unresolved, as the consul reported, due to pervasive Chinese belief that the turmoil at the worksites originated from the Europeans' violent behavior. These conflicts led both sides to regard each other as uncivilized: the Chinese criticized the brutality of European labor practices, while the Europeans disdained the alleged ignorance of fundamental judicial principles.

The consul maintained that the essence of the security dilemma lay in the absence of appropriate and prompt punishment. Given that the Italians were employed by a French company, the shame was destined to be cast upon the French, prompting the consul to argue that the French consulate should handle these cases rather than wait for the Italian consulate's intervention. The Italians' brutality was identified as the primary cause for worker desertions, and it was believed that it would inevitably incite worker rebellion if proper measures were not implemented. As a proposed solution, the consul recommended the construction of a prison in Yunnan, whose expenses would be modest compared to the risk of the entire railway project's failure. This was a pragmatic approach aiming to maintain legal superiority while responding to the practical necessities of an ambitious imperialist endeavor.

Not all French officials shared the same viewpoint on the matter. During a visit to Yunnan in mid-1906 to investigate issues pertinent to the organization of the police force, Indochina Governor Beau arrived at the conclusion that both the French consuls and company representatives were possibly exaggerating the situation.[57] In his assessment, the French gendarme forces stationed in Mengzi and Hekou were performing admirably, despite being numerically inadequate, and were fully respected for their actions and vigor. Governor Beau identified the primary issue as being the Annamites who had been brought into Mengzi to serve the Europeans, describing them as "the dregs of Tonkin cities."[58] He suggested that an identity card system for the Annamites crossing the Tonkin border might be an effective measure, and a similar method could be applied to the railway workers. In addition, he pointed out that the European encampments were prone to regular thefts, largely because the local officials, characterized as "lazy opium addicts," failed to fulfill their obligations to oversee the areas surrounding the worksites. Thus, for the governor, the problem was principally a cultural one. While he acknowledged that Europeans might engage in occasional offenses, he believed that the real problem lay with the Chinese and the Annamites, who were perceived as culturally more predisposed to criminal behavior.

The thefts committed by locals were a recurring point of contention, ranking as the second most aggravating crime in the eyes of the Europeans. Viewed as a direct affront to private property, these thefts were meticulously documented and often escalated into diplomatic negotiation matters between the two nations' representatives. Specific instances of theft, such as the stealing of three horses belonging to Italian contractors on December 17, 1905, and a series of thefts involving horses and cattle in November and December of the same year, were met with particular outrage.[59] During the first half of 1907 alone, European employees of the company reported thirty-five cases of theft, amounting to 48,000 francs in value, leading French officials to secure compensation from the local government for three of these thefts.[60]

According to Kunming consul Leduc, who was expressing the views of the Hekou consul, the thefts and acts of violence against railway entrepreneurs were typically revenge driven, stemming from mistreatment or nonpayment of the workers.[61] Leduc's own observations during a field trip confirmed this assessment. However, when he raised his concerns about the tensions between workers and contractors with the French director of work, the response was dismissive, with the director stating twice that he attached no importance to these facts.[62] Leduc's proposed solution was to exert greater control over the foreign labor force and expand the powers of consular jurisdiction.

Despite these personal convictions, judgments in legal cases tended to favor European staff, particularly if the victims were French. A notable example occurred on October 14, 1908, when Gustave Langrogne's caravan was attacked and pillaged by bandits. Though the crime scene's remote location hindered the investigation, and no suspects were found, the French consulate in Mengzi managed to secure an indemnity from the local administration.[63] This outcome was achieved despite provincial regulations prohibiting travel by foreigners at night and without a Chinese soldier escort.[64] Interestingly, a parallel claim by transportation entrepreneur, Demoulain, who had rented out the horses used by the caravan, was not pursued. The Mengzi consul appeared convinced that Demoulain was trying to take advantage of the incident.[65]

While European personnel could elude the harshest punitive measures through pecuniary settlements or biased legal proceedings, local inhabitants and the Annamites found themselves subjected to draconian sanctions, even for minor infractions such as petty theft. In June 1905, an Italian entrepreneur named Mozzanini claimed that he fell victim to several attacks such as theft, brigandry, and arson.[66] Unsatisfied with French consular officials' pursuit of the matter, he escalated his grievances to higher echelons within the company, ultimately reaching the governor of Indochina. Subsequent inquiries revealed that Mozzanini had lodged two complaints pertaining to theft. Company representatives apprehended three workers in connection with these charges, leading to the conviction of a single Chinese individual.[67] The subprefect of Yiliang sentenced the accused to death, a verdict subsequently deferred due to injuries sustained during apprehension. In a report to the governor, the consuls attributed the issue to Mozzanini's aggressive demeanor.

Within the context of daily interactions, the entitlement of foreigners to extraterritorial privileges precipitated a reimagining of crime and punishment along racial lines. Theft, a crime regarded with utmost seriousness within Chinese jurisprudence, assumed an augmented dimension when perpetrated against foreigners shielded by the provisions of unequal treaties. Consequently, the matter transcended mere legal procedure and invoked diplomatic negotiations. Besides, indigenous methods of punishment, historically ingrained within the Chinese judicial system, became the subject of racial arguments. The juxtaposition of these traditional, ostensibly "barbarian," practices with purportedly modern penal measures such as imprisonment, forced labor, bail, and financial compensation not only drew a stark contrast but also reinforced an arrogant perception of cultural superiority.

Despite the stark power imbalance favoring foreign overseers and the severity of punishments meted out to workers, there were notable instances where railway workers retaliated against their employers with comparable ferocity. For instance, on February 28, 1905, an Italian entrepreneur named Piviotti was murdered, and 500 piastres were stolen from him. Chinese sources attributed the killing to workers from Sichuan who were unable to procure their wages from Piviotti.[68] The workers' satisfaction with his demise was so apparent that company director Guibert reported observing workers celebrating during Piviotti's funeral.[69] During the same year, two other Italians, Buracco and Tiberio, were also assaulted in their residences.

In response to these three incidents, the Italian consul Grimani petitioned the French consulate to lodge indemnity claims with the Qing local government. Viceroy Ding's response was shrewd. While the agreements between China and Italy did not obligate any compensation for losses endured by Italian citizens, he acquiesced to provide modest relief. However, this was conditional on reciprocal claims being acknowledged for Chinese railway workers who had been subjected to mistreatment by their Italian superiors.[70] As a testament to this, Chinese officials narrated an incident near Kunming, involving an entrepreneur, Bourdaret, and his employee, Vial, clashed with their workers demanding due payment. Armed with a revolver and a hammer, the two did not hesitate to use their weapons against the workers. Chinese authorities signaled their readiness to compile an extensive dossier of similar occurrences.[71]

The French consul in Kunming found himself ensnared between the conflicting demands of the Italian and Chinese authorities. He was acutely aware that the Italian consulate would not assume responsibility for the matter, and even if they were to do so, Italy's economic constraints would impede payment of the required indemnities. In his judgement, culpability lay with the company for employing individuals of various backgrounds without adequate scrutiny. In contrast, the company management posited that the monthly subsidy remitted to the provincial government was earmarked specifically for worksite security. They further contended that the ongoing disturbances along the route were indicative of French officials' failure to efficiently allocate these funds, thereby falling short of their obligations.[72]

While French diplomats and company representatives were embroiled in a blame game over the issues at the worksites, Italian consul Grimani dismissed the allegations against his citizens as inconsequential. He articulated a candid explanation for the situation:

> I admit that many Italians treat their coolies in a somewhat brutal way [*d'un manière un peu brutale*], but we must not overlook the fact that among all Europeans, they are the ones who interact most frequently with the natives. The indolent, deceitful, and insolent character of the latter [the natives], along with challenges of mutual comprehension, account for acts of violence that would not otherwise occur. Yet, there is more: you are aware of the thefts occurring along the railway. The burglarized Europeans naturally harbor resentment and are easily infuriated. They feel compelled to exact justice themselves, as local authorities never find the criminals or only penalize those handed over to them.[73]

Here, Grimani framed the issue through racial and cultural lenses. Workers' reactions to mistreatment and their struggles to secure fair compensation were reduced to a mere manifestation of the cultural conduct of "these Asiatiques" (referring to the Chinese and Annamites). Conversely, the Europeans' retaliatory acts were portrayed as a righteous pursuit of justice.[74] Even in instances where Chinese citizens were subjected to violence, the narrative was directed toward safeguarding the well-being and property of Europeans, who were perceived to hold a loftier moral and legal status compared to their Asian counterparts.

This prioritization of European life and property was something that Qing officials were compelled to acknowledge, due in part to the unequal treaty system. Responding to demands from company entrepreneurs, Viceroy Ding granted section chiefs the autonomy to punish the workers on the spot, only reserving the authority to adjudicate severe crimes to local courts.[75] The local government also conceded to the construction of a prison, funded by the Indochina administration. By January 1905, the Mengzi consul was already bemoaning that the prison's surveillance was absorbing half of the city's auxiliary forces.[76] The region's topographical constraints precluded the deployment of these forces elsewhere as needed.

As railway construction progressed, French consuls devised more definitive means of extricating themselves from perplexing incidents involving workers of varying nationalities inflicting harm or death upon one another. In one such instance from April 1907, a Chinese worker killed a twenty-one-year-old Greek company employee named Maltas. The altercation occurred while Maltas was attempting to sell a revolver to the worker for 90 piastres.[77] The Chinese worker offered 70 piastres, and the negotiation concluded with Maltas's death at close range from the very same revolver. The murderer fled to the mountains near the Guangxi border. Although the local governor offered 300 piastres for the criminal's capture, efforts were fruitless. Subsequently, the Greek legation in Paris lodged an indemnity claim against the Qing government, amounting to 20,000 taels.

In situations where Italians were victims to offenses, much like in the case involving the Greek legation in Paris, the French consul in Mengzi was hesitant to pursue the claim. The underlying fear was that such an escalation might imperil French interests in the region.[78] The consul made a distinction between the killing of French citizens, Catholic missionaries in particular, and those of non-French nationals. The individual crimes and crimes perpetrated by organized groups were also different. Under the principles of shared guilt, grave crimes against foreigners would only be subject to indemnity when the liability and guilt of the mandarins or a portion of their staff were demonstrable. Since the lives of missionaries were already safeguarded by existing agreements between China and European powers, the consul concluded that the deaths of two Italians, one Greek, and four Vietnamese subjects over the previous two years were merely common crimes and did not warrant an indemnity. In principle, the same rule was applicable to ordinary French citizens as well. Besides, in the case of Maltas, he was deemed a victim of his own recklessness, as he had violated a consular order banning the sale of arms to the natives. Notwithstanding the consul's personal conviction that the Maltas case did not require indemnity, the Greek legation in Paris continued to seek reparation from the Qing government through French diplomatic channels.[79]

French consuls were growing wearied of the incessant claims made by the company's foreign employees, claims that were mirrored by Chinese authorities. For France, what was at stake was the completion of the railway. Ancillary issues, particularly those not involving French nationals, were considered insignificant compared to the overarching project's grandeur. Moreover, the administration of justice was becoming a problematic matter not only for French consuls but also for all European powers with consulates in China. In May 1907, the French consul in Shanghai reported to the Ministry of Foreign Affairs that out of 156 days of consular service, 115 were dedicated to judiciary services, not including the days spent meditating disputes and consulting with advocates.[80] Both the British and US governments had already established separate courts in Shanghai, and the French press was advocating for a similar division of consular and judiciary services. Ultimately, the French staff engaged in consular service was expected to devote their "precious" time to the expansion of French influence in China.[81]

The French government abstained from implementing any significant measures to regulate consular justice services in Yunnan until the railway's completion. The sole official initiative aimed to alleviate the workload of French consuls in Yunnan was new legislation that transferred judiciary powers from the court in Saigon to the Indochinese Court in

Hanoi for the crimes committed by French citizens in Yunnan. With the completion of the railway, Hanoi would establish direct communication with Kunming and Mengzi.[82] Yet, this new legislation, constrained in its scope, was far from resolving the confusion created by the diverse ethnic composition of the railway's workforce. Further complicating matters was the involvement of other foreign legations in legal disputes. In such a complex environment, the distinction between individual and organized crimes became a primary tool for French consuls, who were reluctant to pursue cases of non-French employees, particularly when broader French interests were at stake.

The focus on organized crimes was not entirely without rationale, especially considering the rise of antidynastic movements and revolutionary activities in Yunnan after 1906. The antidynastic groups led by Sun Yatsen and other revolutionary leaders who had previously been based in Japan were moving to French and British colonial territories adjacent to Yunnan in search of supporters and funds. Parallel to the growth of revolutionary fervor in southern Chinese provinces, incidents of banditry became more frequent, leading to foreign grievances in Yunnan. The Mengzi consul described the situation as a "state of anarchy," while the company managers argued that crimes against foreigners were part of a larger "xenophobic movement" in China.[83]

Several instances highlight the ongoing tensions and threats faced by workers. In December 1907, an Italian contractor named Antoine Valz, age thirty-six, was killed in the Nanxi area while transporting money, with two soldiers unable to stop the attackers. Another Italian contractor, Beneventi, was assaulted in the same area, escaping the initial attack, but succumbing to injuries in a subsequent encounter. The aftermath revealed the bodies of his guard and one Chinese attacker, with only a fraction of the stolen money recovered. A third Italian, Corsini, narrowly escaped a similar assault with the help of a passing Frenchman, who intervened and killed one of the assailants.[84]

According to French officials, the problems in the Nanxi area were exacerbated primarily due to an influx of unemployed railway workers of Cantonese origin. These individuals, struggling to survive on insufficient resources, were involved in acts of banditry, with four Cantonese workers being convicted in the Corsini attack. Meanwhile, the Lolo tribes (of the Yi ethnicity) were reported to pose significant threats to foreigners' assets.

Adding to the complexity, Chinese security forces, despite receiving payment from the company, "lacked rigor and activism," and the soldiers responsible for railway security were accused of collusion with the very groups they were supposed to combat.[85] The commander "Kho," who was in charge of railway area security, was reported to be an "unprincipled" man who constantly demanded money and gifts from contractors. When his demands were not met, railway workers would mysteriously disappear. His officers would ban contractors from cutting trees in the mountains and taking water from nearby lakes and creeks. Qing authorities were at odds with the company over the reason behind the workers' desertions, countering the company's claims about the insecurity in the area with arguments for the company's inadequate supply of rice.[86]

Interestingly, neither the railway company nor French officials in Yunnan recognized the possibility of collective labor resistance among the Chinese and Vietnamese workers until the arrival of antidynastic groups. Part of this oversight can be attributed to a conceptual mismatch between the kinship- or interest-based resistance found among the Chinese workers and the more politicized worker struggles familiar to Europeans. Even if a claim for an organized worker resistance would be more profitable in terms of attaining compensation, equating Chinese and Vietnamese coolies with European workers would have contradicted the underlying tenets of the French civilizing mission. In an era marked by racial capitalism, such a perspective was considered unthinkable.

During the railway's construction, the legal concept of extraterritoriality, defined within the unequal treaty system, functioned as a judiciary device to impose French interpretations of crime and punishment onto the Chinese justice system. This imposition was deeply entrenched in racialized views of the local population and other foreigners. By claiming the superiority of their legal principles, French consular agents could pressure the Qing government into compensating foreign victims of local crimes. Yet, this diplomatic success was starkly contrasted with the ongoing failure to quell workers' widespread defiance.

As the French mission in China undermined the moral and governmental authority of the Qing imperial government, the workers found increased latitude to express their grievances against foreigners, who consistently demeaned them in daily interactions. The complexities of racial and social hierarchy, combined with diplomatic, legal, and economic interests, led to a situation where neither the workers' rights were protected, nor the higher aspirations of the French mission were fully realized. The result was a volatile and tense environment, rife with violence, exploitation, and mistrust.

Conclusion

The French endeavor to connect Indochina to Yunnan with a railway line was an ambitious project, aiming at increasing France's share in the China market. Beyond attracting French capital to the region, the imperialist rivalry over China required France to demonstrate the resilience and merit of its civilizing mission through modernization in fields like economy, education, justice, and medicine. However, the outcome was not as planned.

Instead of showcasing the superiority of systems of justice and fairness, the implementation of extraterritoriality and European methods of punishment produced new racial hierarchies and inequalities. The intermingling of local officials, diverse migrant workers, and European corporate agents exposed the inadequacies and inconsistencies of the French approach, pushing them further into the simplistic categorization of racial and cultural differences.

In Yunnan, as in Indochina and other colonial territories, modern medicine was employed as a tool to exert control and flaunt the benefits of colonial development. Yet, this too fell short of expectations. Despite significant investments in medical facilities and attempts to integrate local populations into these establishments, the high mortality rates among railway workers and the apparent disregard for their well-being undermined the credibility of French claims for superior medical knowledge. Every attempt by French colonists to broaden their cultural and political influence in the region seemed to create new conflict zones and deepen local resentment. Rather than reflecting French grandiosity, these endeavors laid bare the inherent contradictions of the colonial project, ultimately serving to increase layers of antipathy and mistrust among the Chinese populace. The racial categorization, legal dilemmas, and failed attempts at medical superiority all coalesced into a complex environment where France's colonial ambitions were stymied. These ambitions were intrinsically dependent on the effective mobilization of both skilled and unskilled labor, but the negligence, exploitation, and mismanagement of this crucial workforce made it impossible to fully realize the goals of this imperialist project.

CHAPTER 5

Yunnan's Path to Nationhood

Railways, Labor, and Nationalism

DURING THE FIRST THREE YEARS of the construction of the Yunnan–Indochina railway (1903–6), the main impediments to its progress, other than the workers' resistance and mortality, were the physical geography, Qing officials, and the local population. In 1906, a new political actor emerged thanks to the Qing government's attempts to rejuvenate the nation through modern education in Japan and Euro-America. The government-sponsored study-abroad programs produced a new generation of Yunnanese intellectuals and activists who articulated local discontent toward foreign investments and governmental inefficiency into a sophisticated form of nationalist politics that resonated with the local populace. With their participation in local politics, Yunnan turned into a battleground of colonial, imperial, and nationalist ideologies.

In 1902, the Qing government sent ten Yunnan students to Japan for the first time, with numerous others following these in the coming years.[1] Like their Chinese counterparts in Japan, the students from Yunnan quickly became part of the revolutionary movement organized around the Revolutionary Alliance (Tongmenghui) led by Sun Yatsen and other nationalists who aspired to a republican form of government.[2] Initially, the Revolutionary Alliance disseminated its propaganda through its official publication, *Min Bao* (first issued in Tokyo in 1905), but as the movement grew, the leaders decided to encourage the publication of revolutionary journals reflecting China's diverse regions and localities.

In 1906, the leader of the nationalist revolutionary movement, Sun Yatsen (1866–1925), and his companion Huang Xing (1874–1916) personally convened with Li Genyuan (1879–1965), a Yunnanese student who had been sent to Japan in 1904 for military education. The purpose was to convince Li's group about the necessity of a periodical to resist foreign aggression and official corruption in Yunnan.[3] In October of that year, the inaugural volume of the *Yunnan Journal* was published in Tokyo. Up through the Wuchang Uprising in 1911, the opening salvo in the overthrow of the Qing dynasty, the twenty-three volumes of the *Yunnan Journal* circulated among Chinese readers both within and outside China, reaching Japan, Burma, Annam, and Singapore. Throughout its five-year publication period, the *Yunnan Journal* evolved into an influential platform for disseminating news on Yunnan, fostering anticolonial resistance against Britain and France, promoting railroad and mining rights as well as local autonomy, and agitating for the overthrow of the Qing dynasty.

Using articles in the *Yunnan Journal*, this chapter will demonstrate that the Yunnanese nationalists' approach to labor conflicts along the Yunnan–Indochina railway aligned with their broader conception of the creation of a national economy and its implications for local economies. Amid the larger question of nation building and restructuring the economy, Yunnanese nationalists highlighted principles such as economic development, constitutional rule, and local self-government. By applying these principles to the specific context of Yunnan, they formulated an intricate perspective of the local political economy while concurrently aligning Yunnan with an international anticolonial struggle via Vietnamese, Burmese, and Chinese revolutionaries. However, despite successfully crafting a comprehensive blueprint for the project of Chinese nation building, their discussions overlooked the actual needs of the lower ranks of society, whose labor was the foundation upon which the new Chinese nation would be built. For this, among other reasons, their call remained limited to the educated urban elites of Yunnan.

Chinese Nationalist Views on Colonialism and Labor

The popular reactions to foreign interventions in China, which manifested as antiforeignism in the Boxer Rebellion in 1899, evolved into a more structured and elaborate movement in the early years of the twentieth century. Recognizing that random assaults on foreigners, Chinese Christians, or foreign investments served as a pretext for financial reparations and additional concessions, Chinese nationalists began to see restrained collaboration with Western powers as more beneficial than direct confrontation.

Sun Yatsen, a Canton-born physician raised in Hawaii, played a pivotal role in the transformation of Chinese nationalism from a xenophobic current into an organized political movement. Having observed the limitations of government-led modernization, Sun turned to direct action as early as 1894 by founding the Revive China Society in Hawaii and orchestrating an unsuccessful antidynastic uprising in Canton in 1895.[4] His political career as the leader of an overseas Chinese revolutionary movement began with his escape to Japan after this incident. While residing in Japan, Sun participated in the publication of revolutionary newspapers, expanded his ties with secret societies, and revived his revolutionary base in Hong Kong. Between 1903 and 1905, Sun extensively traveled in Europe, the US, and Vietnam to broaden his political network. During this period, he not only engaged with Chinese émigré communities but also established contacts with foreign officials to secure their assistance and recognition, including efforts to reach Indochina Governor Paul Doumer and establish direct communication with French intelligence officers and business figures.[5] Even though Sun's interactions with foreign governments might seem contradictory to the anti-imperialist nature of the Chinese revolutionary movement of the era, Sun was able to convince his peers of his pragmatic strategy and unify various political groups under the banner of the Revolutionary Alliance in 1905.

Chinese revolutionaries' commitment to increasing nationalist consciousness in China was informed by their understanding of China's position in a world dominated by imperialism and colonial competition. In their view, China held a unique status among its counterparts as it was subjugated by both foreign imperialists and the Manchu dynasty that claimed sovereignty over a majority Han population.[6] Sun Yatsen contended that China should be called a "hypo-colony" as it was not enslaved by a single country but all imperialist countries.[7] This predicament, widely debated in a new genre called *wangguo shi* (lost country histories), framed China's survival in a Darwinian world as reliant on a systematic analysis of the world situation as well as acting upon that analysis to metamorphose China into a material site "for the production and performance of new global, national, and local meanings, practices, and histories."[8] While leading nationalist intellectuals articulated their revolutionary vision in *Min Bao*, the *Yunnan Journal* published articles that applied the Revolutionary Alliance's broader perspective to Yunnan's local circumstances.

One of the most urgent themes discussed was colonialism. In the first volume of the *Yunnan Journal*, author Jiang Ze provided a systematic exposition of various types of colonialism (*zhimin zhuyi*).[9] As he narrated, some scholars categorized colonialism according to types of economic activity such as agriculture, commerce, plantation, and mining. Others differentiated between immigration into already populated areas and the opening of new lands for colonial settlement. There were also state-led colonialism and private colonialism. In both temperate and tropical areas, "civilized" countries leveraged their capital to exploit the resources and wealth of others through commerce, agriculture, and industry. Over time, the populations of colonizer countries also began to migrate to these colonized territories for mining and railroad construction. In sum, regardless of the form it took, the purpose of colonialism was to seize a particular land for production and commerce, leading to the domination of a "civilized people" (*wenming guomin*) over a "barbarian race" (*yeman renzhong*). By implication, colonialism was a natural outcome of evolution, which could only be avoided by a solid economic infrastructure and superior military power.

Yunnanese nationalists observed the presence of these colonial processes in Yunnan. First, constant foreign immigration into the province, especially after the beginning of the railway construction in 1903, signaled the initial stage of colonial intrusion. Li Genyuan (courtesy name Xue Sheng), for instance, claimed that French colonists found the climate of Yunnan strikingly similar to that of France.[10] Unlike Vietnam's hot and humid tropical climate, which caused serious health problems among colonists and prompted them to return to their home country within three years, Yunnan's weather was warm, and the climate varied. Li anticipated that upon completion of the Yunnan railway, all the colonists in Vietnam would migrate to Yunnan instead of returning home for recovery. Other authors noted that Europeans involved in the railway construction had already begun buying land for personal use and had opened mines, hospitals, and schools. Given the absence of local investment channels and military forces, the influx of foreign capital and people would inevitably lead to full colonization. Thus, the seemingly "peaceful" means such as land appropriation and civil migration were only the initial phases of Yunnan's colonization.

In addition to the influx of civil colonists, Yunnanese nationalists detected signs of impending military operation. Wary of possible deployment to the Yunnan–Tonkin border, they scrutinized the situation of the French army in Vietnam. Rumors circulated that the French military operations along the border were not targeting banditry, as the French claimed, but rather aimed to expand the French colonial territories. Yunnan's relation to Vietnam mirrored North Manchuria's relation to Russia.[11] In light of the international competition for land and resources, colonizing Yunnan would provide France with a strategic advantage in any potential military conflict in Asia. Likewise, the formation of French police forces to protect the Yunnan–Indochina railway posed a serious threat to the militarily weak province. All these military activities and population movements, coupled with the French involvement in the province's civil affairs, such as medicine, education, and postal services, indicated that Yunnan, though not yet fully colonized, was on the brink of becoming another French colony within less than a decade.

Taking a more radical stance, another contributor to the *Yunnan Journal* posited that the Yunnan–Indochina railway meant the approaching extinction of Yunnan. The author cautioned those who believed the railway would facilitate transportation and improve the provincial economy, arguing that the policy of destroying countries (*mieguo zhengce*) had undergone dramatic changes in the twentieth century. In its new form, it did not require territorial conquest, population massacres, the expulsion of rulers, or the obliteration of businesses. Instead, it worked through "not absorbing land [*zhanling tudi*] but exploiting its essence [*xiqu tudi zhi jinghua*]; not slaughtering people [*shalu renmin*] but annihilating their kind [*miejue renmin zhi zhongzu*]; not banishing officials [*quzhu guanshi*] but leveraging their greed [*liyong guanli zhi tan heng*]; not ruining businesses [*qinrao zhiye*] but usurping their sovereign powers [*an jue zhiye zhi quanli*]."[12] As such, even if France made extensive investments in the province, nationalists viewed them as part of a plan to extinguish China's people, households, and country. The process might unfold gradually, but the end would be swift.

In their resistance against French (and British) colonialism, Yunnanese nationalists drew inspiration from the example of Vietnam. Many articles in the *Yunnan Journal* began with a comparison to Vietnam, or a warning that Yunnan might share the fate of Vietnam in the near future unless the people of Yunnan rallied to protect their country from foreigners and their sovereignty from the reigning dynasty. Their frequent references to Vietnam also originated from personal interactions between Yunnanese and Vietnamese nationalists in Japan. As early as 1905, Phan Boi Chau (1867–1940), a pioneering nationalist leader of the Vietnamese fight for independence, had traveled to Japan to seek military aid for his anticolonial struggle. In Japan, he met with Chinese constitutional monarchist Liang Qichao (1873–1929), who advised him that Japan would not help unless it established its own rule in Vietnam.[13]

During his stay in Japan from 1905 to 1908, Phan acquired considerable knowledge from Chinese reformists and revolutionaries. Most importantly, he abandoned the idea that Japan, a country he considered to be of the same kind, would rescue Asian nations from European imperialism. Chinese activists in Japan, in turn, learned much from Phan, especially from his writings on the Vietnamese experience of colonialism. Liang Qichao published Phan's *History of the Loss of Vietnam*, which circulated widely in China as a crucial text on anticolonial struggle. To rouse the "sick nations of East Asia" against national extinction and the perils of European colonialism, the *Yunnan Journal* published Phan's "A Letter from Abroad Written in Blood" in 1907.[14] In this piece, Phan argued that the population of Vietnam was a burden to France, which only needed the country's abundant land-based resources, not its limited local manufactures. If France could wipe out the local population from the colony, the colonizers could effortlessly enjoy these local resources without the inconvenience of providing for the locals.

Here, it is important to note that Phan's discussion about the extinction of his kind (*wo ren zhong*) serves as a complex metaphor for both the potential physical eradication of the Vietnamese and the loss of their sovereignty, including the erasure of their unique cultural, political, and social identity as a nation. In this formulation, the loss of country (*wang guo*) did not require the annihilation of the people as living beings. This interpretation is supported by Phan's dialogue in the preface of *Questions to Young Adolescents*:

> QUESTION: Today, is our country still there or is it already lost?
> ANSWER: We have already lost it!
> QUESTION: How strange! The land is there! The people are there! Why do you say we have lost our country?
> ANSWER: In order to have a country, you must have three elements: first, of course, is the land; second, the people; and third, the self-determination (meaning that we are masters of our destinies). Self-determination is, however, the most important ingredient. In fact, if the territory is there, but we do not have the right of self-determination, then the territory belongs to others, not to us. You should think about it. Does our country have an ounce of self-determination?[15]

In this piece, Phan underscored that self-determination was the most critical element in the existence of a country. Without sovereignty, the physical existence of land and people alone do not suffice to constitute a nation. Still, he acknowledged the rhetorical potency of invoking the threat of mass killing and colonial oppression to stimulate awareness and action among his fellow countrymen.

Considered together with previous discussions in the *Yunnan Journal*, both Phan and Yunnanese nationalists were deciphering the changing face of colonialism years before Lenin systematically dissected imperialism as the highest stage of capitalism. According to Lenin, the convergence of interests between banks and industrial capital culminated in monopolistic finance capitalism, which entailed geopolitical conflict over the exploitation of labor across the world.[16] The analyses in the *Yunnan Journal* also predated the adoption of terms like "neocolonialism" and "semicolonialism" by Third World activists to delineate distinct forms of colonial domination.[17] As to the historical development of colonialism, authors of the *Yunnan Journal* stated that European nation-statism (*minzu guojia zhuyi*) turned into national imperialism (*minzu diguo zhuyi*) in the early nineteenth century and quickly spread to America, Australia, and Africa.[18] From that moment on, universal principles of equity and justice (*gongli*) were supplanted by the survival of the fittest (*yousheng liebai*), reflecting the harsh realities of global power politics.[19] They argued that Europeans, wielding brute force, brought destructive influences to Asia and undermined sovereign nations through commerce, colonization, loans, and mining. These were often couched in benevolent pretexts such as protection and development, but the real goal, as perceived by these nationalists, was to carve up (*guafen*) countries and exploit the fruits of the people's labor (*zhigao*). In the twentieth century, these goals were achieved even without territorial aggression, through financial means and investments in railroads and mines.

Phan echoed these themes in his writings, equating the loss of his country to the dispossession of the nation's labor because the country was created "by the hard labor of the muscle of thousands upon thousands of millions, spending the flesh and blood of thousands upon thousands of millions, organizing the rice fields of thousands upon thousands of millions."[20] Vietnam was lost because its rulers did not respect the people's labor and lived lavishly, while the people starved, with rotten hands and scorched feet. Thus, his narrative frames the Vietnamese people as the rightful owners of their country, given that their labor had created and sustained it.

Along the same lines, Phan also appealed to the idea of the country's building by collective effort across Vietnam and China. He claimed that it was the Han Chinese (*hanzu*) immigrants from the provinces of Yunnan, Guangdong, and Guangxi who introduced the Vietnamese to advanced agricultural methods and increased the quality of the Vietnamese land during the earlier dynasties. He posed the rhetorical question: how could they [the Chinese] consent to the appropriation of their labor and wealth by the French?[21] During his stay in Japan, Phan made similar appeals to the Japanese to incite opposition against French colonization in Vietnam. In this instance, however, he stimulated Japanese national pride by pointing out that Japan's silence on Vietnam's colonization ran counter to its show of strength in China's northwest against Russia.[22] In the case of Yunnan, where France employed thousands of Chinese and Vietnamese workers, Phan seemed to consider the labor connection a more pertinent aspect to highlight.[23]

Yunnanese nationalists were similarly sensitive to French labor exploitation. For the first issue of the *Yunnan Journal*, they dispatched a special agent to inspect the working conditions at the railway construction sites. The agent reported from the Hekou border that the French compelled every Vietnamese above eighteen years of age to contribute labor toward railway construction.[24] Those who refused faced incarceration or execution by gunfire. He personally witnessed the execution of two Vietnamese and the amputation of two others. He noted that Chinese workers were mostly regular recruits who did not suffer as much as their Vietnamese counterparts. According to this report, only laborers from Yunnan's Chuxiong county received treatment akin to the Vietnamese's because villagers in this area were obliged to pay exorbitant fines if they defied the government-issued work orders. Laborers who agreed to work on the railway had to pay officials for their travel expenses, and many perished on their way back home due to hunger, disease, extreme cold, or other hardships of travel. The reporter himself found the corpses, one near a dike and another under a big tree, of two people who had died a few days earlier and were covered with flies and mosquitos. Overwhelmed with grief, the reporter bought two coffins and hired a local man to bury the deceased. In the end, he could not help but get choked up and kowtow before those bodies.

Many authors who narrated the working conditions along the railway employed a similarly emotive tone and emphasized the plight of

FIGURE 5.1 Workers toiled in groups under the supervision of foreign employees assisted by an interpreter. ©Archives Cité du Train–Patrimoine SNCF.

the Vietnamese workers who, unlike their Chinese counterparts, had no power to resist their colonial patrons. This was due, in part, to the weak yet still extant sovereign rule of the Qing state that afforded some degree of protection to Chinese workers. Nevertheless, the recognition of Chinese workers' relative autonomy does not suggest that the *Yunnan Journal* endorsed the Qing state. Quite the contrary, the journal used accounts of Chinese workers' suffering as a means of highlighting the government's impotence, hence using them for its antigovernment propaganda.

Besides, the *Yunnan Journal* was not the only platform where people expressed their discontent with the official handling of railway affairs. One Yunnanese scholar named Chen Rongchang (1860–1935) castigated the Yunnan governor for luring the villagers of Dali and Chuxiong into railway work by promising extra payments from the government budget.[25] There is, however, scant evidence to suggest that Qing officials coerced locals into working on the railway. In reality, French officials and company representatives lamented the lack of support from local officials, for which they had to collaborate with foreign and Chinese intermediaries to recruit workers in distant provinces. François, the French consul in Kunming, made the following observation on Viceroy Ding's attitude toward France:

> Because the mandarins see the railroad as the first step toward the occupation of their province, they fight against its construction by all their means. . . . The former viceroy Wei also had similar concerns but at least he was aware that leaving the convention unexecuted would cause further troubles, so he acted with sincerity.[26]

Despite the profound antipathy toward foreign enterprises harbored by the higher echelons of the provincial government, the railway treaty obligated the local administration to cooperate, specifically on matters of labor recruitment and land appropriation. For instance, during the work season of 1905–6, the Yunnan Railway Bureau sought approval for recruiting three thousand men from various prefectures of Yunnan.[27] While the official directive generally safeguarded workers' salaries and welfare, the scheme that positioned officially appointed foremen as overseers of workers' recruitment and retention for a minimum of six months likely precipitated Chen Rongchang's accusations.

In this state-regulated recruitment strategy, foremen essentially became investors by depositing funds amounting to a minimum of 1,000 Chinese yuan to start procuring labor. If recruits deserted the worksites before the termination of their contracts, foremen were obligated to cover recruitment fees and travel expenses within twenty days. In case of payment delays, the consulate had the authority to enlist local officials to collect the outstanding amount from responsible parties on their behalf. In sum, workers' desertion had significant financial ramifications for recruiting agents, extending up to the top of the administrative hierarchy, thereby compelling officials and recruiters to suppress workers when deemed necessary.

Another purpose of the sensational plea voiced on the pages of the *Yunnan Journal* was to turn the shared hardships of the railroad workers into the building blocks of a unified anticolonial struggle. In his call to the Yunnanese, Phan explained why France had not occupied Yunnan. The first reason was Yunnan's lack of a harbor, which rendered the transport of French arms and soldiers into the province impractical. Second, the proximity of British forces in neighboring Burma meant that any French encroachment would be met with vehement British resistance. Due to these concerns, France had no chance other than using the Yunnan–Indochina railway as a Trojan horse for gradual colonization in Yunnan. Despite the gradualist and seemingly civilian nature of French colonial scheme, recent military reorganizations along the Tonkin border should be monitored carefully as they could signal a potential military operation.

In addition, Phan apprised his readers that, in September 1906, the French and Chinese authorities agreed on several restrictions on the Vietnamese railroad workers in response to frequent complaints about their unruly behavior. Per this agreement, only Vietnamese with guarantees and identification cards from the French embassy were allowed entry into Yunnan. Once they crossed the border, these workers were required to report to their workstations immediately, stay in worker dormitories, and refrain from interacting with the Chinese populace. Violators of these conditions were subject to severe punishments.

Phan interpreted these regulations as indicative of France's colonial ambitions in Yunnan, with the situation likely to exacerbate once the railway was completed. Against French efforts to segregate Vietnamese workers from the Chinese, Phan advocated for the solidarity of these two groups to counteract French colonialism. Phan was optimistic that the Vietnamese would join an uprising if the Yunnanese rose against the railway. In other words, their liberation hinged on their unity. As Phan eloquently put it, "while the Vietnamese grip the French throat, the Yunnanese hit their back; while the Yunnanese restrain the French arms, the Vietnamese hold their shoulders. [By so doing,] the Yunnanese will maintain, and the Vietnamese will recover their independence."[28]

Although Phan's call to his Yunnanese fellows was well received, Chinese nationalists' approach to Vietnam was ambivalent. In articulating the French notion that safeguarding colonial rule in Vietnam was contingent on the occupation of Yunnan, author Wu Yi noted, "We cannot maintain China unless we preserve Yunnan; we cannot maintain Yunnan unless we restore [*huifu*] Burma and Vietnam."[29] It remains unclear if by "restore," the author implies reinstating Chinese rule or attaining independence. In another piece, author Li Fu proposed reclaiming Burma and Vietnam as part of a national salvation strategy: "What this journal would genuinely celebrate be to annul the mining treaty with Britain and France, buy back the Yunnan–Indochina railway, construct the Yunnan–Sichuan and Yunnan–Burma railways [with native capital], establish local self-government, implement universal education and conscription, bolster the economy, and expel British and French influences from the Red River area. A step further, to retrieve [*shouhui*] Annam, and restore [*huifu*] Burma."[30]

Similar ideals emphasizing solidarity with colonized nations were echoed after the foundation of the Yunnan Dare-to-Die Society in 1907. The society was a militia group conceived in reaction to the government's ineptitude in shielding the province against foreign incursions. In a pamphlet declaring the society's mission, Zhang Chengqing proposed that Yunnan "severe ties with the Beijing government and instigate a revolution grounded in people's patriotic love for their country, province and race [*zhongzu*]; open the province's mines, construct the Yunnan–Sichuan and Yunnan–Burma railways and buy back the Yunnan–Indochina railway; augment the knowledge, discipline, and strength of the people; and deploy five million soldiers with a do-or-die spirit to Annam, Burma, and India to regain their independence. If this is not achieved, the 15 million Yunnanese, akin to their counterparts in Burma, Annam, and India, will disgracefully be reduced to slavery like cattle and horses [*niuma nuli*]."[31] Two supportive letters also extolled the foundation of the society as a beacon for all Chinese patriots, with the avowed aim of "overthrowing the barbarian government [*yeman zhengfu*] internally and eliminating the ruthlessness of the white race [*baixi renzhong*] externally."[32]

Thus, contrary to Phan Boi Chau, who emphasized mutual aid and solidarity between Yunnan and Vietnam, many Chinese nationalists displayed a sense of superiority, envisioning either reclaiming Vietnam from Western oppressors or extending unilateral assistance to the Vietnamese in their struggle for independence. This condescending attitude was likely rooted in their Sinocentric worldview that perceived Vietnam as a country that had once lived under the rule of Chinese emperors until it was "lost" to France. In this perspective, a resurgent China could restore Vietnam to its former status, facilitate its progress, and foster its freedom under the guidance of a modernized China.

Another factor contributing to nationalist ambivalence was the conviction that Vietnam had been lost due to the ignorance of the Vietnamese themselves. When Phan Boi Chau met Liang Qichao in Japan, Liang's advice to him was to make publications and send Vietnamese students to Japan to heighten nationalist consciousness in Vietnam. However, unlike Liang Qichao or Sun Yatsen, Phan lacked an affluent Vietnamese diaspora to back his revolutionary endeavors. By the end of 1907, the number of Vietnamese students in Japan exceeded one hundred, but this was a modest figure in comparison to the population of overseas Chinese students.

An ideological disparity also existed between the two groups. When Phan approached Chinese revolutionaries, the Revolutionary Alliance had long been advocating for republican rule, while Phan believed in the necessity of preserving the Vietnamese monarchy as a unifying force, at least until the French rule was ousted. In the eyes of many Chinese revolutionaries, the perceived intellectual "backwardness" within the Vietnamese revolutionary vanguard, not to mention among the impoverished and uneducated masses, suggested that the Vietnamese were the victims of their own "slave mentality," and had thereby lost their country. The Chinese, in contrast, still had the chance to empower themselves against colonial influences and assist others. Thus, a simultaneously transnational and ethnocentric perspective through which late-Qing Chinese nationalists construed the modern subjecthood in relation to the West as well as to the colonized others, including "China's familiar Other," shaped the political imagination across borders.[33]

Nationalist Political Economy and Yunnan

If labor held such a pivotal role in nationalist propaganda from both the Chinese and Vietnamese perspectives, why did the Revolutionary Alliance leadership turn a blind eye to the idea of mobilizing the miners and railway workers in Yunnan as a strategy against French colonialism? Were they uninformed about worker strikes and socialist politics in the West, or did they make a conscious choice to avoid worker mobilization?

The existing scholarship on Chinese labor history proposes that labor assumed a central role in Chinese movement politics only during the May Fourth Movement. This anti-imperialist and cultural movement originated in student protests in Beijing on May 4, 1919, and led to the birth to the Chinese Communist Party. Indeed, even reformist scholars like Liang Qichao and Kang Youwei (1858–1927) were cognizant of the increasing worker activism and Marxist political theories in the West, despite the fact that Chen Duxiu (1879–1942) first translated and published *The Communist Manifesto* in full in 1920. During his stay in London in 1896–97, Sun Yatsen witnessed numerous worker strikes and social injustices characteristic of nineteenth-century Europe. Upon his arrival in Japan in 1897, unionization was gaining traction among Japanese workers, and *The Communist Manifesto* was available in Japanese translation.[34] In other words, his testimony of class struggle and burgeoning radical theories shaped his thinking as he defined his antidynastic struggle and formulated his seminal work, *The Three Principles of the People* (nationalism, democracy, and people's livelihood).

Scholars generally concur that Sun Yatsen incorporated the principle of people's livelihood (*minsheng zhuyi*) to the alliance program as a counterpart to European socialism. Yet, as Arif Dirlik contends, "socialism in the Revolutionary Alliance conception was not an alternative to capitalism but a means to control it."[35] Although Sun acknowledged that the principle of people's livelihood, as it pertained to the emergence of the subsistence question when machine production replaced human labor and hence induced unemployment, was the main theme of socialism, he interpreted conflicts among different socialist groups as a sign of the fallibility of Marx's emphasis on material forces as the determinant in history. Instead, as he would later propose, following American thinker Maurice William (1881–1973), the struggle for a living in a very physical sense as a more accurate formulation of the social problem.[36] In his words in 1924, subsistence or "people's struggle for existence is one of the laws of social progress and is the central force in history."[37] Unlike Marx, Sun did not see an inherent conflict in the interests of workers and capitalists. On the contrary, he believed that if capitalists enhanced the living conditions of workers, then workers would produce more for capitalists, and their salaries would naturally increase.

Sun's critique of Marxist class theory was not purely philosophical. When he witnessed worker strikes in Euro-America and Japan, he perceived them not as indications of a dynamic society but rather as signals of unhealthy development. Despite their technological and industrial advancements, Western countries had failed to cultivate happiness among their populations. Since his political strategy hinged on the assumption that China should use its latecomer position to its advantage by circumventing the mistakes of more advanced countries, he regarded socialism as a valuable means to avoid the pitfalls of capitalism on the path toward China's national unification. This was especially true if it were implemented through policies of government ownership of transportation and communications, direct taxation, and socialized distribution.

Despite their diverging political views, constitutional reformists shared with republicans the belief that class conflict was not a pressing issue in China. For example, Liang Qichao believed in the irrelevance of class because China did not have an aristocratic class, a consequence of the equal distribution of hereditary lands. Since China's growth relied on the investments of the affluent, the country's priority needed to be the simultaneous protection of both the rich and the poor.[38] Similarly, Sun, in his application to the Socialist International in Brussels in 1905, informed his European colleagues that the conditions of Chinese peasants and workers were not as dire as those of their European counterparts. Because production in China was less mechanized compared to Europe, exploitation of one class by another was a matter of the future. Sun believed this could be prevented through the efforts of the Revolutionary

Alliance backed by the international community.[39] Hence, while class conflict was a peculiarity of Europe for Liang, Sun viewed it as a contingent outcome of industrial production relations, which could be avoided with state-centric socialist measures in an underdeveloped county like China.

For Sun, the primary means of overcoming the capitalist tendency toward inequality was the introduction of a land tax, inspired by the land value tax proposed by nineteenth-century American political economist Henry George (1839–1897) as "the remedy" to "the persistence of poverty amid advancing wealth" and to industrial depressions.[40] George identified land as "the source of all wealth" because it was "the substance to which labor gives the form."[41] Since land did not originate from human labor and was naturally limited, it offered its owners the opportunity to monopolize it as a natural resource, to which others had natural entitlement. Following George's proposal to relinquish private land ownership as a solution to the social oppression caused by monopolization in capitalist societies, Sun and other Revolutionary Alliance intellectuals advocated for government ownership of the country's land as a productive resource.[42] In the scheme of Chinese republicans, the land tax (or rent) would eliminate a major obstacle to industrial production by making national land available for use by a larger group of people, thus preventing its monopolization and future speculation. After all, money spent on land purchase was of an unproductive kind. Revolutionary intellectual Hu Hanmin (1879–1936), for instance, argued that money used for purchasing land was a waste of capital—an act against capital accumulation—that could otherwise be employed in productive or value-generating ventures.[43]

Lü Zhiyu (1881–1940), one of the founders of the Yunnan branch of the Revolutionary Alliance in Tokyo and a writer under the pen name Xia Shao, also endorsed the public ownership of the country's land for communal benefit.[44] In discussing the problem of national sovereignty, he delineated the duties of the state as making use of the country's land, developing people's livelihood, expanding their sovereign rights, and protecting the country against foreign aggressions. In other words, from a nationalist viewpoint, the building blocks of a state were economic development (development of land, in particular) and protection of national territories. Notably, the author employed the term "land" (*guotu*) to indicate not just national borders but also a source of livelihood and economic value. In the first sense, *guotu* was articulated as "territory," and in the second, as land. In this sense, what the authors of the *Yunnan Journal* propagated included but also went beyond the concept of "territorial nativism," as delineated by Manu Goswami in her analysis of Indian nationalism.[45] While Indian nationalists waged a struggle against foreign control of their land and resources, with land playing a vital role in shaping national identity, the Chinese nationalist depiction added complexity to this relationship. For them, land was not merely a matter of identity and heritage; it represented a more fundamental concern related to survival and subsistence.

Building on J. J. Rousseau's theory that a society comes into being when people give up their individual interests for the common good, Xia argued that public ownership of the country's land could only be legitimized if the ruler was elected or chosen by the populace and utilized the country's land for the benefit of all. If the ruler used the land for his personal gain or surrendered it to foreigners, it meant that the social contract was broken. Xia stated:

> China's land belongs to the four hundred million Chinese people, and Yunnan's land belongs to the ten million Yunnanese. No other people can sell/buy or lend/borrow this land. Unless the Chinese are completely exterminated or China sinks into the waters of the Pacific Ocean, our sand, rocks, grass, and wood all belong to us [*guomin*].[46]

Starting from the premise that the Qing government lacked legitimacy due to its failure to recognize national land ownership and protect national borders, Xia reformulated the relationship between the state, society, and the country's land. First, *guotu* as the source of food, clothing, and shelter was not merely national borders; it also referred to resources extractable from the land either through productive activities such as mining and agriculture or through connective features like trade zones and railroads. By ceding these local sources of national revenue in

Yunnan to Britain and France, the Qing government violated the people's sovereign rights, and condemned them to enslavement under foreign rule.

Second, the legitimacy of the central government's rule was dependent on local and national economic activities being carried out by native capital without unjust foreign intervention. The government was responsible for providing conditions for fair competition and creating an environment conducive to the growth of national capital in the form of public and private initiatives. Third, the country's administrative division into eighteen provinces turned them into disjointed entities without organic contact with one another. The unequal allocation of provincial tax obligations functioned as a divisive factor, engendering the perception that wealthier provinces were subsidizing the poorer ones, thereby promoting regionalism. Hence, the path toward national unification and economic development went hand in hand with a comprehensive reform in the tax system. Fourth, since the country—with its land and people—was not the emperor's private property, he had no authority to isolate the country or randomly limit its trade to the borders of his choosing. People should be free in their interactions with the outside world, especially if they aimed to advance their economic prospects.

From a more explicit Georgist standpoint, Xia observed that when new trade zones were opened, foreigners bought lands in these areas at low prices. After certain improvements, the Chinese were then compelled to pay higher amounts to rent or buy back these pieces. This pattern also applied to railroad routes and mining areas, which appreciated in value after foreign involvement. Considering the central government's fragility and the corruption of local officials, he deemed it most appropriate to delegate land protection to a civil initiative. He proposed the establishment of a land-protection institute to oversee the usage of the nation's land and prevent foreigners from purchasing it. The same institute would also be authorized to penalize individuals—with the death penalty, if necessary—who illicitly sold their lands to foreigners. Likewise, local officials who sold or lost lands to foreigners in border areas were to be reported to the central authority for punishment. It was crucial for the institute to cooperate with the government to inspect railroad and mining areas so that changes in land value were effectively managed.

Constitutional monarchist Liang Qichao was highly critical of the revolutionary proposal for government ownership of the country's land. He firmly believed that private property and personal gain were the main factors motivating people for further work and investment. For Liang, China's pressing issue at the time was production, not distribution, whereas the republican revolutionaries maintained that interests on capital, wages for labor, and rents on land collectively made a great impact on production processes. To elucidate this point, author Yan Yi, while discussing Yunnan's primary economic activities, listed railways, mining, agriculture, sericulture, husbandry, tea cultivation, forestry, textile, and commerce as interconnected links in a single economic chain.[47] While mining was a critical determinant in the provincial economy, the transfer of mining rights to foreigners deprived locals of any economic benefits from the region's rich natural resources. Even if locals conducted the extraction, foreigners could balance their deficits and profits by inflating transportation fees, for they had ultimate control over the railroads. Hence, it was impossible to separate production from distribution and circulation, just as it was unfeasible to perceive the economy in a fragmentary manner. It would only make sense if it was viewed as a unity of organically interacting components.

The nationalist views on foreign railway investments in China were a logical extension of their economic understanding. On one hand, Revolutionary Alliance intellectuals advocated for the nationalization of all railway lines to secure absolute control over the national economy. On the other hand, unlike Liang Qichao, who vigorously argued for the protection of native capital to resist foreign domination of the economy, they found foreign investments beneficial, especially given the fact that China lacked native capital to enhance its industrial infrastructure. Railways were crucial tools for enriching the nation through domestic and international trade. Regardless of whether they were built by foreign or native capital, their service to the national economy would not diminish. Indeed, foreign entities often proved more efficient than the Chinese in building railways.[48] In addition, since wages and rents paid by foreigners would increase national revenue, what China needed was not an outright rejection of foreign investments but a robust government that safeguarded its national interests against foreigners. If the government owned the country's land and became the most prominent capitalist, the country and native capitalists would gain further advantages over foreign entities.[49]

In view of the impact of distribution and circulation on production, Yunnanese nationalists believed that leveraging foreign-built railways, which were meant to benefit foreign industrialists and merchants, for the benefit of Chinese commercial expansion was a more logical strategy than completely rejecting them.[50] With this reverse tactic, they hoped to improve Yunnan's mining activities and the human resources of the mining profession through modern technical education. After all, mining was the lifeblood of the provincial economy, pervading popular memory with tales of hard labor, productivity, and work ethics.

Like mining, sericulture, another labor-intensive industry, stood to significantly benefit from the foreign-built railways without requiring considerable investment. In 1908, author Shao Ling drew attention to the potential profitability of silk, a luxury item.[51] Although there were some silk-producing countries like Japan, Italy, and France, their land was limited and labor expensive. In stark contrast, China was the world's largest silk producer, boasting a vast and inexpensive labor force. Taking a leaf from the Japanese model, Chinese peasants should be systematically trained in silkworm cultivation. If Chinese students trained in Japan were strategically assigned to their provinces, silkworm cultivation could see significant progress in a decade. Coupled with the introduction of new techniques and the training of a female labor force, government efforts to sign commercial treaties with foreign countries could bolster exports.

Author Jia Yuan also proposed sericulture as a lucrative alternative to opium cultivation in Yunnan.[52] He stated that even though people were inclined to grow opium poppy, the provincial income from opium constituted only one-third of the potential profits from mulberry farms. Raising silkworms was an easy and highly profitable activity that could be popularized without disrupting farming seasons. Jia claimed if locals converted their poppy fields into mulberry gardens and applied modern techniques, they could easily export their products to France via the Yunnan–Indochina railway. Taking inspiration from Japan, Italy, and France, who opened new schools to teach modern silk production techniques, Yunnan could develop a self-sufficient economy. In addition to sericulture, Yunnanese intellectuals also recommended other labor-intensive tasks like ice making, stonework, sculpting, and can production as replacements for poppy cultivation. While these simpler industries could easily be promoted with the improvement of individual skills and production techniques, advanced industries would necessitate machinery, engineering, and capital.[53]

The juxtaposition between Yunnan's lack of capital, technical education, and certain human qualities such as ambition and open-mindedness, and China's abundance of land and labor oriented the focus of Revolutionary Alliance intellectuals toward agriculture and peasantry as the building blocks of a national economy. In their initial discussions, they considered the peasantry as an obstacle to the nation-building project due to the conservatism and lack of national consciousness among peasants. Shao Ling, for instance, listed the qualities of peasants as follows: they were impoverished and uneducated, which made them narrow-minded and shortsighted, possessing no innovative vision for their production techniques. Their geographic dispersion led to minimal communication with each other and the outside world. They were simple minded, and hence the things they produced were not intricate. Because these qualities rendered them the biggest demon (*mozhang*) to the progress of civilization (*wenming jinbu*), all great powers had to craft complex agrarian policies centered on peasant associations and rural schools.[54] If similar associations were established in China, they would serve to the protection of peasant rights in the market while simultaneously encouraging them to cooperate with big landowners. On a broader scale, peasant associations were expected to negotiate directly with the government and maintain economic balance through their negotiation power, as was the case in developed countries like Japan, Germany, and Italy, where agricultural policies were framed in consultation with peasant associations. According to Shao, if centrally planned and professionally trained by these associations, peasants would constitute the core of Chinese nation building.

Gradually, the debates on agriculture, initially revolving around the issue of peasantry and then the importance of civil initiative and central planning in peasant education and market regulation, evolved into a more systematic approach to agrarian policy under the banner of "agrarianism" (*zhong nong zhuyi*), with obvious inspiration from the Physiocrats. In 1910, author Zhen Ge noted that despite scholarly emphasis on the profitability of industry over agriculture, "there is no industrialized country in the world which did not first develop its agriculture."[55] Britain, for instance, not initially renowned for its agricultural production, made North America its agricultural base. When North America gained independence, Britain moved its agriculture to India, thanks to the wealth and resources from North America. Similarly, Russia prioritized building railroads into Siberia, Afghanistan, and Persia before their defeat in the Russo-Japanese War of 1905. However, after the war, they formulated a policy of expanding into Mongolia, Tibet, and further south into India to enlarge their agricultural base. According to Zhen, everyone in the world, except China, recognized the importance of farming. They utilized scientific knowledge and other modern techniques to enhance productivity, understanding that a stable supply chain for commerce and industry could only be guaranteed through improvements in agriculture.

Zhen's analysis radically differed from Shao's in that he did not see the peasantry as an impediment to modern development. Rather, following Sun Yatsen's theory of people's livelihood, Zhen contended that a country's existence hinged on its people, the source of labor, knowledge, and vitality. Since people's survival relied on the permanent supply of food, clothing, and housing, and since all these material sources originated from agricultural production, Zhen argued that agriculture was the essence of a country. This was why China had to adopt agrarianism as its course of action toward developing a modern economy.

As Zhen Ge formulated it, agrarianism could embark on two different paths. Its horizontal implementation was exemplified in the United States, where a physiocratic policy motivated people to open even rocky highlands to farming. Its vertical application was evident in countries like Germany and Belgium, where governments incentivized people to expand agricultural fields by leaving the profits from the land to those who utilized them. In these countries, governments supported settled communities in addressing their daily concerns, and nomads were granted land with full cultivation rights. Since a country's land was (ideally) the communal property of all, the government had the authority to distribute it among its populace to promote agricultural production. Furthermore, farmers were not just producers; they also defended the country when required. As more people engaged in farming, the number of vagabonds would decrease, leading to a more peaceful and prosperous country with minimal wasteland. Hence, irrespective of the method employed—whether expansion into wastelands or utilization of unused lands—"agrarianism first benefits people; secondly enriches the country, and finally strengthens the state so that it can catch up with the world."[56] In sum, contrary to Shao's view that regarded the peasantry as a deficiency to be eliminated through modern education and government mentorship, Zhen perceived them as a natural resource to be fostered for the creation of a strong nation-state.

Insofar as the nationalists contended against the monopolization of the country's land by individual landowners, they also resisted the monopolization of international trade by certain countries. Drawing on a social Darwinist perspective, they noted the fiercely competitive and uneven nature of the world market, asserting that only those with unified commercial spheres could survive the international competition.[57] For instance, Britain had managed to subsume India by employing the East India Company and expanded its influence globally through commercial syndicates. Conversely, the Jews, despite their advanced commercial and financial abilities, were globally dispersed due to a lack of unity as a nation-state.

The author, who wrote about international trade, identified a burgeoning consciousness among Chinese business circles. When the US banned Chinese immigration, the Shanghai Chamber of Commerce responded by boycotting US products. The same approach could be adopted on a larger scale to further defend the commercial interests of Chinese entrepreneurs abroad. For Yunnan, the author recommended establishing the Yunnan Chamber of Commerce, which would oversee the region from eastern Yunnan to Rangoon, the capital of Burma, with particular emphasis on Burmese trade. The chamber would be empowered to directly negotiate with the British government on trade regulations and the protection of Chinese merchants in Burma. The chamber also required the support of the Chinese government, even to the extent of declaring war if peaceful means proved useless in resolving commercial disputes. The chamber should strive to dismantle the British monopoly in sectors like kerosene, banking, and transportation.[58] In sum, the growth of a regional and national economy depended significantly on the collaboration of different social actors, as well as on the government's protection of commercial rights. Paradoxically, much of this anticolonial proposal mirrors the methods of colonial countries.

As these examples illustrate, Chinese nationalist notions of the economy were not solely driven by a simple desire to enhance the well-being of the populace. Rather, the economy was construed as a social bond uniting China's diverse population around the ideals of a strong state and affluent society, characterized by constitutional rule, national markets, civil society, and modern education. The strength of this national bond corresponded to the extent to which China's local particularities were taken into account, especially if China was to secure a strong foothold in the modern global economy. With its abundant mineral resources and strategic location, Yunnan was integral to the Chinese nation-building project. However, its development necessitated liberation from both the intrusive operations of imperialist powers and the pressure and mismanagement of the Qing central government.

Local Self-Government and Yunnanese Nationalists

It was not only the nationalists who thought about the prospect of China's political system. Having witnessed the superior military capabilities of the West, the Qing central government had long been searching for ways to keep the country intact and the dynasty in power. As republican propaganda started to permeate a larger section of society, the central government responded by initiating another round of reforms, which included opening a national assembly designed to incorporate diverse voices from China's eighteen provinces into the political discourse. Some historians argue that regardless of their limitations, these assemblies represented the first examples of democratic practices in China in that they acted to counterbalance the absolute rule of provincial governors and offered platforms through which popular will could exert some influence over decision-making processes.[59] However, Revolutionary Alliance intellectuals were swift to critique the government program, viewing it as a top-down initiative that would serve to further empower local elites. Still, it is worth exploring why Yunnanese nationalists, who were staunch advocates of local self-government, opposed local assemblies, which might have assisted in the realization of Sun Yatsen's earlier plan of creating an independent state in south China to topple the Qing government.

The idea of "self-government" (*zizhi*) had long been in the background of Chinese political thought and practice, especially in defining the relation between the imperial center and local administrations. Even during periods when the empire functioned as a centralized bureaucratic entity, a significant section of the ruling elite endorsed the idea that the autonomous rule of localities by appointed officials would enhance the stability of the central government.[60] Nonetheless, in the context of the late nineteenth century, pro-Qing intellectuals, including Liang Qichao and Kang Youwei, offered a novel interpretation of this concept, conceiving the institution of local self-government (*difang zizhi*) as the foundation for China's transition to a constitutional regime without rejecting the role of the central government.[61] In their formulation, local self-government was integral to the construction of a modern nation-state because it was through such self-governance that the populace would assume responsibility for their own lives and the country's challenges. On this ground, they reconfigured the long-debated relationship between central control and local autonomy in a way to ensure that even the smallest units of society were incorporated into the national body politic through the mechanism of local self-government. Sharing the neo-Confucian notion that every individual is capable of self-cultivation, and that effective governance hinges more on self-discipline than on laws and institutions, Liang posited that once individuals achieved self-mastery, local self-government would then form the bedrock of constitutional rule.[62] Hence, before developing robust government institutions, it was deemed crucial to foster and encourage self-discipline among the populace by granting them increased autonomy and responsibility in political affairs, while simultaneously enhancing opportunities for access to modern education.

Beginning in 1904, the concept of local self-government gained nationwide significance with the participation of antidynastic groups in debates responding to government preparations for constitutional rule—known as the "new policy" (*xinzheng*) debates. In the reformist press, there were a concurrent emphasis on the concept's Chinese origins in the feudal system of ancient China, and on its manifestation in the West as a basic platform of societal participation in national governance.[63] Through a comparative analysis of these models, both the constitutional monarchists and the republicans concluded that China's path to nation building had to pass through local self-government, which they found to be the ultimate means of cultivating people and developing the economy. However, there was neither a clear definition of the term nor a definitive idea about how it should be implemented. In 1905, the Revolutionary Alliance, in its founding statement, described local self-government as the second stage of its revolutionary plan—martial law—during which the people's will would be expressed through provincial councils, before the enactment of a permanent constitution.[64]

The Yunnanese intellectuals associated with the Revolutionary Alliance began outlining their perspectives on local self-government from the first volume of the *Yunnan Journal* in 1906. In an article titled "On the Essence of Local Self-Governance," author Mo Zhihun emphasized the importance of properly articulating the relationship between a country's people and its state.[65] Mo indicated that the state (*guojia*) and its people (*renmin*) depended on each other for survival. The continuation of nations and countries was based on the population's understanding of this intimate relationship. In "civilized countries," people viewed their state akin to how an infant sees its mother, recognizing that their mutual prosperity could be achieved against the natural laws of evolution only through the vigorous efforts of both parties. In contrast, in less developed countries, state affairs were considered as separate from the individual, giving rise to a belief that people had no rights or responsibilities in the country's management, and that governance was solely the duty of bureaucrats.

According to Mo, China was still in the league of undeveloped countries for not having institutionalized a parliament and local self-government. If government hesitation in ushering constitutional reform policies was a stumbling block, the primary cause of failure was the absence of a nationalist consciousness among the people. In developed countries, people enjoyed self-government—that is, an independent state and individual political rights—whereas in China, corrupt officials handed the country over to foreign powers without considering the voice of the people. This double subjugation of Chinese people to both a corrupt government and imperialist foreigners formed the basis upon which the people of Yunnan had to build their fight for local self-government.

The analysis of this piece makes it evident that the call for local self-government as articulated in Yunnan's revolutionary press was not a separatist cry despite the fact that Sun Yatsen saw the establishment of an independent state in southern China as a tactical move preceding the overthrow of the dynasty and the reunification of the country under constitutional rule.[66] As the author relayed from a Japanese scholar, the tenets of local self-government included the state's independence to make decisions with its own populace, the congruence of personal and public interests, and the recognition of individual rights and responsibilities. By obliterating the division between the state and society, the author was addressing the population inhabiting the national territories (*guotu*) as the agents of national sovereignty. They were no longer the "folk" (*min*) of traditional Chinese political thinking, but rather the "citizens" or "country people" (*guomin*) of an ideal modern nation-state. Their inclusion within the national territories made them such, regardless of their lineage, ethnic, or religious identification.

As illustrated in this example, Yunnanese nationalists deemed local self-government a necessary step in the path toward nation building. It would liberate individuals and localities from the constraints and obligations of the dynastic government. By establishing provincial associations abroad and highlighting their local circumstances through publications, the nationalists propelled their provincial identities to the forefront of a patriotic struggle. To them, Chinese provincial identities mediated their identification with the Chinese land, envisioned to function as a cohesive socioeconomic entity.[67] In this sense, the nationalist goal was not to segregate Yunnan from the imperial center, but rather to develop it as a self-reliant unit within a holistic, organically integrated entity.

Likewise, they conceived local self-government and the central state as mutually reliant. Without governmental protection of national territories, localities would forfeit their land and resources to foreigners, as in the case of the Yunnan–Indochina railway. Conversely, without the development of local economies, the state (whether dynastic or constitutional) would lose its revenues and sources of legitimacy. The government could only endure the tribulations of natural evolution in a Darwinian sense by transforming local actors into active agents in politics and the economy. In this regard, like earlier Chinese scholars who saw local self-government as a means to reinforce dynastic rule by integrating localities into its own functioning, Yunnanese nationalists perceived local self-government as a potential tool for mobilizing local populations toward the territorial and economic unification of the country.

For the purpose of national unification, Yunnanese nationalists dismissed all divisive factors within localities, such as class, religion, and ethnicity. Xia proposed that the local mines should be managed through local cooperation: the rich would invest the capital, the educated would contribute ideas, and the poor would supply labor. The author ruled out any potential conflicts of interest among these groups. As to the ethnic minorities living in the border areas under local chiefs, Xia surmised that their troubles mostly arose from the cruelty of the Qing-appointed officials. With the establishment of a civil land-protection institute, these disputes would be impartially monitored, and the rights of local chiefs would be preserved. It was part of the nationalist economic strategy to encourage migration from densely populated provinces to these sparsely populated border regions to promote cultivation. Hence, even while the author argued for respecting and studying local lifestyles, his economic planning paradoxically necessitated a degree of social engineering. There was no plan, nor even consideration, of how to harmonize the demands of a modern economy with the local ways of life.

Everyone harbored distinct political motives for endorsing local self-government. While nationalists found it useful as a first step for forging a national subject who would rationally work for the common good, the Qing government was increasingly alarmed about losing popular support due to Western imperialist intrusions. Particularly after Japan's triumph over Russia in 1905, it became evident that a significant overhaul of the imperial administrative system was a dire necessity to reclaim local elites back under the imperial rule. These elites were expected to fill the void created by the inability of the central government to deliver local services.[68] Bearing these factors in mind, the imperial court launched a reform program known as the "New Policy." The term "self-government" (*zizhi*), used by constitutionalists, was a direct adoption from the German-inspired ideas of Japanese prime minister Yamagata Aritomo (1838–1922).[69]

The crux of the New Policy reforms lay in the establishment of a National Assembly, organized from county- to provincial-level assemblies. After a brief closed-door discussion among higher-ranking officials, and largely based on the suggestion of Zhili governor Yuan Shikai (1859–1916), the Qing dynasty decreed in September 1907 to establish a National Assembly. In October, provincial governors were instructed to establish provincial assemblies, composed of bureaucrats and gentry, which were envisioned more as advisory boards than local parliaments.[70] In July 1908, the court promulgated the Charter for Provincial Assemblies and Charter for the Election of Provincial Assemblymen, which accelerated the establishment of government bureaus to prepare for the elections and assemblies.

The reform directives from the central government took effect in Yunnan immediately. The initial wave of local reforms entailed the restructuring of the administrative units and offices, followed by the creation of new departments focused on police and commercial services. The Yunnan Provincial Office for Self-Government was established in 1908, helmed by representatives from the bureaucracy and gentry. The office organized units to study self-government theory and conduct social surveys.[71] Advisory boards for commercial enterprises were also set up the same year. By the time of the dynasty's overthrow in 1911, Yunnan had successfully instituted both provincial and county-level self-government bureaus.[72]

The Revolutionary Alliance leadership, notably Sun Yatsen, who radically opposed constitutional monarchy, elaborated on the government preparations for constitutional rule in the way they approached the question of local self-government.[73] In late 1908, Xia Shao, whose reasoning on the necessity of local self-government we have just reviewed, severely criticized the government- and gentry-led efforts for the creation of a national assembly. Xia contended that constitutions and parliaments could fulfill their purposes if they emerged from the people's national consciousness and sovereign thinking. He argued that the provincial assemblies initiated by the Qing government had been designed to use the power of the Chinese people for the dynasty's benefit and for a select number of elites who stood to gain from potential parliamentary positions.

In formulating this argument, Xia's main targets were the constitutional monarchists, led by Kang Youwei and Liang Qichao, who were competing abroad with Sun Yatsen's Revolutionary Alliance for funds and ideological hegemony. Xia cited a letter sent by Chen Jingren (1868–1939), the son of a prominent overseas Chinese leader in Singapore and a disciple of Kang Youwei, to the imperial bureau in charge of constitutional preparations. He denounced the expectations of the constitutional monarchists, stating that their sycophantic overtures to the government would not result in a Japanese-style parliament where they could promote their personal interests. While Chen's letter praised government attempts and appealed for the expedited progression of the reform program, Xia noted the conspicuous absence of constitutional rights, such as the right to life, equality, freedom of speech, or the right to organize and petition. He claimed that "this gang of scoundrels" (*huqun goudang*) was duping the Chinese into a plot designed to empower the government by helping it raise taxes and conscript soldiers.[74] Xia further contended that since China lacked an aristocracy, these individuals were trying to form a new class of nobility (*guizu*) through the creation of a cabinet similar to the British/Japanese House of Lords (*guizu yuan*). Xia opined that the upper echelons of society, desirous of joining this new nobility, and those in local advisory boards and local self-government bureaus, who attained their positions through personal networks and family wealth (except for a few), were awaiting opportunities to enrich themselves through these channels. For Xia, then, the issue was not the inefficiency of institutional reforms, but the possibility of new class stratifications that could prove disastrous, given the pervasive corruption among China's ruling elites.

In constructing a parallel with the Japanese board of senior statesmen (*genrô*), Xia observed that its members were instrumental in Japan's modernization. In China, on the contrary, the counterparts to these individuals were responsible for instigating the massacre of their fellow citizens and facilitating Japanese domination of East Asia. Xia's sarcastic commentary emphasized that, with nobles like these, China could certainly boast the world's most formidable House of Lords! Xia continued his satire by ridiculing Chen's claim that China's parliament was different from those of other nations, and that no political theorist could prescribe the optimal path to constitutional rule in China. To Xia, China's distinctiveness was clearly manifest in its practice of local self-government: the head of the local self-government bureau was an ordinary scholar, its advisory board was chosen by individuals with personal endorsements, and the entire process was contingent on the approval of the provincial governor. Anything but the will of ordinary citizens was reflected in these bureaus.

Contrary to the Chinese exceptionalism argument of the constitutional monarchists, Xia subscribed to the universalism of human rights, including political rights and freedoms. Without these, he believed that a constitution and a parliament would only bolster monarchic rule and empower a small group of elites at the expense of common people. He asserted that autocracy took many forms, and constitutionalism could easily devolve into one such form if the populace did not enhance their understanding of sovereign rights. The same author who previously advocated for the unified struggle of society's lower and upper strata for national salvation was now warning the poor peasants and workers against the malevolence of an avaricious gentry. Despite his antipathy toward the gentry and the implied reference to social conflict, Xia chose not to exacerbate these conflicts. To him, such conflicts were not inherent to social relations; instead, they were mere anomalies resulting from people's lack of national consciousness, regardless of their social status.

The way Revolutionary Alliance intellectuals situated Yunnan within a broader Chinese national context underlines that the nationalist notion of local self-government was diametrically opposed to separatist and divisive politics. In 1907, author Wu Yi explained how societies transition from inorganic to organic states gradually.[75] Initially composed of discrete parts, these small units eventually coalesce into a larger whole through the interplay of laws, education, rituals, agriculture, and industry. As societies mature, a shared social life emerges, until external attacks occur. Wu, in his analysis of other countries' administrative models in comparison to China's, proposed that a federal structure would best accommodate the needs of a vast country like China. He noted that, due to limited transport technologies, the imperial army cannot protect the borders against foreign invasions, while foreigners could easily reach their destinations through their cross-border railways.

Yunnan, for instance, did not possess a sizable army due to the restrictions from the central government. In case of a foreign attack from Annam or Burma, the intruders could swiftly use the Yunnan–Indochina railway to deploy their weapons and troops, while the Qing central government would struggle to mobilize its forces. If Yunnan, the gateway to southwestern China, were to be conquered, other parts of the country would quickly follow. Worse still, as per established international agreements, if one country occupied China, others would be permitted to do the same. Thus, Wu concludes, Yunnan, as an integral and indispensable part of China's national unity, should be allowed to manage its local resources in line with the local community's needs, including the investment in a local army. With these considerations in mind, the autonomous rule of Yunnan was justified only to the extent that it served the protection and development of the country.

Conclusion

As the twentieth century dawned, China was beset by distinct circumstances. The encroachments of imperialist and colonialist powers not only instigated a redefinition of the Qing imperial government's sovereignty but also gave birth to new political actors seeking to uphold China in a world governed by the rule of the survival of the fittest. Amid intense capitalist competition, Chinese nationalists proffered the concept of a Chinese national subject, an individual primed through self-discipline and modern education to subordinate personal interest for the nation's collective welfare. The envisioned postdynastic republican state would then foster an environment conducive to realizing this ideal subject's potential, characterized by civil initiative, local self-governance, fair competition, and the protection of native capital through taxation, commercial treaties, and commercial and industrial infrastructure.

Chinese nationalists, in their pursuit to elevate Yunnan to the epicenter of the national struggle for self-determination, adopted a developmentalist and social Darwinist outlook. This perspective, which prioritized nation building over the everyday hardships of common people, forestalled them from identifying labor as the cornerstone of China's sociopolitical overhaul. Notwithstanding their warnings about the new class hierarchies potentially arising from the Qing government's New Policy reforms, figures like Sun Yatsen and numerous republican revolutionaries settled on the idea of responsible citizenship, inspired by a slanted view of the Japanese model, as opposed to mobilizing working masses for a potentially divisive class struggle. As we will see in the discussion of the railway-rights movement in the next chapter, their calls for labor mobilization were primarily directed toward an interracial context, with the foreign colonizer, whether French, British, or Manchu, being the primary target of such protest.

CHAPTER 6

Nationalist Activism and the Completion of the Railway

THIS CHAPTER SEEKS TO ADDRESS the question of the nature of activism embraced by Yunnanese nationalists between 1906 and 1911, considering both the economic and political aspects. The nationalist activism during this period can be seen through two interconnected dimensions, which were closely tied to the nationwide struggle against the ruling dynasty and the challenges posed by imperialism. The first dimension focused on the anti-imperialist arguments put forth by the Revolutionary Alliance. As we saw in chapter 5, Alliance intellectuals believed that railways were crucial for territorial integration and economic prosperity, as they would facilitate domestic and international trade networks. However, the loans acquired by the central government for railway projects resulted in unearned profits for imperialist powers through interest rates, while also jeopardizing national security by granting foreigners control over China's railway system. Thus, despite their direct opposition to the ascendancy of local elites through government-led preparations for constitutional rule, the nationalists did not hesitate to join the movement for railway rights, which was led by a coalition of Qing-friendly gentry and bureaucracy.

The second dimension of nationalist activism was centered on the antidynastic political agenda of the Revolutionary Alliance. While collaborating with bureaucrats and gentry to reclaim control over foreign-built railways and construct new railway lines, the nationalists did not abandon their primary goal of overthrowing the ruling dynasty. With the nationalist wind behind their back, they intensified their armed struggle in southern provinces to initiate a wave of uprisings that would ultimately bring an end to the dynasty's autocratic rule.

Historians have approached the movement for the recovery of railway rights from different angles. Chinese socialist historiography interprets this movement as a significant phase of the bourgeois revolution in China (the foundation of the republic in 1912 is understood to be the bourgeois revolution that predated the socialist revolution of 1949). On the other hand, Western scholarship had predominantly sought to identify the sprouts of democracy within the mass mobilizations of this period.[1] Despite their fundamentally different viewpoints, both perspectives share the common belief that social mobilizations during this period were characterized by "elite activism."[2] Although lower layers of society participated, the tone of mass politics was determined by elite groups, including bureaucrats, merchants, landowners, intellectuals, and other educated segments (referred to as the *bourgeoisie* in socialist terms and the *elite* in nonsocialist historiography). This social stratum emphasized maintaining a "civilized" opposition to foreigners, in contrast to the earlier acts of violence against foreign lives and properties, such as the Boxer Rebellion.[3]

This chapter agrees with the aforementioned approaches in recognizing the detachment of late-Qing elite mobilizations from the lower ranks of society. However, it shifts the focus from the intended outcome of political mobilization, whether democracy or socialism, to the limitations of nationalist developmentalism and its political implications. In so doing, the chapter suggests that the failure of nationalist mobilizations in this period was not solely due to the inability to establish a unified nationalist politics with democracy and civic institutions at its core. Rather, the failure can be attributed to the neglect of diverse political subjectivities that emerged from people's everyday interactions within the distinct circumstances of the early twentieth century. Subjectivities among railway workers were multifaceted and cannot be simply contained within the categories "nationalist democratic" or "economic developmentalist." The late-Qing elite failed to acknowledge these nonhegemonic tendencies. Due to this shortcoming, neither Chinese nationalists (revolutionary or reformist) nor Western imperialists fully grasped the political significance of everyday forms of resistance within diverse local settings, particularly those deemed "uncivilized." Moreover, due to this oversight, the unresolved sociopolitical tensions of the late Qing period carried over into the next revolutionary phase that started with the foundation of the republic. This chapter will outline the history of the recovery of the railway rights movement in Yunnan and end with a brief discussion of how, by the end of the long construction process, France was still far from rendering itself a hegemonic power in the region.

The Movement for the Recovery of Railway Rights in Yunnan

Beginning with the successful campaign to regain control of the American Canton–Hankou railway concession in 1904–1905, the movement advocating for the recovery of railway rights evolved into a nationwide crusade against foreign investments in China.[4] This movement, led by patriotic officials, students, and gentry, and interpreted by Chinese scholars as a precursor to the republican revolution in 1911, rapidly spread to other provinces, including Zhejiang, Sichuan, Anhui, and Shandong.[5] The initial purpose of the movement, when the government launched it, was to transfer the rights to build railways to private unions or companies founded by provincial entrepreneurs. By acquiring foreign loans through private means, the government aimed to create a national railway network without political liabilities.[6] Therefore, while the Qing government was at the center of diplomatic negotiations for reclaiming control over foreign-built railways, local investors emerged as the primary financial beneficiaries of the planned railway projects.

Over time, this model, advocating for private ownership as a strategy to circumvent foreign involvement in the railway industry, intensified tensions between the Qing government and local elites, as provincial railway unions were established wherein these elites held significant vested interests and the line between these interest groups and government authority was not clearly demarcated. In 1911, when the government decided to nationalize the Chengdu railway—initiated with local capital but not completed within the designated timeframe—local discontent erupted into violent social upheaval, marking the initial phase of events that ultimately led to the overthrow of the dynasty by the end of that year.

The movement for railway rights gained momentum in Yunnan when the British government expressed its intention to construct a railway connecting Burma and Yunnan, as a counterpart to the French railway stretching from Haiphong to Kunming. In the face of Russian and Japanese rivalry in northeastern China, Britain and France had reached an agreement on October 2, 1905, which stipulated that the Hankou–Sichuan railway, along with a potential extension of the Yunnan railway into Sichuan, would be built by an Anglo-French syndicate.[7] Similar to France, Britain was hoping to connect its Burma colony with the Sichuan market through the railways constructed under this Anglo-French partnership.[8]

To Chinese nationalists and railway-rights activists, the Anglo-French entente served as further evidence of European powers' joint commitment to carve up Yunnan, enslave its people, and ruin local society.[9] Upon learning about the British intentions, Chinese students in Japan and at the headquarters of the Yunnan–Sichuan Railway Company initiated a campaign against the British scheme.[10] Numerous telegrams were sent to Beijing and publicized in the *Yunnan Journal*, arguing that there was no treaty between China and Britain that granted British businesses the right to build the Yunnan–Burma railway. They emphasized that railway construction was a matter of national sovereignty. The case of the Yunnan–Indochina railway, which had been lost to the French due to a lack of timely planning of local actors, served as a clear example. Having learned from this lesson, the railway activists urged Qing officials and the Yunnanese gentry to prevent British involvement in the issue before it became too late.[11]

The idea of purchasing the Yunnan–Indochina railway from France emerged in the midst of discussions on how to prevent the British from constructing the proposed Tengyue railway from Burma to Yunnan. By buying back the almost completed French railway, the Qing government aimed to demonstrate its commitment to eliminating all foreign involvement in railway construction. In January 1907, the vice-president of the Chinese Foreign Affairs Bureau invited the French minister in Beijing to discuss the recovery of the Yunnan–Indochina railway. Initially, the French Ministry of Foreign Affairs responded negatively for several reasons. First, they believed that China lacked sufficient funds to pay for the railway, and that applying for a foreign loan would increase China's dependence on another foreign power. Second, transferring the railway before its completion would raise doubts about French capabilities, as had already been criticized in the Chinese press on multiple occasions. Third, it would eliminate the possibility of extending the French railway into Sichuan, which was seen as a potential lucrative trading hub.[12]

In the meantime, Chinese students in France initiated a campaign for the retrocession of the Yunnan railway. Offended by the colonial exposition in 1906, where French organizers exhibited products from Yunnan under the label of "Yunnan" in Chinese characters, implying that Yunnan was their colonial territory, and irritated by frequent publications in the French press on Yunnan's wealth and resources, the students concluded that Yunnan was under serious threat from French expansionism.[13] Even if they were willing to cooperate with foreign engineers in building new railways, the students demanded that the chief engineers of the planned railways be selected from among Chinese students who had received education abroad.

As part of the same campaign, the Yunnan–Sichuan Railway Company embarked on a search for funds to finance the construction of the Sichuan and Tengyue (Burma) railways, as well as the repurchase of the Yunnan–Indochina railway, which required a total of 10 million taels. Considering the limited financial resources of the province, the company understood that raising this amount through individual contributions would take eight to ten years.[14] Xiliang, the patriotic viceroy of Yunnan and Guizhou provinces, who had previously initiated the Sichuan–Hankou railway union with local capital, sought assistance from the Qing government but received no help.[15]

Another potential strategy involved expediting the establishment of self-government bureaus in local counties so that they could effectively monitor property and professions in each household and impose railway taxes accordingly. However, this approach also required considerable time for implementation. Consequently, before these methods could be realized, the Yunnan–Sichuan Railway Company decided to seek the aid of officials of Yunnanese origin, who served in different parts of China.

In collaboration with the managers of this Chinese company, Governor Xiliang reached out to these officials through a letter where he likened the dire situation of Yunnan to "a burning house or a drowning man."[16] He accused those who refused to help of lacking patriotism.

The French consul in Canton viewed Xiliang's efforts as merely "naïve," firmly convinced that the Chinese side would never be able to amass enough funds to buy back the railway or construct new lines.[17] Nevertheless, Xiliang remained persistent in his endeavors. He pressured the local gentry, urging them to purchase railway shares, and slightly increased land taxes beginning with the lands owned by Christian churches.

While the governor was actively taking practical steps to nationalize railways, the nationalist press continued to highlight the French scheme of colonizing Yunnan through indirect means. In November 1907, the *Yunnan Journal* published a report written by their agent, who was dispatched to the province for a firsthand investigation.[18] Overall, the agent's report was in line with the prevailing arguments of the nationwide campaign against foreign-built railways. According to the report, the Yunnan–Indochina railway was the pivot of French colonialism in Yunnan. Its main purpose was to clandestinely transfer French munitions into the province. The railway guards, predominantly situated in Mengzi, were seen as the vanguards in the service of French expansionism. And French agents were suspected of planning to use Vietnamese immigrants as a means to establish colonial infrastructure in Yunnan.

Aside from these general arguments against the French scheme, the agent shared his personal observations about the harsh working conditions of the railway workers to raise awareness among the locals about the cruelty imposed by foreign forces. The working conditions were described as extremely challenging, with workers facing a tropical climate characterized by unbearable humidity, continuous fumigations to combat diseases, and contaminated water and soil. The terrain included mountains, cliffs, and rocky areas that were difficult to work on. Moreover, the workers received low salaries, paid high prices for rice, and had to deal with brutal foremen. The agent highlighted the plight of sick workers who were sent back to their hometowns, only to face death from hunger or disease shortly after their departure. The roadsides were scattered with the bodies of these deceased workers. In response to the grim situation, compassionate local communities had established "coffin societies" to provide free coffins for the dead and ensure they were buried properly. However, their benevolent efforts could only help half of those in need. Even if the reporter did not state it explicitly, his descriptions hinted at the view that these dead bodies were symbolic of the decline of Chinese national strength and dignity.

The agent's observations also revealed that the workers faced significant challenges in receiving their payments. Foreign employers, aware of the mortality rate among the workers, deliberately withheld their salaries until the middle of the month so that the salaries could be confiscated in the event of their death. As a result, conflicts with the employers over incomplete payments were frequent, and in many instances, these disputes escalated to physical violence, with workers being beaten or shot. The presence of armed Vietnamese, French, and Italian guards further exacerbated the oppressive atmosphere. These guards would punish workers they perceived as "idling around" with fists or flying kicks. The workers lived in fear and distress whenever they encountered these "yellow-faced guards in Western uniforms" (*yangzhuang er mianhuang*). The reporter conveyed that Westerners (*xiren*) treated Chinese railway workers with little regard, no better than cattle and horses (*niuma*).

Throughout the text, the reporter consistently referred to the employers as "the French" (*faren*), even though only a limited number of actual French individuals were business owners. In reality, it was mostly Italian contractors who were in charge of construction and resorted to violence against the workers. However, for the reporter, foreign contractors, regardless of their national identity, represented the epitome of European cruelty against the colonized people of Asia. Consequently, the reporter framed the conflict as a confrontation between the yellow race and the "Latin people/race" (*lading minzu*).

Despite his animosity toward "French" business owners in Yunnan, the reporter did not shy away from criticizing his fellow Chinese compatriots. He viewed the Chinese foremen and members of the railway inspection committee as more culpable for the workers' suffering than the foreign personnel. These collaborators were deceived by French promises and held hopes of receiving official ranks and salaries if France were to turn Yunnan into their protectorate. With its accusations against the corrupt character of officials, the agent's report raised doubts about whether a national company would have provided better working conditions.

Similarly, the workers themselves were also seen as making sacrifices, exchanging their "precious lives and bodies" (*zui baoshan zhi shengming xuzhi*) for money. The agent's report does not clearly suggest that the workers should boycott France or quit working on the railway. Instead, his argument seems to be directed elsewhere. He acknowledged that since the Yunnanese lacked the resources to complete the railway on their own, and given the significance of railways in creating a national economy, there seemed to be no alternative but to wait for the completion of the project. Hence, it becomes evident that the overt concern shown for the workers' well-being might have been more of a rhetorical strategy, appealing to antiforeign sentiments rather than genuine proworker solidarity.

By implication, the nationalist writings conveyed the notion that the railway workers were not active subjects but passive objects in the anticolonial struggle. They were portrayed as enduring suffering at the hands of Westerners, and their ubiquitous struggles for dignity or survival were not seen as constituting a genuine political struggle for the observers. For Yunnanese nationalists aligned with the Revolutionary Alliance, their intellectual and nationalist agenda represented the authentic political struggle. In this context, the author of the piece that included the field report suggested that a solution to the lack of nationalist consciousness among the foremen and workers could be achieved through modern education (*rexin jiaoyu*). This proposal implied that true politics could only emerge with the rise of nationalist consciousness, and that meaningful political action was only possible when such consciousness was cultivated.

In early 1908, after the French railway company was bailed out by the French government with an additional subsidy of 53 million francs, the French mission in China revised its initial refusal to hand over the

Yunnan railway to the Qing government. During a brief conversation in the capital, Qing Foreign Minister Zhang Zhidong inquired about the French government's stance on the recovery of the Yunnan railway. Zhang proposed that if the Qing government could revoke the French concessions in the region, it would strengthen China's position to resist British demands to extend the Burma railroad into Yunnan.[19] Considered this way, the Chinese intention to purchase the Yunnan railway appeared less irrational to the French side.

The change in the French attitude was further bolstered by a report prepared by the Mengzi consulate, which indicated that the construction of the railway had turned out to be "a disastrous affair" from a financial perspective, and selling the railway might cover at least some portion of its costs.[20] Several reasons were cited for the failure of the railway project up to that point. First, the actual cost of the partial construction had already exceeded the estimated cost of the entire project by 40 million francs, even before completing all the work. Second, due to the railway being built on a different route than originally planned, the line bypassed the most populous and commercially vibrant regions of the province. This meant reduced profits from cargo services. When factoring in the estimated operation and maintenance costs, it became evident that the railway was financially unviable.

The Mengzi consulate was not oblivious to the political implications surrounding the railway project, but they admitted that the changing political climate, marked by the rising tide of nationalism in China, would make it increasingly difficult to operate the railway. The prevailing nationalistic sentiment in China viewed domestic railways as beneficial but considered the foreign-built ones as detrimental to national interests, as they could potentially serve the agenda of foreign intruders. On the other hand, transferring the railway to China before its completion carried the risk that the project might never be finished and the French ambitions to penetrate China would be permanently thwarted. To navigate this delicate situation, the Mengzi consul proposed "alluding to the nationalistic spirit of the Chinese, which was manifest to the highest degree" at the time, and initiating negotiations immediately while the Chinese authorities were still unable to accurately assess the actual costs and profits of the railway. The consul suggested finalizing the sale for the postconstruction period, sacrificing some portion of the costs if the Qing government guaranteed favorable conditions to French businesses for future railway operations.[21]

The apprehension about the railway's ability to generate expected returns was not confined to the French representatives in Yunnan. An English-language periodical published in Beijing expressed similar concerns and described the railway's prospects in a similarly pessimistic manner. The article concluded that it was unreasonable to expect China to take over a project of this scale, which they characterized as a "white elephant."[22] According to the author, the railway might eventually be viewed as a significant blunder on the part of France.

Chinese nationalists were not concerned about the potential profitability of the railway; instead, they viewed it as a symbol of Yunnan's anticolonial struggle. The propaganda for the railway's recovery was so fervent that nationalists firmly rejected any arguments to allocate local resources to the planned, as-yet-unbuilt Yunnan–Sichuan railway, preferring to use those resources to purchase the partially constructed Yunnan railway. As the completion of the railway approached in 1910, authors of the *Yunnan Journal* continued to emphasize its significance in the context of a new version of colonialism where intensified exploitation was prioritized over territorial expansion. They believed that the fate of Yunnan and all Chinese provinces was tied to the retrocession of the Yunnan railway.[23] Remarkably, railway-rights activists did not address workers and peasants as key players in the retrocession struggle. Rather, the nationalist mobilization campaign primarily targeted intellectuals, educated youth, merchants, gentry, industrialists, and military personnel.

The exclusion of railway workers from the political activism of the time was not due to a lack of awareness of social movements or class struggle. In the same volume of the *Yunnan Journal*, an author using the pen name Hua Sheng situated the problem of the Yunnan railway within a broader discussion of capitalist development in China.[24] In the section where the basics of railway-rights recovery policy (*jiuzhi ce*) was introduced, Hua Sheng identified the government responsible for the recovery of railway rights while viewing (civil) society as the real site of resistance against foreign-led capital expansion. In Hua Sheng's formulation, the nineteenth century was the age of machinery where those with access to big capital (*ziben*) could afford new industrial technologies and dominated worldwide production. That is, the quality and amount of production was proportionate to the power of capital. As big capital expanded and pressured small capital, manual production was replaced by machinery; the rich got richer and the poor poorer, giving rise to social tensions between these two groups, between labor and capital, and to ideologies like socialism (*shehui zhuyi*) and communism (*gongchan zhuyi*). In contrast, Yunnan's advantage was seen as deriving from its lack of capitalist social stratifications, attributed to the absence of big capital necessary for developing local industries. However, with the completion of the Yunnan–Indochina railway, the author anticipated an influx of foreign capital into the province, potentially leading to new social problems. To address this, Hua Sheng emphasized the role of local joint ventures, such as the Yunnan–Sichuan Railway Company, as a means to mitigate the negative impacts of capitalism (*ziben zhuyi*) before new social problems emerged.

From a nationalistic perspective, an inherent aspect of the issue was the perceived backwardness of Yunnan as a multiethnic border province with limited monetary resources. The development of the province was attributed to the efforts of the Han race—the author used the phrase "our Han race" (*wo hanzu*), which was considered superior and had initiated progress in the region, previously inhabited by so-called primitives (*yemanzhi*).[25] "Who would have thought that there was also a white race (*baizu*) even superior to the Han?"[26] Despite the hard work of the Han population, Yunnan remained economically underdeveloped, heavily reliant on the neighboring province of Sichuan for its survival. This dependence was partly attributed to the government's policy of isolating itself from the outside world, promoting an uncivilized antiforeignism, and passively allowing natural evolution to dictate outcomes. The nationalist perspective argued that such a geography required active intervention from advanced political forces, specifically the government and gentry, to integrate the province into the global economy through railways and other local investments. This approach was seen as necessary to propel the development of capitalism in the region.

However, this nationalist perspective exhibited a condescending attitude toward lower classes, including peasants, workers, and ethnic minorities in Yunnan. They were perceived as lacking capital and therefore sidelined in local politics, with little or no leading role. This condescension and neglect of the lower classes and ethnic minorities would later lead to the failure of the revolutionary gambit of the Hekou Rebellion in 1908.

The Hekou Rebellion, April–May 1908

As described in the previous chapter, Sun Yatsen was a strong proponent of direct action from the early days of his revolutionary career. During the Boxer uprising in 1900, he negotiated with Li Hongzhang (1823–1901), the viceroy of Guangdong and Guangxi provinces, about the possibility of creating a separate state in the south as a protest against the Qing court's decision to support the Boxers and declare war on foreigners. Around the same time, Sun also attempted, albeit unsuccessfully, to see the Indochina governor to obtain French help in establishing an independent government in southern China.[27] While Li eventually abandoned the separatist plan and returned to his official duties, the idea of using Canton and southern China as a revolutionary base remained a principal strategy of Sun's antidynastic movement.[28]

Before unifying diverse revolutionary groups under the banner of the Revolutionary Alliance, Sun made significant efforts to seek the assistance of foreign governments in the region. Initially, Japan, which had been the breeding ground of Chinese student activism, supported Sun's revolutionary activities. However, Japan later shifted its stance toward a more cooperative policy with the Qing government, hoping that its social and political reforms would serve as a model for the Qing's modernization efforts. Between December 1902 and May 1903, Sun spent six months in Hanoi with the hope of replacing the diminishing support from Japan with French assistance. Unfortunately, Sun's stay in Vietnam did not yield significant results, except for establishing some personal contacts.

Sun's visit to Paris in 1905 was more successful. He met with several ministry officials, including Raphaël Réau, who would later serve as the consul of Mengzi.[29] These official contacts were followed by further communications with the French Intelligence Service on China, established under the direct management of the Ministry of War to monitor the situation and Japanese activities in southern provinces. Until the Intelligence Service was suppressed in October 1906, Sun and his associates closely collaborated with its members, particularly with Captain Boucabeille, despite objections and warnings from the French diplomatic mission in Beijing.[30] Boucabeille and his team saw in Sun's struggle a potential for a Chinese version of the 1789 French Revolution.

In March 1907, at the request of the Qing government, Japan expelled Sun Yatsen. Sun and the Revolutionary Alliance leadership had no option but to return to their original southern base to intensify their struggle against the dynasty. First in Saigon and then in Hanoi, Sun, accompanied by his long-time fellows Huang Xing (1874–1916) and Hu Hanmin, continued to expand their network with discreet support from the French expansionists until March 1908 when he was banished from the French territory because of two insurrections he organized at the southern borders.[31]

Sun's objective in provoking these local and sporadic insurrections was to spark an antidynastic rebellion that would spread throughout the southern provinces with the help of sympathetic provincial commanders and secret societies. To achieve this, he sent his comrade Huang Xing to Guangxi to mobilize secret societies and orchestrate an uprising in Yunnan. On April 29, 1908, Sun's field commanders Huang Mingtang (1866–1938), Wang Heshun (1869–1934), and Guan Renfu (1873–1958) crossed the Yunnan–Tonkin border and captured the border city of Hekou with the help of sympathetic Qing forces. In their efforts, they killed a border garrison commander who refused to cooperate and cut the telegraph lines to disrupt communication with the provincial center. Subsequently, they advanced northward to seize the city of Mengzi.

On May 1, the rebel leader Huang Mingtang issued a proclamation to the international community that guaranteed foreigners' life and property, recognized the concessions granted to foreign powers by treaties, and condemned any foreign support for the Qing government.[32] He also sent a letter to the French railway company, informing them that their trains could freely cross the border, except when carrying Qing imperial troops and weapons.[33] In the meantime, the Chinese community in Vietnam engaged in fundraising and propaganda in support of the rebellion, negotiating loans from French banks to purchase French arms.[34] However, Huang Xing, who was returning to Hanoi to bring in arms and money, was arrested by French border police en route.[35] Sun's attempts to provide assistance from Singapore also proved unsuccessful. On May 26, Qing imperial troops dispatched by Viceroy Xiliang suppressed the rebellion. Six hundred revolutionaries fled to Tonkin and were deported to Singapore and French colonial territories.

The rebellion's initiation in Hekou, the first station of the Yunnan railway in China, coupled with the ongoing Chinese efforts to reclaim the Yunnan railway from the French, has led Chinese nationalist historiography to depict the rebellion as a reaction to France and its railway.[36] On the other hand, some scholars with a more anti-Qing stance consider the cooperation between the Qing and Indochina governments to suppress the rebellion as a betrayal of the ruling dynasty.[37] In reality, by 1908, the railway had already begun partial operations in southern Yunnan and was essential to provide communication between revolutionaries across the China–Vietnam border. As part of the cycle of antidynastic uprisings, the rebellion primarily targeted the ruling dynasty's control over the southern provinces rather than specifically attacking French nationals or the railway. It has even been suggested that Mengzi Consul Raphaël Réau provided arms from Indochina to support the uprising.[38] Hence, in addition to Huang's foreign-friendly proclamation and letter to the company, the discreet contacts between Chinese nationalists and French citizens indicate that the revolutionaries, notwithstanding their anticolonial ideology, did not see France as their main enemy.

French archival records reveal that French officials in Yunnan, including Consul Réau, were sympathetic to Chinese revolutionaries as long as they did not inspire Vietnamese nationalists with a vision of shared revolution or attract the attention of Qing imperial troops, which could lead to unrest among the local and foreign populations. Complaints from the railway company detailed that soldiers confiscated horses used in railroad construction and impeded the transport of rice designated for railroad workers and cement required for urgent works. Allegedly, soldiers plundered the tomb of a Frenchman in search of jewelry, representing a common harassment to Europeans.

An inspector assigned to the Nanxi area by the Mengzi consul observed that some military posts were entirely composed of former railway workers. The company lost approximately one thousand workers in the Mengzi area, with some fleeing to avoid forced conscription. The inspector learned that the local government provided a small monthly stipend and daily rice supply to these ex-coolies.[39] Soldiers employed workers for transporting arms, baggage, food, and injured individuals. Incidents were reported where soldiers coerced Vietnamese workers to push a lorry in the telegraphic service, and in another instance, a worker was beheaded for not properly cooking rice. Soldiers were also reported having forcefully evicted Vietnamese workers from their huts and harassed them with swords and clubs.

In addition to the Vietnamese, Chinese workers from Guangdong and Guangxi provinces also received harsh treatment from Qing officers. Because these two provinces were regarded as hotbeds of antidynastic activity, all railway workers from these provinces were suspected to be potential rebels. Soldiers even threatened to exterminate all workers from these provinces after the rebellion.[40] As a result, a quarter of the workers in the second section of the railway had fled by early May. While it remains unclear whether they joined the rebellion, contractors asserted that their foremen chose to leave because they felt threatened by the presence of troops.[41]

Throughout the rebellion, French authorities communicated with Qing officials multiple times to urge them to exercise caution in deploying armed forces. In response, French subjects were accused of favoring the revolutionaries and allowing the revolutionary militias to use company trains.[42] Qing officials possessed records of earlier contacts between Chinese nationalists and French officials promoted by Boucabeille's intelligence service in addition to the widely circulated but unproven plans of some Indochinese officials to use the border disturbances as a pretext for military intervention into China. However, given the international and domestic circumstances at the time, the annexation of Yunnan was not a feasible option for French policymakers. Instead, seeking an indemnity for the losses suffered during the disturbances appeared more advantageous to the Indochinese colonial economy than territorial expansion.

Initially, French officials in Yunnan maintained a neutral stance, but they eventually had to cooperate with the local administration to avoid conflict with the Qing government. Prior to the outbreak of the rebellion in Hekou, the Mengzi *daotai* had informed the French consul of a planned rebellion in the area. Qing intelligence officers alleged that many coolies employed by the railway company were affiliated with the rebellious group. In response, the consul requested the company personnel to help the police search for rebels and permitted the police to arrest any suspects at the worksites to prevent any suspicious individuals from entering the province. Based on its own inspection, the company sent sixty workers identified as former rebels to Tonkin.[43] On similar grounds, another group of two thousand Chinese and Vietnamese workers were sent to Hanoi under the supervision of their foremen and the gendarme forces.[44]

Despite the Qing government's claims of widespread railway worker involvement in the rebellion, British and French consular records indicate that worker participation in the rebellion was minimal. Even after the defection of Qing soldiers, the number of rebel forces was at most around five thousand. The leaders of the rebellion reported that three hundred rebels who had previously participated in an uprising in the area were overseas Chinese living in Vietnam, and another two hundred revolutionaries had impersonated coolies.[45] The quick suppression of the rebellion and Viceroy Xiliang's adept handling of the situation also support the argument of low participation.

During the nationalist campaign to reclaim the railways from foreign control, Viceroy Xiliang had garnered support from patriotic gentry and educated youth. Similarly, by persuading the central government not to implement reorganization policies toward ethnic tribes along the border, Xiliang managed to maintain their loyalty, especially that of the Shan and Miao chiefs from whom the revolutionaries expected significant help.[46] Rebel leader Wang had long been known for his inability to get along with these ethnic tribes.[47] And finally, Xiliang's firm resistance against Anglo-French demands to exploit Yunnan's mines won the sympathy of Gejiu miners. Neither the miners nor the intellectuals working for railway rights in different parts of the province joined the rebels in Hekou. They likely found the viceroy's efforts to combat foreign railways and the opium trade more aligned with their nationalist sentiments than the antidynastic call of the Alliance leadership, which was openly associated with the French, the "wicked" employers of the railway workers. Nevertheless, their anticolonial propaganda reinforced resentment against foreign enterprises and their labor recruitment practices.

Sino-French Relations After the Hekou Rebellion

The cooperative attitude of the French border police and the Indochina administration in apprehending the leaders of the revolutionary movement was appreciated by the highest levels of the Qing government. However, the tone of postrebellion negotiations took a different course as both sides demanded compensation for the damages they had incurred during the turmoil.[48] Qing local officials accused France of helping the rebels, pointing to the involvement of some French individuals in the rebellion. In response, the French side claimed that the railroad construction had suffered great losses due to forced conscription of workers and maltreatment of foreign subjects in the region. They argued that holding the French government officially accountable for the actions of its individual subjects was impractical.

While Hekou was retaken from the revolutionary forces within a month, the revolutionary turmoil persisted. Yang Zhenhong (1874–1909) and Huang Yuying (1885–1912), key revolutionary leaders, had met with Sun Yatsen in Singapore, where the strategic importance of Yunnan for the revolutionary action plan was once again emphasized. Following the death of the Guangxu Emperor in December 1908, Yang Zhenhong entered Yunnan through Burma to lead rebel groups, including rebels from different ethnic groups, in Yongchang County (modern Baoshan) in the western part of the province.[49] Although the Qing forces defeated the revolutionary forces in the west, they continued their chase southward toward the Indochina border and throughout villages inside the Tonkin borders.

The skirmishes between the imperial troops and revolutionaries on both sides of the border cost the lives of a French officer and numerous Vietnamese soldiers. The continuous battles severely damaged the railway construction sites and caused commercial losses to many European entrepreneurs. The Qing government did not object to the indemnity claims made on behalf of the soldiers and civilians killed or injured during the operations of the regular forces. The indemnity received by the Indochina government was substantial enough to compensate the soldiers and Vietnamese villagers and strengthen the police forces in Tonkin.[50] For the family of Lieutenant Weigand, the only European casualty during the operation in Phalong (Vietnam), a compensation of 75,000 francs was provided. However, the lives of the six deceased Vietnamese soldiers were not valued as highly; each Vietnamese soldier's family received 500 piastres for their losses.[51]

The main point of contestation between the Chinese and French sides during the negotiations was the compensation demanded by the railway company. The company made a claim for 2,728,628 francs, and the total claims made by the entrepreneurs amounted to an additional 503,458 francs. During the negotiations between the representative of the Chinese Foreign Affairs Bureau and the French minister in Beijing, Chinese officials were adamant in their stance: "China will not spit out a penny to compensate a company that supported a rebellion in Yunnan."[52] The Chinese delegate accused the railway company, which was financially strained, of aiding the revolutionaries in obtaining an indemnity from the Qing government. The company directors were also accused of transporting arms and ammunition of the revolutionary forces on company trains. Additionally, the French border patrol was criticized for turning a blind eye to the infiltration of rebel groups despite earlier warnings from Qing authorities that a group of rebels was gathering in Laocai.

Although the French minister rejected the accusations made by the Qing delegate, he expressed moments of embarrassment while responding to their charges. He believed that the support offered to the

Chinese revolutionaries in Indochina was a result of an unfortunate policy, which has led to France being considered "the second most detested power in China after Japan."[53] The formal meeting between the parties also included an informal conversation, during which the Qing delegate inquired about their "final price" (*dernière prix*). In response, the minister informally suggested that the price might be reduced if the Qing government agreed to transfer lands for a French establishment in Tongkou, Zhili.[54]

While the French minister in Beijing aimed to utilize the company's claims as a bargaining chip to obtain further concessions from China, French officials in Indochina had a different approach. They were focused on refuting the compensation claims made by their own subjects. The claims were carefully examined first by a chief engineer of control services assigned by the Indochinese government, and then by a representative of the Ministry of Foreign Affairs. The Indochina governor strictly warned these controllers that granting an indemnity to the company could set an "unfortunate precedent" that might be used against the colonial government in the future.[55] Despite the fact that these claims were based on Article 58 of the convention signed in 1901, according to the governor, the company would have been entitled to an indemnity only if their losses were caused by a French operation in Yunnan, which was not the case.

Echoing the governor's concerns, the Ministry of Foreign Affairs representative, Veroudart, prepared detailed reports arguing that the losses claimed by the company and entrepreneurs were "exaggerated," and the attitudes of the revolutionaries toward Europeans and the railway were "perfect."[56] Even if he admitted that individual contractors suffered losses due to worker escapes and worksite disorganization, Veroudart deemed the company's claims for labor recruitment costs to be inconsistent and unsubstantiated.[57]

The company's initial claims for compensation were substantial, asserting that around four thousand Chinese and nine hundred Vietnamese workers had quit the worksites in panic during the incidents. They demanded indemnity for the evacuation costs—workers were transported on trains to Hanoi— and recruitment expenses incurred to bring these workers from their hometowns. Moreover, the company was planning to recruit more workers from Vietnam in October 1908, and they needed funds for this new round of recruitment.[58] Veroudart firmly rejected these claims and recalculated the company's actual loss at 620,000 francs.

For the Qing government, paying the indemnity was not solely a matter of treaty compliance but also a strategic move to extend its sovereign power beyond Chinese territories and suppress what they perceived as a major domestic threat to imperial rule. In January 1909, they made the French government sign a convention for the repression of revolutionary movements at the China–Vietnam borders.[59] With this convention, France agreed to cooperate with Chinese authorities by sharing intelligence and taking active measures to prevent the gathering of antidynastic and revolutionary groups. They also agreed to prohibit and repress any revolutionary propaganda through public press in Indochina. If necessary, the authorization granted to local newspapers would be revoked. This prohibition covered several revolutionary books and periodicals, including the *Yunnan Journal*.[60] Other convention articles ruled that the rebels who fought against Chinese security forces would be disarmed and interned as refugees in French territories. These refugees would be expelled after a certain period to be determined by the French government and banned from travel in French territories and protectorates. All measures were to be taken to prevent the reentry of these individuals into Chinese territories. Only those who had committed ordinary crimes were to be submitted to Chinese authorities.

The deal reached by the Qing and French governments was a disputable gain for both sides. The Qing government added another burden to its already crumbling economy, but it could at least exert its sovereign power against rebellious groups. While the Qing court had adeptly manipulated foreign interests against each other, the nationalist movement, fueled by popular support, proved more challenging to control through traditional imperial governance. The nationalists were the first political group seeking to mobilize the Yunnanese for a programmatic antidynastic campaign. Although they ultimately failed, it became evident that the popular xenophobia manipulated at opportune times to the advantage of the imperial government had slipped through the fingers of officials and turned into an internationally recognized movement that prioritized overthrowing the Manchu dynasty as a first step toward the country's liberation from imperialist aggression. Surprisingly, the railway workers, initially protected under official treaties as a symbol of Qing imperial sovereignty against foreign governments, became the target audience for these competing political ideologies.

For the French side, the agreement demonstrated that the Qing government remained capable of exerting control over its peripheries thanks to the imperial efforts in military modernization. Meanwhile, the defensive and balance-seeking policy of the French Ministry of Foreign Affairs in China had caused the country to fall behind other competing powers. The Yunnan railway, originally initiated to advance French commercial interests in China, had become a burden due to its enormous financial and human costs. Even if French diplomats did not care whether the railway workers were involved in revolutionary activism, the daily troubles at the worksites had tarnished France's prestige by delaying the railway's completion.

France and the Railway Company After the Hekou Rebellion

Amid discussions on the retrocession of foreign-built railways and revolutionary uprisings, the Yunnan railway commenced full operations in April 1910. Even then, the nationalists continued to hope for an intervention from above that would lead to victory in their efforts to reclaim railway rights. In 1910, Tang Shouqian (1856–1917), the head of the Zhejiang Railway Bureau, was appointed to lead the provincial railway bureau in Yunnan after a contentious struggle for the self-construction of railways in Zhejiang. Author Can Xue from the *Yunnan Journal* depicted Tang as a national hero who did not hesitate to sacrifice his career for the recovery of railway rights—appointment to Yunnan was understood as a career demotion since it was on the periphery of the Qing Empire.[61] While his departure was a loss for Zhejiang province, the people of Yunnan welcomed him as a savior. In the meantime, Viceroy Xiliang informed French representatives that China had decided not to purchase the railway. Using the local railway funds to build the Sichuan and Burma lines was more realistic than using them to rescue a bankrupt foreign company. The Yunnanese students abroad continued to oppose foreign railway initiatives, successfully preventing Britain from building the Tengyue railway. However, this campaign did not precipitate an immediate victory for their antidynastic cause on the ground.

The Hekou rebellion further strained the relationship between the French government and the railway company. In May 1908, the arbitrage commission evaluating the company's claims from the Indochina government held the company accountable for amounts exceeding the original estimated construction costs. The company, facing liquidation after the commission's decision, was saved by an additional subsidy from the French government. The situation was complicated by the allocation of work to individual contractors, creating further challenges in the relationships between the government, the company, and the Italian contractors.

The company's claims for compensation after the Hekou rebellion marked the coup de grâce for government–company relations. French diplomats in the region had accustomed to the company's tendency to turn every incident into a matter of indemnity. However, given the complexities in international politics and excessive costs associated with the railway project, the company's excessive claims became increasingly intolerable. Apart from the assertive attitudes of the company's management, the Italian contractors had begun to act freely, as if it was their own government that showed all those efforts to advance their commercial interests, the French diplomats thought.

In early 1909, as the railway approached completion, the French consul in Kunming presented a report to the French Ministry of Foreign Affairs on the "Italian threat," where he blamed the Italians for making undue profits from a French investment, despite lacking the technical qualifications and expertise of superior French engineering.[62] He pointed out that while French engineers had performed the more labor-intensive and challenging aspects of the work, they had left with far smaller savings compared to the Italians. For instance, contractor Bossolo, known as the "emperor of Namti," had amassed 900,000 francs, and another contractor, Mozzanini, who had arrived in the province with no financial

FIGURE 6.1 The Yunnan section of the railway was completed in 1910. ©Archives Cité du Train–Patrimoine SNCF.

resources, returned home with a profit exceeding 500,000 francs, according to the records of La Banque de l'Indo-chine. These figures take on an even more egregious aspect when one reflects on the plight of the destitute railway workers, who were condemned to death due to inadequate access to food, shelter, and medical care.

Beyond the material profits, the rising activity and influence of the Italians in Yunnan posed a potential threat to French influence in southwest China. Dr. Mozzanini, for instance, independently signed a contract with Commander "Che" for treating imperial soldiers. An Italian named Aurély represented the Indochinese Commercial Union in Kunming and oversaw establishing commercial relations with Italy, France, and Germany. Contractor Bozzolo proposed building the perpendicular lines of the Yunnan railway to the local government while an employee of contractor Vitali offered technical services to the Chinese railway bureau at discounted rates that were unimaginable to the French.

In an effort to counter Bozzolo's railway proposal, the French consul attempted to persuade a French contractor to make a competing offer. Through negotiations with local officials, he managed to secure a three-month extension to prepare the new proposal. However, to his dismay, he later discovered that the French contractor in question was in Tonkin and preparing to return to France soon. Even after France significantly improved the infrastructure of the province, French entrepreneurs were still not enthusiastic about directly serving the interests of the empire. The Italian threat in Yunnan extended to cultural aspects as well, with Asti, an Italian sparkling white wine, replacing French champagne on the festive tables of Chinese officials and notables.[63] These developments signaled a significant shift in the dynamics of power and influence in the region compared to the time when France first initiated the railway project in the late nineteenth century.

In 1910, a new point of tension arose between the company and French representatives in Yunnan concerning the repatriation of railway workers from Vietnam, and Guangdong and Guangxi provinces. Qing official communications with the French consulate in Kunming indicated that approximately four hundred Cantonese workers were living on the outskirts of Kunming in dire conditions, residing in straw cabins, and suffering from famine, cold, and disease.[64] The ones who could afford a hostel had left their possessions to the hostel owners before being expelled from these inns. The local officials feared that these workers could either succumb to famine or become a social threat in the city.

The company's manager, Maxime Getten (1857–1934), argued that the responsibility for repatriation did not fall on the company, as there was no written statement obliging them to do so. His argument held validity. In contrast to overseas labor contracts, there was no provision outlining the workers' return expenses for domestic recruits. The company intended to retain approximately one hundred workers for future work in the Nanxi area, and the rest were beyond their concern. The French consul in Kunming, Flayelle, responded assertively and with a threat. He pointed out that the company was facing a group of men—referring to the workers—belonging to "a bellicose and bandit-friendly race" with the potential to form gangs along the railway, jeopardizing its infrastructure and possibly attacking passengers.[65] Flayelle warned that obtaining indemnities from the local government in such circumstances might not be straightforward, as the authorities could accuse the company of not taking necessary precautions to prevent gatherings of these unruly workers. In sum, as in the overseas coolie trade, he held the company responsible for the decommissioned Chinese workers.

The situation regarding Vietnamese ex-workers also posed challenges. The gendarme forces in Mengzi and Kunming were arresting and repatriating Vietnamese workers without matriculation cards. Flayelle argued that many Vietnamese men of "dubious morality" had come to the region due to the railway construction, causing disturbances post-construction. Consequently, their repatriation was seen as necessary.[66] Simultaneously, the consul requested that Vietnamese merchants who had established businesses along the railway be allowed to stay, in acknowledgement of the hospitality shown toward thousands of Chinese immigrants within French territories.

Following Flayelle's warnings, the company directors changed their approach and initiated the repatriation of the Chinese ex-workers. They dispatched Bodin, the railway's chief engineer, to Kunming to organize the repatriation process. Bodin kept around three hundred workers in the Nanxi region for future work and sent others back to their hometowns in Guangxi and Guangdong.

In the meantime, the metropolitan elites, in the comfort of their urban lives, were still debating the feasibility of extending the Yunnan railway into Sichuan. Commander Oilone, who visited Yunnan in mid-1909, observed the province's vast cultivable fields, grassy mountains, and numerous human residences as indicators of its potential for railway development.[67] According to the statistics, the province had a population of 12 million. The railway could serve this massive population and enormously benefit from the province's copper, tin, silver, and coal deposits. While the "Yunnan myth" was still alive to deceptively dazzle the foreign traveler, the commander argued against prolonging the line to Sichuan for a different reason. Unlike earlier proponents who sought to reach the Sichuan market, Oilone reasoned that connecting Yunnan to a larger inland network would divert trade volume from the Sino-French Yunnan–Haiphong route to a fully Chinese Yunnan–Sichuan route. This, he believed, would harm French diplomacy and commercial transactions through Tonkin. Therefore, keeping Yunnan isolated from inland routes and connected solely to Tonkin would better serve the interests of French merchants and industrialists. As a result, the Yunnan–Indochina railway evolved from an initiative to enlarge French commercial networks in China into a means to monopolize limited trade with Yunnan through the French colony of Tonkin. Apparently, the challenging and painful construction process served to dampen the ambitions of French colonialists, despite their initial allure by the prospects of Yunnan.

Conclusion

The final years of the Yunnan–Indochina railway construction were marked by the surge of Chinese nationalism, manifested in the struggle for railway rights and scattered armed rebellion, culminating in the Hekou rebellion of May 1908. The Qing government's efforts to regain control over railway concessions by shifting railway initiatives to private hands and provincial unions inadvertently fueled a nationwide anti-imperialist movement led by reformist and revolutionary nationalists. This movement saw the transformation of antiforeign sentiment into anti-imperialism, representing an evolution in China's nationalist discourse.

Despite their patriotic fervor, the provincial railway unions faced challenges in expanding the railway lines due to limited financial resources and managerial issues. While they successfully mobilized urban populations in various provinces, their failure to establish organic connections with lower-ranking members of society hindered their progress. Amid the ongoing struggle for railway rights, Sun Yatsen and the Revolutionary Alliance, following their expulsion from Japan in 1907, adopted a new strategy of inciting local rebellions in southern provinces against the Qing dynasty. These rebellions, depicted as part of the anti-imperialist milieu by Chinese nationalist historiography, also exhibited a strong antidynastic character, even surpassing their antiforeign disposition. Notably, archival documents indicate discreet support from French colonialists in Indochina for Sun Yatsen and his revolutionary movement.

Ultimately, the attempts to buy back the Yunnan–Indochina railway and launch border rebellions aiming at weakening the dynasty resulted in the failure of the nationalists in Yunnan. If modernization of Qing imperial troops played a role, the main reason for the failure lay in the nationalists' inability to create a coalition of local forces, including disgruntled officials, ethnic tribes, peasants, miners, and railway workers. Their Han-centric, developmentalist discourse and limited conceptualization of politics centered on educated citizens with national consciousness fell short of harnessing the full political potential inherent in people's everyday encounters.[68]

Conversely, France did not reap the expected benefits from its ambitious investment. The strained relations between the railway company and the French government escalated to a total collapse after the Hekou rebellion. As construction costs mounted and the company faced liquidation, it became evident that Yunnan was not the El Dorado they had hoped for, nor was the railway a financially rewarding venture. Despite the accomplishment of superior French engineering, at the cost of thousands of lives, the unfulfilled political significance of the railway continued to overshadow its economic value. In the following years,

France was able to generate significant profits from cargo traffic between Vietnam and Yunnan, but the railway's unachieved political promise persisted. French scholar Bruguière argued that the Yunnan–Indochina railway held limited economic value without its promise of colonial expansion.[69] As the postcolonial era dawned, this promise vanished, leading to France selling the railway to China in 1945.

Today, the Yunnan–Indochina railway's story stands as a complex interplay of nationalist aspirations, imperial interests, and alternative political imaginations, and continues to profoundly influence the region's historical narrative. Bruguière's assertion regarding the political significance is indeed valid, bearing in mind that colonialism rested heavily on labor exploitation. The railway's construction process unequivocally demonstrated that Chinese workers would not acquiesce to an exploitative labor regime under French rule. With a defiant labor force, the Yunnan railway would have engendered more conflict than profit in an increasingly radicalized China.

Epilogue

ON MARCH 31, 1910, THE inauguration of the Yunnan–Indochina railway was marked in Kunming with a daylong ceremony organized under the auspices of Getten, the director of the French Railway Company. The event commenced in the morning with the formal reception of the viceroy of Yunnan and Guizhou Provinces at the Kunming railway station. Following a brief tour of the festively adorned station buildings, Chinese dignitaries and esteemed guests were escorted to a banquet. Here, representatives of both the French and Qing governments delivered speeches in celebration of the occasion.

Henry Bourgeois, the delegate of the Ministry of Foreign Affairs in Yunnan, articulated that the completion of the railway was emblematic of not only the "crowning of a remarkable work in every regard," but also a testament to the resolve that "when France and her children embark on a task, they see it through despite all obstacles."[1] In expressing his gratitude, he hailed the arduous and persistent efforts of men across all ranks who had labored for many years, defying scientific constraints in the pursuit of progress, and enabling them to exclaim: "No more Namti!" This was a reference to the perilous Nanxi valley, where numerous Europeans, as well as thousands of Chinese and Vietnamese workers, perished. Strikingly, none of the speakers explicitly acknowledged these individual sacrifices or named those lost, instead directing their thanks to the director of the company for the monumental achievement.

Amid the semblance of grand diplomatic courtesy, the railway lay like a scar through the mountains, bearing witness to the strife and fatalities among those who had toiled on the project. What, then, was the promise of the railway, and what was the ultimate outcome?

The case of the Yunnan–Indochina railway endures as a simultaneously typical and unique example of colonial developmentalism and imperialist rivalry of the late nineteenth and early twentieth centuries. Typical in the sense that its construction process unveiled the tensions between the metropolitan and colonial representatives of the French empire, revealing the fragility of colonial institutions and ideology, and calling into question the universal applicability of bourgeois values and categories, especially within the specific context of a locale where indigenous populations robustly resisted the dominance of these values in unforeseen and innovative ways.[2]

Similar to colonial endeavors in other regions, French activities in Yunnan, notwithstanding the province's noncolonial status, were carried out by a group of men (and their female family members) whose economic, political, and personal interests often proved more conflicting than harmonious. Even if these actors may have united around a bourgeois ideal of civilization, defined by private property, industrial production, and free trade, among other principles, their interpretations of the surrounding sociopolitical landscape differed significantly. For example, the Indochina governor, Doumer, perceived the annexation of Yunnan as a logical extension of French colonial expansion. In contrast, French foreign ministers, regardless of their expansionist ambitions, saw it as a precarious venture that could potentially precipitate military conflict with Britain. These diverging viewpoints and tensions between colonial and metropolitan perspectives suggest that French colonial theory was neither monolithic nor static, nor was its practice immutable. Instead, influenced by the resistance of local actors, the strategies employed by other colonial powers, and experiences in various colonial territories, both theory and practice were subject to continuous evolution across time and space. In essence, French colonialism was a complex amalgamation of theories, ideals, values, and practices, always in the making.

With all its underlying instability and vulnerability, French colonialism sought to create along the Yunnan railway a dominion where France would have ideally exerted control over the labor and movement of indigenous populations without engaging in the risks of direct military intervention. However, even before the fulfillment of these colonial aspirations, local Yunnanese and railway workers from other Chinese provinces quickly challenged the French claims of universality (pertaining to development, modernization of production, expansion of commerce) by withdrawing their labor and bodies from the perilous operations of capitalist development. These acts, although unorganized and perhaps motivated by a basic instinct for survival, rather than fitting into the conventional narratives of class politics, left a profound impact on French colonial history.

Apart from the immediate and long-term consequences of labor resistance on construction and French colonialism, the manner in which railway workers defended their physical integrity against French colonialism's offenses revealed to French colonizers that labor was not a mere commodity to be consumed and disposed at the end of a workday. Instead, it necessitated continual efforts to sustain and augment its productive ability. Even if wages and labor contracts provided a legal framework for French employers to utilize Chinese labor, reproducing the labor force—in the sense of maintaining workers' diligence, health, regular attendance, and overall vitality—proved an unattainable goal within this legal landscape.

Due to the inherent limitations of wages and contracts in preserving the labor force, France had to embark on an extensive social project centered on controlling the laboring body. The intricacy of the emerging power dynamics and the pervasiveness of worker defiance illustrate that the turbulent process through which worker subjectivity emerged in Yunnan cannot be simply explained as a "transition to wage labor." Rather, it demands an intricate examination of the complex relationship between nation and labor, land and livelihood, and bare life and politics.[3]

Paradoxically, the French recognition that labor was both a unique and universal commodity laid the groundwork for the Chinese worker, a peculiar and cultural object of French imagination, to be depicted as an embodiment of labor as a universal category.[4] Within this transformation, the Chinese worker was made comparable, if not equal, to the European worker, produced within a European bourgeois context. Even if the outcome of this comparison might have been the reaffirmation of

European cultural superiority in colonial discourse, the same universality provided Chinese workers with new opportunities to carve out a niche within the tensions of capitalist development and colonial rivalry. It is hard to define this niche as the site of class, class consciousness, or the labor movement, whose limits were determined by workers' discretion in whether to realize their productive capacity within modern production relations. In a context where the categories of true politics (imperial, nationalist, colonial, socialist, etc.) were in the process of making and not yet strictly defined, the railway workers were able to turn their lives, their "labor as capacity," into sites of struggle, hence of politics, regardless of their recognition by other political actors.

The labor conflicts also unmasked the racial underpinnings in the developmentalist and universalist economic narratives of Chinese nationalists and French colonists. In their quest to legitimize a nationalist agenda against the ruling dynasty and in dialogue with Western economic and political theories, Chinese nationalists adopted a condescending attitude toward ethnic minorities in Yunnan and the colonized peoples of East and Southeast Asia. According to Chinese nationalists, the backwardness of these peoples in developing a national consciousness compatible with the ideals of a modern economy rendered the Han Chinese, with their not-yet-lost sovereignty over Chinese territories, the sole leaders of an anticolonial struggle in the region. This racial and social Darwinist undertone, rather than uniting the local communities around anticolonial ideals, distanced them and laid the groundwork for subsequent ethnic conflicts.

By the same token, the emphasis on the notion that land constituted the foundation of livelihood, coupled with the propaganda for "territorial nativism," overshadowed the labor question and facilitated the absorption of the railway workers' resistance into a nationalist narrative in subsequent historiography. This territorial nativism led to an extension of the so-called Chinese national revival beyond the majority Han Chinese, fueling ethnic conflicts in various periods of Chinese history.

The failure to recognize the political potential inherent in the workers' daily struggles also confined nationalist political activism to an elite circle, generating new tensions that reverberated throughout the turbulent Republican years (1912–1949), until the Communist Party successfully rallied the support of the peasant and worker masses. During this period, the Beijing government's initiative to send Chinese workers abroad during World War I emerged as another instance of the Chinese workers' role in asserting national sovereignty.[5] This new exposure to Europe, during a time when the continent was engulfed in a capitalist-driven war, introduced workers to European radical ideas, including communism and class struggle. Drawing on these multifaceted experiences, workers in the 1920s utilized the metaphor of "cattle and horses" to broaden their critique of labor exploitation.[6] This new iteration extended beyond the realm of interracial contexts and encapsulated labor exploitation by capitalists more broadly, encompassing Chinese capitalists in addition to foreign employers.

In addition to these overarching conclusions, the Yunnan–Indochina railway has etched a significant mark on Yunnan's social and economic history. As contemporary Chinese scholars have posited, Yunnan's industrial development can be traced back to the railway. In 1909, Viceroy Xiliang founded the Gejiu Tin Business Stock Company, engaging a German engineer to supervise production, thereby introducing Western managerial technics and machinery into the region. The same year, an electric generator company was established in Gejiu, and Kaiyuan (Lin'an) saw the opening of its first machine repair factory. Following the initiation of the railway's operations, the province also introduced its first gas lamp and papermaking and printing machines, transported from Shanghai via the Yunnan–Indochina railway.[7]

During the Japanese colonial occupation in 1937, the Yunnan railway drew attention as the exclusive channel for conveying international aid to China. France, however, was reluctant to place the railway at the service of the Chinese nationalist government, apprehensive of provoking an outright conflict with Japan.[8]

After completion of the railway, there also appeared a negative trend in the province's economic activities. The escalating importation of foreign textiles, specifically cotton and wool, precipitated a severe downturn in the local textile industry. Only during the Japanese occupation in northeastern China in the 1930s, when economic activity moved to the country's inner regions as part of a strategy to create a "Great Rear Area" (*dahoufang*), did the Yunnanese economy experience brief growth.[9] Besides textiles, other Western manufactured goods flooded the Yunnan markets, usurping local handicraft industries. Throughout the interwar period, Kunming's streets were replete with stores bearing signs proclaiming "foreign made," a phenomenon later interpreted by Chinese socialist historians as the emergence of a comprador class.[10] An anomalous exception to this domination of imports occurred during World War I, when European powers acquired Yunnan's tin in unparalleled quantities.

Controversy regarding whether the railway imparted a negative or positive impact on the provincial economy must be contextualized within the evolving political and diplomatic landscape of China. What is pertinent to this discussion is the realization that even though current scholarship endeavors to highlight the railway's economic contributions and recast the railway workers' tragedy as collective memory—evoking imagery of imperialist incursion and anticolonial nationalism without reference to production relations—the latent capacity to resist capital remains entrenched in the workers themselves. While the resistance of the Yunnan railway workers may seem to some as sporadic, unorganized, and consequently negligible, its intrinsic connection to the workers' lives and bodies renders it worthy of transcending generations as an exceptionally political and universal story.

Notes

Introduction

1. Villechénoux and Reynaud, "Précis d'une monographie d'un coolie," 265–91.

2. A meter-gauge railway is a narrow railway with a track gauge of 1,000 mm or 1 meter. European colonial powers often used meter-gauge railways in mountainous areas for light passenger and freight traffic.

3. Cheng, "Dang'an jilu xia de dian-yue tielu" [The Yunnan–Vietnam railway in archival records], 40.

4. Villechénoux and Reynaud, "Précis d'une monographie d'un coolie," 278.

5. Villechénoux and Reynaud, "Précis d'une monographie d'un coolie," 279.

6. Villechénoux and Reynaud, "Précis d'une monographie d'un coolie," 279.

7. Villechénoux and Reynaud, "Précis d'une monographie d'un coolie," 279.

8. Villechénoux and Reynaud, "Précis d'une monographie d'un coolie," 279.

9. Meister, *"In den wilden Bergschluchten widerhallt ihr Pfeifen,"* 124.

10. Meister, *"In den wilden Bergschluchten widerhallt ihr Pfeifen,"* 129.

11. There are varying speculations about the number of workers employed and the number who perished during the railway's construction. The figures I present are my own estimations, derived from a comparison of numerous archival sources.

12. China suffered several military defeats that forced the country into an unequal treaty system. Britain defeated China in two (opium) wars, the first in 1839–42 and the second in 1856–60. France emerged victorious in the Sino-French War of 1884–85, followed by China's defeat in the Sino-Japanese War of 1895. The last blow came when allied foreign forces suppressed the anti-Christian Boxer Rebellion in 1900, forcing China to pay an enormous indemnity.

13. For the changes in trade deficit between China and Britain after the Opium Wars, see Wong, *Deadly Dreams*. For the global economic impact of the opium trade, Trocki, *Opium, Empire and the Global Political Economy.*

14. Salt, silk, and opium remained the main items of commerce in Sichuan, but they were exported abroad or to other parts of the empire in raw forms. Feuerwerker, "Economic Trends in the Late Ch'ing Empire, 1870–1911," 36, 43.

15. Zelin, "The Rights of Tenants in Mid-Qing Sichuan," 499–526.

16. Shi, *Agricultural Development in Qing China*, 54–55, 67, 198–99.

17. Wong, *China Transformed*, 47.

18. Lai, *Indentured Labor, Caribbean Sugar*, xi.

19. Li, *Migrating Fujianese.*

20. Statistical Department of the Inspectorate General of Customs, *Treaties, Conventions, etc. Between China and Foreign States*, 161.

21. Statistical Department of the Inspectorate General of Customs, *Treaties, Conventions, etc. Between China and Foreign States*, 240.

22. Gyory, *Closing the Gate*.

23. Colleen Lye employs the term "Asiatic racial form" to distinguish the Asia in European colonial imagery from the concept of "America's Asia." The latter emerged as a racial category in the nineteenth century with the importation of Asian labor to the US and evolved through the contradictory tropes of the "yellow peril" and the "model minority." In this sense, it includes the idea of Euro-American anxiety over Asia's potential for boundless success. Lye, *Racial Form and American Literature, 1893–1945*.

24. Ngai, *The Chinese Question*.

25. Williams, *Returning Home with Glory*.

26. Chan, *Diaspora's Homeland*.

27. For the Qing Empire's borderland management in Yunnan, see Bello, *Across Forest, Steppe, and Mountain*; Giersch, *Asian Borderlands*.

28. Atwill, *The Panthay Rebellion*.

29. Herman, "Empire in the Southwest: Early Qing Reforms to the Native Chieftain System," 47–74.

30. Giersch, *Corporate Conquests*.

31. For a discussion of revolutionary renditions of rights and citizenship in the late Qing period, see Zarrow, *After Empire*, 195–206.

32. In *The Birth of Biopolitics*, Foucault explores the distinction between the "subject of rights" and the "subject of interest" within liberal economic theory. This distinction is important to understand the individual's relation to the state. Foucault, *The Birth of Biopolitics*, 267–89.

33. In late-Qing intellectual debates, equal citizenship and democracy were central themes, but they all included a mistrust of Chinese people's ability for self-governance due to their lack of intellectual resources. Peter Zarrow attributes this totalizing view of the nation to the scientific racism of the day, "which equated a people with the ruling elite." Zarrow, *After Empire*, 157.

34. Chesneaux, *The Chinese Labor Movement, 1919–1927*, 131.

35. Chesneaux, *The Chinese Labor Movement, 1919–1927*, 119–22.

36. Kawashima, *The Proletarian Gamble*.

37. Marx, *Grundrisse*, 267.

38. Marx, *Grundrisse*, 272.

39. Robinson, *Black Marxism*.

40. Bruguière, "Le chemin de fer du Yunnan."

41. Rousseau, "An Imperial Railway Failure," 1–17.

42. François, *Le mandarin blanc*. Jorge Amat's documentary, *Through the Consul's Eyes*, includes François's personal video recordings of China. Réau and Marchant, *Lettres d'un diplomate en Chine au début du Xxe Siècle*; Marbotte, *Une*

chemin de fer au Yunnan. Engineer Albert Marie's family has donated his archive to the Institute of South Asian Studies in Singapore. Based on this collection, Vatthana Pholsena published a photo essay: "Technology and Empire: A Colonial Narrative of the Construction of the Tonkin–Yunnan Railway." The memoirs of engineers Georges-Aguste Marbotte and Albert Marie became the basis of a recent book: Bernard, Locard, and Marbotte, *Le chemin de fer du Yunnan*.

43. Duan, *1910 nian de lieche* [The train of 1910]; Miao, "Fa diguozhuyi yu dian-yue tielu [French imperialism and the Yunnan–Vietnam railway]; Zhuang, "Qiantan dian-yue tielu dui yunnan shehui jingji de yingxiang [On the Yunnan–Vietnam railway's impact on the economy and society of Yunnan].

44. Yunnan sheng zong gong hui gongren yundong shi yanjiu zu, *Yunnan gongren yundong shi ziliao huibian, 1886–1949* [Documents on the Yunnan labor movement].

45. Sun, "Fan-ya tielu jianshe yu dian-yue tielu lishi wenhua baohu" [The construction of the trans-Asian railways and the historical and cultural protection of the Yunnan–Vietnam railway]; Wang and Fan, "Dian-yue tielu yu dian dongnan shaoshu minzu diqu gongyehua hudong guanxi pingshui" [The Yunnan–Vietnam railway and industrial development in ethnic regions of southeast Yunnan]; Wang, Peng, and Fan, *Dian-yue tielu yu dian dongnan shaoshu minzu diqu shehui bianqian yanjiu* [The Yunnan–Vietnam railway and social change in the ethnic regions of southeast Yunnan], Duan, *Dian-yue tielu: kuayue bainian de xiao huoche* [The Yunnan–Vietnam railway: The small train that spans a hundred years].

46. Although the "Belt and Road Initiative" has been proposed by current Chinese president Xi Jinping, the idea of reviving ancient Chinese commercial routes, both inland and maritime, has long been on the Chinese diplomatic agenda.

47. Peng, *San guo yanyi, bainian migui–Dian-yue tielu de lishi tuxiang* [The story of three kingdoms and the one hundred years of meter-gauge train—The historical image of the Yunnan–Vietnam railway].

48. Wu, *Yanshen de pingxingxian–Dian-yue tielu yu bianmin shehui* (Extended parallel lines—Dian-Vietnam railway and borderland community); Wu, "Zuowei jiben jiyi yu ziwo yanxu de wuzhi wenhua yanjiu–Yi dian-yue tielu weilie" (A research on substance culture as collective memory and self-continuance—Taking the Yunnan–Vietnam railway as example).

49. Fan, *Bisezhai*.

Chapter 1

1. Fauvel, "La main d'œuvre chinois dans nos colonies," 115–16.

2. Bruguière, "Le chemin de fer du Yunnan: Paul Doumer et la politique d'intervention française en Chine, 1889–1902," 277.

3. Lee, *France and the Exploitation of China, 1885–1901: A Study in Economic Imperialism*.

4. Laffey, "Municipal Imperialism in France: The Lyon Chamber of Commerce, 1900–1914," 8–23.

5. Laffey, "Lyonnais Imperialism in the Far East 1900–1938," 225–48.

6. Bonin, Hodeir, and Klein, *L'Esprit économique impérial (1830–1970): Groupes de pression et réseaux du patronat colonial en France et dans l'empire.*

7. Doumer, "Journal officiel de la République française. Débats parlementaires. Chambre des députés: Compte rendu in-extenso," December 16, 1898, 2442.

8. Daughton, *In the Forest of No Joy: The Congo-Océan Railroad and the Tragedy of French Colonialism.*

9. Dupuis, *A Journey to Yunnan and the Opening of the Red River to Trade*; Garnier and Delaporte, *The Mekong Exploration Commission Report, 1866–1868: A Pictorial Journey on the Old Mekong: Cambodia, Laos, and Yunnan*; Garnier, *Further Travels in Laos and in Yunnan.*

10. He, *Gebishi tielu: Yunnan ren yin yi zhihao de cun gui tielu* [An inch-gauge railway that the people of Yunnan take pride of], 20.

11. Walsh, "The Yunnan Myth," 272–85.

12. Singaravélou, "L'Empire des économistes: L'enseignement de 'l'économie coloniale' sous la IIIe République," 121–34.

13. Geenens and Rosenblatt, *French Liberalism from Montesquieu to the Present Day.*

14. The building of the Beijing–Hankou railway is another example from China. Lee, *France and the Exploitation of China*, 109.

15. Lee, *France and the Exploitation of China*, 184–85.

16. Remer, *Foreign Investments in China*, 76.

17. Remer, *Foreign Investments in China*, 99.

18. Dubois, "L'Arsenal de Fuzhou et la presence militaire française au Fujian (1869–1911), 91–102.

19. Brocheux and Hémery, *Indochina: An Ambiguous Colonization, 1858–1954*, 23.

20. Laffey, "The Lyon Chamber of Commerce and Indochina During the Third Republic," 325–48.

21. Brunat, *Exploration commerciale du Tonkin. Report presented to the Lyon Chamber of Commerce*, 11.

22. Pila, Séance extraordinaire du 28 Mai 1891. Rapport de M. Ulysse Pila sur son second voyage d'études commerciales au Tonkin, 11, 13.

23. Klein, "Une culture impériale consulaire? L'exemple de la chambre de commerce de Lyon (1830–1920)," 350.

24. Méline served as the sixty-fifth prime minister of France from April 1896 to June 1898 after Léon Bourgeois. Trang, "Paul Doumer: Aux origins d'un grand project, le chemin de fer Transindochinois," 124.

25. Doumer, *Situation de l'Indo-Chine 1897–1901: rapport*, 60.

26. Doumer, *Situation de l'Indo-Chine 1897–1901: rapport*, 3–4. For a discussion of Doumer's governorship, see Lorin, *Paul Doumer: Gouverneur General de l'Indochina, 1897–1902.*

27. Doumer, *Situation de l'Indo-Chine 1897–1901: rapport*, 3–4.

28. Brocheux and Hémery, *Indochina*, 120–28.

29. Sasges, "State, Enterprise and the Alcohol Monopoly in Colonial Vietnam," 133–57.

30. De Lanessan, *L'expansion coloniale de la France*, 581.

31. Geddes, "Opium and the Miao: A Study in Ecological Adjustment," 8–9.

32. Trocki, "Drugs, Taxes, and Chinese Capitalism in Southeast Asia," 92.

33. Descours-Gatin, *Quand l'opium finançait la colonisation en Indochine: L'élaboration de da Régie Générale de l'opium, 1860 à 1914*, 95–96.

34. Cooke, "A Chinese Businessman in 1860 French Cochinchina: The Making of Wang Tai (1828–1900)," 1–33.

35. *China Imperial Maritime Customs: II. Special Series: No 9*, 49.

36. An Asian unit of weight that corresponds to approximately 60 kg.

37. Additional Commercial Convention, June 26, 1887, Article V.

38. Claré, "Juger aux marges de l'Indochine: le cas des trafiquants d'opium de Lào Cai (1902–1940)," 83–104.

39. Descours-Gatin, *Quand l'opium finançait la colonisation en Indochine*, 191–92.

40. Descours-Gatin, *Quand l'opium finançait la colonisation en Indochine*, 209.

41. Sasges, "State, Enterprise and the Alcohol Monopoly in Colonial Vietnam," 145.

42. Bardoux, "M. Doumer and His Work in Indochina," 613–15.

43. Report presented to the Chamber of Deputies, Jun 24, 1901, NS 496.

44. Report presented to the Chamber of Deputies, Jun 24, 1901, NS 496.

45. Commercial Report for 1901 by O. Tiberi, the assistant in charge at Mengzi Customs Office, *L'Echo de Chine*, March 9, 1903.

46. Report on opium trade in China, *L'Echo de Chine*, January 23, 1904.

47. Réau to Bapst, July 9, 1906, NS 584; *China Maritime Customs Decennial Reports I*, 276.

48. Descours-Gatin, *Quand l'opium finançait la colonisation en Indochine*, 213.

49. Lin, "Late Qing Perceptions of Native Opium," 117–144; Bello, "The Venomous Course of Southwestern Opium: Qing Prohibition in Yunnan, Sichuan, and Guizhou in the Early Nineteenth Century," 1109–42.

50. Beau to Delcassé, June 3, 1902, NS 584.

51. Prince Qing (of the First Rank) was an official title given to Qing princes in the peerage system. Prince Qing mentioned here is Yikuang (1838–1917), a Manchu politician who was made a first-rank prince by Empress Dowager Cixi in 1894. During the Boxer Rebellion (1899–1900), Yikuang was the head of the pro-foreign faction in the court and fought against the Boxers. He accompanied Li Hongzhang during the peace negotiations with the Eight-Nation Alliance after the joint European forces suppressed the rebellion.

52. In February 1905, the US Senate held a hearing about the campaigns against British opium trade in China. The purpose was to put international pressure on Britain to terminate the Nanjing Treaty that legalized opium traffic in China. *Senate*

Documents, no. 135, 58th Congress, 3rd Session, "Report of Hearing by the American State Department on Petitions to the President to use his Good Offices for the Release of China from Treaty Compulsion to Tolerate the Opium Traffic." The submission of the Philippine Report to Congress, on March 12, 1906, was another phase of anti-opium campaign in the US.

53. Reins, "Reform, Nationalism and Internationalism: The Opium Suppression Movement in China and the Anglo-American Influence, 1900–1908," 101–42.

54. For the translation of anti-opium edicts and other official measures, see Wright, "The International Opium Commission," 828–68.

55. The report by Réau, March 20, 1908, NS 507.

56. Dispatch from His Majesty's Minister in China Forwarding a General Report by Mr. Leech Respecting the Opium Question in China, China no. 2 (1908), National Archives of the UK: FO 881/9139.

57. China Maritime Customs Decennial Reports I, 276; Piaud, "Opium et intérêts français au Yunnan (1906–1937)," 197.

58. "Le prix d'achat de l'opium," 284.

59. Descours-Gatin, *Quand l'opium finançait la colonisation en Indochine*, 245–59.

60. In the Fashoda Incident, France had to withdraw from its Fashoda expedition in Egypt, which it started against Britain in 1898. In the end, France ceded control of Egypt to Britain in return for dominance over Morocco. Following the incident, French anxiety over British colonial rivalry was commonly called the "Fashoda syndrome."

61. Fang, Xu, and Mu, *Yunnan shiliao congkan* [Collections of historical sources of Yunnan], 501–3.

62. Lee, *France and the Exploitation of China*, 202.

63. Lee, *France and the Exploitation of China*, 190–203. Doumer was planning to use potential disturbances by the Muslim and Miao minorities as a pretext to annex the province. Tixier, "La Chine dans la stratégie impériale: le rôle du Quai d'Orsay et de ses agents," 79.

64. Andrew, *Theophile Delcassé and the Making of the Entente Cordiale: A Reappraisal of French Foreign Policy, 1898–1905*, 26–91.

65. Cited in Lee, *France and Exploitation of China*, 211.

66. There was no treaty provision for the creation of a French consulate in Kunming, so François was appointed as consul général honoraire.

67. John Hay to Thiébaut, Washington, July 3, 1900, Ministère des Affaires Étrangères, *Documents Diplomatiques: Chine, 1899–1900*, 64–66.

68. Ministère des Affaires Étrangères, *Documents Diplomatiques: Chine, 1899–1900*, 241; Bruguière, "Le chemin de fer de Yunnan," 267–69.

69. Report prepared by the Colonial Commission in charge of examining the bill for the approval of the convention finalized by the Indochina government for the construction of the Haiphong–Yunnan-sen Railway, presented by Deputy Maurice Ordinaire on June 24, 1901, NS 496.

70. Report prepared by the Colonial Commission in charge of examining the bill for the approval of the convention finalized by the Indochina government for the construction of the Haiphong–Yunnan-sen Railway, presented by Deputy Maurice Ordinaire on June 24, 1901, NS 496.

71. Cited in Bruguière, "Le chemin de fer de Yunnan," 265.

72. Bruguière, "Le chemin de fer de Yunnan," 140.

73. Bruguière, "Le chemin de fer de Yunnan," 140.

74. Delcassé to Decrais, July 10, 1902, NS 235.

75. Delcassé to Beau, September 17, 1901; October 24, 1901, NS 496.

76. Company administration to Delcassé, April 9, 1902, NS 497.

77. Interpretation of the agreement is based on a comparative reading of the Chinese and French versions of the text.

78. The Hanoi Exposition (November 3, 1902–February 26, 1903) was designed and organized by Paul Doumer to demonstrate his accomplishments in Indochina. Hanoi was the centerpiece of Doumer's policy of centralization and colonial urbanization. One of the major themes of the exposition was the riches of China, which would be carried to the French economy by way of the Yunnan railway. For a detailed account of the Hanoi Exposition, see Vann, "'All the World's a Stage,' Especially in the Colonies: L'exposition de Hanoî, 1902–1903," 181–91.

79. Contre-projet de règlement du chemin de fer remis par le Vice-Roi Lin-Chao-Nien, March 24, 1903, NS 499.

80. Note sur les modifications apportées au projet de règlement, March 31, 1903, NS 499.

Chapter 2

1. Todd, *A Velvet Empire: French Informal Imperialism in the Nineteenth Century.*

2. Fourniau, "Politique coloniale ou 'politique mondiale': Doumer et le Yunnan," 55.

3. Bélard accompanied Guillemoto and Leclère during their railway route survey in 1899 and published a report on mining the same year, NS 441.

4. Report by Leclère, "Projet de chemin de fer de Haiphong à Yunnan-sen: Ressources minières du Yunnan," 1901, NS 496.

5. "Rapport de l'ingénieur des mines," by Leclère July 31, 1899, NS 441.

6. Robert Lee gives a detailed account of how the French "Syndicat minier du Yunnan," founded in May 1899, was transformed into the Anglo-French Yunnan Syndicate. Lee, *France and the Exploitation of China*, 256–66.

7. "Syndicat du Yunnan: Details of the Concession Obtained from the Chinese Imperial Government," *The Financial News*, September 27, 1902.

8. Memorial by Wei Guangtao concerning the expanding mining activities of the Anglo-French syndicate, May 20, 1902, in Fang, Xu, and Mu, *Yunnan shiliao congkan* [Collections of historical sources of Yunnan], 532–33.

9. Telegram by Wei Guangtao concerning the ban on Chinese businesses in Gejiu, September 1902, in Fang, Xu, and Mu, *Yunnan shiliao congkan* [Collections of historical sources of Yunnan], 533.

10. Telegram by the foreign relations office concerning the businesses in Gejiu and revisions on the mining agreement, September 1902, in Fang, Xu, and Mu, *Yunnan shiliao congkan* [Collections of historical sources of Yunnan], 533.

11. Giersch, *Corporate Conquests*, 128–37.

12. "Agreement for the Yunnan mining concession, June 21, 1902," in MacMurray, *Treaties and Agreements with and Concerning China, 1894–1919*, 913.

13. Sun, "Mining Labor in the Ch'ing Period," 45–61.

14. Atwill, *The Panthay Rebellion*, 22.

15. For a detailed account of work practices and superstitious beliefs among mine workers, see Golas, "Mining," 387–410.

16. Dejean de la Bâtie to Delcassé, September 20, 1899, NS 441.

17. *L'Echo de Chine*, June 22, 1903.

18. François to Delcassé, November 24, 1903, NS 236. Based on Chinese sources, des Forges contends that Zhou's escape to the mountains after the rebellion in 1903 was facilitated by the reluctance of local officials to punish him, owing to his considerable popularity. He also asserts that Zhou led the miner bands that were expected to join the revolutionary forces in 1908 but instead joined the Qing army in charge of suppressing the very rebellion they were once expected to support. Des Forges, *Hsi-Liang and the Chinese National Revolution*, 103–26.

19. Fan and Wang, "Zhou Yunxiang yu Gemindang" (Zhou Yunxiang and Sun Yat-Sen's Revolutionary Party), 119–27.

20. The French translation of Zhou Yunxiang's letter to Sainson, attached to the letter of François to Delcassé, July 9, 1903, NS 236.

21. The French translation of Zhou Yunxiang's letter to Sainson, attached to the letter of François to Delcassé, July 9, 1903, NS 236.

22. Li, *Yunnan jindai jingji shi* [Economic history of Yunnan], 99.

23. Giersch, *Corporate Conquests*, 137–40.

24. Yi, "Yunnan da shiye jia zhao laoren zhuan" [The story of Yunnan's great entrepreneur Mr. Zhao]. 157–61.

25. The National Archives of the UK, FO 228/2640.

26. *China Maritime Customs Decennial Reports I*, 280. C. F. Brown does not mention any foreign-run mine apart from a Japanese mine during his visit in December 1908–May 1910.

27. The tael was a Chinese currency. 1 French franc was equal to 3.73 taels in 1901 and 3.40 taels in 1911.

28. The report by Grillières, attached to the letter of François to Delcassé, March 17, 1903, NS 236.

29. The report by Grillières, attached to the letter of François to Delcassé, March 17, 1903, NS 236.

30. The French translation of Ding's letter to François, April 10, 1903; Dubail to the French Ministry of Foreign Affairs, February 21, 1903, NS 236.

31. François, *Le mandarin blanc: souvenirs d'un consul en Extrême Orient, 1886–1904, temps & continents.*

32. François to Delcassé, March 24, 1903, NS 236.

33. Telegram from Hanoi, May 23, 1903, NS 236. In the meantime, the French government refused the Chinese request to transfer Qing troops from Nanjing via Tonkin to suppress the rebellion. Telegram by Dubail, May 24, 1903; Doumergue to Delcassé, May 30, 1903, NS 236.

34. Rene Bouiller, the general secretary of the railway company, to the French Ministry of Foreign Affairs, May 26, 1903, NS 498.

35. Altan, "Yirminci Yüzyıl Başında Çin'de Fransız Sömürgeciliği, Yunnan Müslümanları ve Osmanlılar [French colonialism, Yunnan Muslims, and the Ottomans in early twentieth-century China]," 50–56.

36. Landau, *Pan-Islam: History and Politics*, 1–5.

37. Burke, "Pan-Islam and Moroccan Resistance to French Colonial Penetration, 1900–1912," 97–118; Landau, "Documents on Pan-Islamic Activity in France near the End of the Ottoman Empire," 64–100.

38. The dispatch by Paul Beau, dated August 28, 1901, MAE 26, PAAP13, 154–55.

39. Malsagne, *Au cœur du grand jeu: la France en Orient: Charles-Eudes Bonin (1865–1929), explorateur diplomate.*

40. Beau to Delcassé, June 18, 1902, MAE 26, PAAP13, 203–4.

41. D'Agostini, "French Policy and the Hajj in Late-Nineteenth-Century Algeria: Governor Cambon's Reform Attempts and Jules Gervais-Courtellemont's Pilgrimage to Mecca," 112–41.

42. François to Delcassé, March 17, 1903; April 14, 1903, NS 236. The opening sentence of Courtellemont's article on northern Yunnan is as follows: "Assigned by the governor general of Indochina for a mission to investigate Yunnan, I wanted to take advantage of my presence in the northern part of the province to discover the great bend of the Blue River described by explorer Bonin." Gervais-Courtellemont, "La Grande Boucle Du Yang-Tseu-Kiang," 266.

43. François to Delcassé, April 14, 1903, NS 236.

44. Gervais-Courtellemont, *Voyage au Yunnan.*

45. Sainson to Dubail, July 5, 1903, attached to the letter by François to Delcassé, July 9, 1903, NS 236.

46. François to Delcassé, August 31, 1903, NS 236.

47. François to Delcassé, August 31, 1903, NS 236.

48. Beau to Doumergue, July 3, 1903, NS 499.

49. Beau to Doumergue, July 3, 1903, NS 499.

50. Beau to Doumergue, July 3, 1903, NS 499.

51. Beau to Doumergue, July 3, 1903, NS 499.

52. Leduc to Delcassé, August 16, 1904, NS 501.

53. French missionaries were active among Chinese Muslims, albeit not very successful in conversion. Israeli, "The Cross Battles the Crescent: One Century of Missionary Work Among Chinese Muslims (1850–1950)," 203–21.

54. Sainson to Beau, September 28, 1904, NS 501.

55. Dubail's note on Algerian guards, April 26, 1905, NS 502.

Chapter 3

1. [The railway is the way to hell]. This saying emerged when France built the railway to Salonika in the Ottoman Empire. "The Railway of Yunnan," *The North China Daily News*, June 28, 1906.

2. De Montjau, *De l'émigration de Chinois: Au point de vue des intérêts Européens*, 14.

3. Fauvel, "La main-d'œuvre chinois dans nos colonies," 116. For the details of the conditions of coolie deployment on Réunion Island, see Stanziani, "Beyond Colonialism: Servants, Wage Earners, and Indentured Migrants in Rural France and on Réunion Island," 64–87.

4. Fauvel, "La main-d'œuvre chinois dans nos colonies," 116.

5. Fauvel, "La main-d'œuvre chinois dans nos colonies," 116.

6. Fauvel, "La main-d'œuvre chinois dans nos colonies," 116.

7. The initial Chinese recruits for Réunion originated from Southeast Asia. They were a defiant group, unafraid to resort to violence if subjected to mistreatment. Until 1908, Chinese workers in Réunion resisted their employers in various forms, including absenteeism, petitioning, and open revolt. Kam, *L'Engagisme chinois: révoltes contre un nouvel esclavagisme*, 35–39; 60–69.

8. The piastre was a silver-based currency used in French Indochina from 1885 to 1952. In 1890, 1 piastre equaled to 4.14 francs, and in 1902, 2.21 francs.

9. François to Delcassé, November 20, 1903, NS 499.

10. Réau, "Note sur le chemin de fer du Yunnan," December 1905, NS 503.

11. Réau, "Note sur le chemin de fer du Yunnan," December 1905, NS 503.

12. Réau, "Note sur le chemin de fer du Yunnan," December 1905, NS 503.

13. Martínez, "'Unwanted Scraps' or 'An Alert, Resolute, Resentful People'? Chinese Railroad Workers in French Congo," 79–98.

14. Extract from Sainson's report dated November 30, 1903, NS 500.

15. Vetch's relationship with the consul was perceived as problematic by many of their contemporaries, but it reached a scandalous apex when Mrs. Vetch departed from Fuzhou, found to be pregnant with Claudel's child. Chiovenda, "Portrait d'un engagiste: Les premières opérations de recrutement de Francis Vetch et Paul Claudel à Madagascar et à la Réunion (1901)," 231–43.

16. Fauvel, "La main-d'œuvre chinois dans nos colonies," 118.

17. Benton and Liu, *Dear China: Emigrant Letters and Remittances, 1820–1980*, 171–72.

18. Extract from the letter of Dufour to the French vice-consul in Beihai, November 8, 1903, NS 500.

19. The French vice-consul in Beihai to Dufour, December 8, 1903, NS 500.

20. The dollar currency used in Hong Kong and Guangdong area.

21. The French vice-consul in Beihai to Delcassé, January 26, 1904, NS 500.

22. The Chinese Foreign Relations Office to Dubail, attached to the letter dated June 30, 1904, NS 501.

23. Dubail to Delcassé, June 30, 1904, NS 501.

24. Casenave to Delcassé, June 4, 1904, NS 501.

25. The British government became the first to formalize an official treaty with the Qing government for coolie emigration and continued to amend the terms of coolie recruitment as needed. However, the establishment of these rules and regulations did not necessarily translate into improved treatment of workers on British and other plantations. Ngai, "Trouble on the Rand: The Chinese Question in South Africa and the Apogee of White Settlerism," 59–78. For a comparison of French and British practices of coolie employment, see Stanziani, "Local Bondage in Global Economies: Servants, Wage Earners, and Indentured Migrants in Nineteenth-Century France, Great Britain, and the Mascarene Islands," 1218–51.

26. Casenave, June 4, 1904, NS 501.

27. Implementing a universal contract labor law was still incomplete and on French colonists' agenda as late as 1929. Martínez, "Unwanted Scraps," 86–87.

28. Casenave to Delcassé, June 4, 1904, NS 501.

29. Lindner, "Indentured Labour in Sub-Saharan Africa (1870–1918): Circulation of Concepts between Imperial Powers," 59–82.

30. Gaston Kahn to Dubail, May 4, 1905, NS 502.

31. Note by Casenave, May 8, 1905, NS 502.

32. For a discussion of "coolie as commodity" and how the British worked to create a free labor market in China, see McKeown, "The Social Life of Chinese Labor," 62–83.

33. Stanziani, "The Abolition of Slavery and the 'New Labor Contract' in French Equatorial Africa, 1890–1914,", 236.

34. Stanziani, "The Abolition of Slavery and the 'New Labor Contract' in French Equatorial Africa, 1890–1914,", 239–40.

35. The idea of a free labor market was not the same everywhere. For instance, in the Straits Settlements, British entrepreneurs viewed government intervention against the monopoly of Chinese brokers as essential for the maintenance of a "free" labor market. McKeown, "The Social Life of Chinese Labor," 75–79.

36. Leduc to Delcassé, December 5, 1904, NS 501.

37. Yunnan Railway Office's memorial to the Yun-Gui Viceroy for the recruitment of three thousand workers, in Zhuang, Wu, and Li, *Dian-yue tielu shiliao huibian* [Documents on the Yunnan–Vietnam railway], 20.

38. Leduc to Delcassé, February 2, 1905, NS 501.

39. Company administrator Genty to Delcassé, February 22, 1906, NS 689.

40. "Réponses au rapport de la sous-commission du chemin de fer du Yunnan: recruitment des coolies," 1907. Bibliothèque Nationale de France, FOL-V-6956 (3).

41. Hu-Dehart, "Chinese Coolie Labor in Cuba in the Nineteenth Century: Free Labor or Neo-slavery?" 67–86.

42. Cohen, "The Chinese of the Panama Railroad: Preliminary Notes on the Migrants of 1854 Who 'Failed,'" 309–20; Yun, *The Coolie Speaks: Chinese Indentured Laborers and African Slaves in Cuba.*

43. "Note sur le recrutement des coolies pour le chemin de fer de Laokay à Yunnansen," November 2, 1905, annexed to the letter of the railway company to the Ministry of Colonies, November 13, 1905, NS 689.

44. Leduc to Delcassé, December 5, 1904, NS 501.

45. Leduc to Delcassé, November 27, 1904, NS 501.

46. Company director Jules Gouin to Delcassé, November 26, 1904, NS 501.

47. Letter of P. Badie, the apostolic missionary, to P. Oster, the attorney of the Yunnan mission in Kunming, December 11, 1904. The date of the incident is unclear. NS 501.

48. The French Consul in Fuzhou to the French Ministry of Foreign Affairs, January 5, 1906, NS 504.

49. The French Consul in Canton to Dubail, May 4, 1905, NS 502.

50. Robert L. Irick, *Ch'ing Policy Toward the Coolie Trade*, 1847–1878.

51. Confidential telegram of Yunnan viceroy to the customs *daotai*, August 2, 1905, NS 502.

52. Dubail to Delcassé, May 31, 1905, NS 502.

53. Clémentel to the company, December 18, 1905, NS 689.

54. Leduc to Delcassé, June 15, 1905, NS 502.

55. Dupont to Leduc, May 25, 1905, NS 502.

56. Prince Qing to Dubail, September 15, 1905, NS 502.

57. The Proclamation of Viceroy Cen Chunxuan, December 1, 1905, NS 503.

58. Telegram sent by the viceroy of Yunnan, quoted in Cen's proclamation, December 1 1905, NS 503.

59. Letter of Governor Cen to the French consul in Canton, January 17, 1906, NS 504.

60. Kahn to Beau, March 13, 1906, NS 504.

61. The Minister of Colonies to the Ministry of Foreign Affairs, May 2, 1906, NS 504.

62. Flayelle to the Mengzi consul, March 10, 1906, NS 504.

63. Flayelle to the Ministry of Foreign Affairs, March 18, 1906; Flayelle to the Mengzi consul, March 10, 1906, NS 504.

64. A piece titled "Striking Injustices" was published in *Der Ostasiatische Lloyd* in 1905. I use the partial French translation attached to the official correspondence between Dubail and Rouvier dated October 20, 1905, NS 503. An example from the Anglophone press was D. W. Crofts, "A Grave Scandal," in *North China Daily News*, June 20, 1906. French citizens were also involved in the debate through their letters to *North China Daily News.*

65. Sibeud, "Une libre pensée impériale? Le Comité de protection et de défense des indigènes (ca.1892–1914)," 57–74.

66. Daughton, "The 'Pacha Affair' Reconsidered: Violence and Colonial Rule in Interwar French Equatorial Africa," 493–524; Pedersen, "Alsace-Lorraine and Africa: French Discussions of French and German Politics, Culture, and Colonialism in the Deliberations of the Union for Truth, 1905–1913," 9–28.

Chapter 4

1. Singaravélou, *Tianjin cosmopolis: une autre histoire de la mondialisation.*

2. Blanc, "Vectors of French Cultural Imperialism: Training in Medicine and Pharmacy at the Schools of Hanoi and Dakar (1904–1953)," 122–33; McClellan, "Science, Medicine, and French Colonialism in Old-Regime Haiti," 36–58.

3. Bretelle-Establet, *La santé en Chine du Sud, 1898–1928.*

4. Lebon to the Ministry of Foreign Affairs, April 13, 1898, NS 651.

5. The Ministry of Colonies to the Ministry of Foreign Affairs, April 7, 1898, NS 651.

6. Bretelle-Establet, "Resistance and Receptivity: French Colonial Medicine in Southwest China, 1898–1930," 174–75.

7. Note by the Ministry of Colonies, July 20, 1898, NS 651.

8. Report by Dr. Magunna, January 9, 1908, NS 650.

9. Report by Dr. Magunna, January 9, 1908, NS 650.

10. General Pennequin had said "Le sanatorium du Tonkin est au Yunnan." Cited in Doumer, *Situation de L'Indo-Chine*, 8.

11. Paul Doumer, *Situation de L'Indo-Chine*, 8.

12. Clavel, *L'Assistance médicale indigène en Indo-chine: organisation et fonctionnement*, 497.

13. Du Halgouet to Dubail, March 19, 1905, NS 651.

14. Report by Dr. Ayraud, the chief physician of the Kunming Hospital, for the year 1904, NS 650.

15. Report by Dr. Ayraud, the chief physician of the Kunming Hospital, for the year 1904, NS 650.

16. Medical report for 1907, prepared by Dr. Magunna, attached to the letter dated February 18, 1908, NS 650.

17. Dr. Dinan, *Notice sur la propriété fébrifuges*, 13–15.

18. Company directors Guibert and Gouin to the Ministry of Foreign Affairs, June 19, 1902, NS 496. The company directors asked the ministry to assign Dr. Regnault to the position as a ministry cadre though they were willing to pay for his expenses. That was the condition of Dr. Regnault to accept the position.

19. The resume of Dr. Regnault attached to his acceptance letter, May 4, 1902, NS 496.

20. Ackerman, "The Intellectual Odyssey of a French Colonial Physician: Jules Regnault and Far Eastern Medicine," 1084.

21. "Le chemin de fer du Yunnan," *La Dépêche Coloniale Illustrée*, June 30, 1908.

22. Compagnie française des chemins de fer de l'Indochine et du Yunnan and Société de construction de chemins de fer indo-chinois, *Le chemin de fer du Yunnan*, 124.

23. Compagnie française des chemins de fer de l'Indochine et du Yunnan and Société de construction de chemins de fer indo-chinois, *Le chemin de fer du Yunnan*, 125.

24. Extract from the medical report by Dr. Barbezieux for 1903, NS 500.

25. Report signed by Billecocq, the government commissaire, April 24, 1906, ANOM, GGI/65 989.

26. Letter by Sainson, November 30, 1903, NS

27. Letter by the French resident in Thanh-Hoa, June 2, 1907, ANOM, GGI/66 003.

28. Rochaix, "La Lutte contre le paludisme" [The fight against malaria].

29. "Le chemin de fer du Yunnan," *La Dépêche Coloniale Illustrée*, June 30, 1908, 182.

30. "Le chemin de fer du Yunnan," *La Dépêche Coloniale Illustrée*, June 30, 1908, 183.

31. Monnais, "Rails, Roads, and Mosquito Foes," 198.

32. Medical report by Dr. Magunna for the consular hospital in Kunming, January 29, 1908, NS 650.

33. Report by Dr. Feray for 1908, attached to the letter of Bourgeois to the Ministry of Foreign Affairs, May 28, 1909, NS 650.

34. Report by Dr. Barbezieux, NS 651.

35. Sainson to François, October 29, 1903, NS 651.

36. Leduc to Rouvier, July 13, 1905, NS 650.

37. Bourgeois to the Ministry of Foreign Affairs, October 5, 1908, NS 650.

38. Medical report by Dr. Feray for September 1908, October 25, 1908, NS 650.

39. Bretelle-Establet, "From Extending French Colonial Control to Safeguarding National Prestige," 82.

40. Bourgeois to the Ministry of Foreign Affairs, November 21, 1908, NS 650.

41. Reporter, "Kan! Kan! Kan! Faguo yunnan zhi zhimin jiankang" [Look! Look! Look! French colonial medicine in Yunnan], 361–62.

42. Bourgeois to the Ministry of Foreign Affairs, March 26, 1909, NS 650.

43. Che to Bourgeois, June 10, 1909, NS 650.

44. In 1904, French officials made several attempts to purchase land in Kunming for the purpose of creating a European concession, but local officials rejected them because the existing treaties between China and France did not include provisions or regulations for concession areas. Leduc to Delcassé, October 15, 1904; December 29, 1904, NS 501.

45. Pholsena, "Technology and Empire," 547.

46. Pholsena, "Technology and Empire," 549.

47. French exterritorial rights were regulated by the Sino-French Treaty of Huangpu, signed on October 24, 1844. Cassel, *Grounds of Judgment: Extraterritoriality and Imperial Power in Nineteenth-Century China and Japan*, 54.

48. All the examples summarized in this section are from a correspondence between the French consul in Kunming and Delcassé, April 10, 1905, NS 502.

49. A subsequent correspondence indicates that Cagnotti was arrested in Yen Bay (Vietnam) where he impersonated a French citizen named Pujol. A case was opened for his crimes in China, and he was sentenced to three-month imprisonment for his resistance to security forces. He was recorded as an insubordinate man and submitted to military authorities. Vaselle to the Ministry of Foreign Affairs, December 22, 1905, NS 503.

50. The criminal court record in Hanoi, NS 503.

51. Vaselle to the Minister of Foreign Affairs, December 22, 1905, NS 503.

52. Réau, "Note sur le chemin de fer du Yunnan," December 1905, NS 503.

53. Du Halgouet to the minister in Beijing, March 7, 1905, NS 502.

54. Du Halgouet to the minister in Beijing, January 31, 1905, NS 501.

55. Du Halgouet to the minister in Beijing, January 31, 1905, NS 501.

56. The company administration to the Ministry of Foreign Affairs, April 20, 1904, NS 500.

57. The governor-general to the Minister of Colonies, May 28, 1906, NS 505.

58. The governor-general to the Minister of Colonies, May 28, 1906, NS 505.

59. Guibert to Réau, December 22, 1905, attached to the letter of Leduc to Rouvier, January 13, 1906, NS 504.

60. Réau to Bapst, July 20, 1907, NS 506.

61. Leduc to Delcassé, April 10, 1905, NS 502.

62. Leduc to Delcassé, April 10, 1905, NS 502.

63. The Mengzi *daotai* to Bradier, October 22, 1908, NS 694.

64. Bourgeois to Bradier, June 19, 1909, NS 694.

65. Bradier to Boissonnas, August 5, 1909, NS 694.

66. Leduc to Rouvier, October 17, 1905, NS 502.

67. Broni to Guibert, August 9, 1905, NS 502.

68. Leduc to Delcassé, April 10, 1905, NS 502.

69. Guibert to the consul, March 2, 1905, NS 502.

70. Leduc to Rouvier, October 16, 1905, NS 503.

71. Leduc to Rouvier, October 16, 1905, NS 503.

72. The company perspective cited in a letter by Leduc to Rouvier, October 17, 1905, NS 503.

73. Grimani to Leduc, December 13, 1905, NS 503.

74. Dubail to Rouvier, October 30, 1905, NS 503.

75. Leduc to Delcassé, May 6, 1905, NS 502.

76. Réau to Dubail, January 11, 1905, NS 501.

77. Réau to Pichon, March 2, 1908, NS 662.

78. Réau to Pichon, March 2, 1908, NS 662.

79. Letter to the Greek legation in Paris, April 18, 1908, NS 662.

80. Note pour le ministre, May 22, 1907, NS 599.

81. "La Justice Consulaire de France en Chine," *L'Echo de Chine*, March 10, 1908, NS 599.

82. "Projet de loi" discussed in the Chamber of Deputies on October 22, 1907, NS 599.

83. Réau's report on the crimes against the Italians, April 25, 1907; the company directors to the Ministry of Colonies, March 10, 1908, NS 507.

84. Réau to Arnold, December 30, 1907, NS 507.

85. Réau to Arnold, December 30, 1907, NS 507.

86. Réau's report on the crimes against the Italians in Yunnan, April 25, 1907, NS 507.

Chapter 5

1. Zhou, *Wan qing liu ri xuesheng yu jindai yunnan shehui* [Chinese students in Japan in the late Qing period and modern Yunnan society], 1.

2. In the third issue of *Min Bao*, Hu Hanmin included "building a republic" (*jianshe gonghe zhengti*) as one of the six principles of the magazine. Hu, "Min Bao zhi liu da zhuyi" [The six principles of Min Bao].

3. Li and Shi, *Xinhai geming zai yunnan* [The 1911 revolution in Yunnan], 22.

4. Bergère, *Sun Yat-sen*, 49–59.

5. Wilbur, *Sun Yat-sen: Frustrated Patriot*, 60–67.

6. Zou, "The Revolutionary Army," 32–38.

7. Sun, *San-min chu-i: The Three Principles of the People*, 17.

8. Karl, *Staging the World: Chinese Nationalism at the Turn of the Twentieth Century*, 16.

9. Jiang, "Lun zhimin zhi zhonglei" [On the types of colonialism], 16–19.

10. Xue, "Faren yu yunnan" [The French and Yunnan], 361.

11. The gradual expansion of Russia into Manchuria began after the first Sino-Japanese War (1894–1895).

12. Yi, "Wei dian-yue tielu zaocheng jinggao quandian" [A warning to Yunnan on the completion of the Yunnan–Vietnam railway], 515.

13. Duiker, *The Rise of Nationalism in Vietnam, 1900–1941*, 40; Karl, *Staging the World*, 164–66.

14. Chao, "Yuenan ren zhi haiwai xue shu" [A letter from a Vietnamese abroad written in blood], 627–39. A translation of the second part of this text is available in Dutton, Werner, and Whitmore, *Sources of Vietnamese Tradition*, 353–69.

15. Lâm, *Colonialism Experienced: Vietnamese Writings on Colonialism, 1900–1931*, 80.

16. Lenin, *Imperialism: The Highest Stage of Capitalism*, 58–69.

17. Lenin's *Imperialism: The Highest Stage of Capitalism* was first published in 1916, and Nkrumah's *Neo-Colonialism: The Last Stage of Imperialism* was first published in 1965. In a recent study on Chinese railroad workers employed at the

Transcontinental Railroad, Manu Karuka has defined this process through which indigenous lands were appropriated in the United States as "railroad colonialism." Karuka, *Empire's Tracks: Indigenous Nations, Chinese Workers, and the Transcontinental Railroad.*

18. Fei, "Yunnan shibai zhi da yexin jia Li Wenxiu zhuan" [The story of ambitious Li Wenxiu], 339.

19. Xia, "Yunnan zhi jianglai" [The future of Yunnan], 261.

20. Dutton, Werner, and Whitmore, *Sources of Vietnamese Tradition*, 354.

21. Chao, "Ai yue diao dian" [Grief over Vietnam and condolence for Yunnan], 641–42.

22. Marr, *Vietnamese Anticolonialism, 1885–1925*, 113.

23. Phan's view on seeking foreign assistance for independence, as well as China's role in Vietnam's development, was distinct from his fellow Phan Châu Trinh (1872–1926), another leading figure of Vietnamese nationalism. Phan Châu Trinh viewed the pre-French era in Vietnam as akin to Chinese colonialism, given that the ruling dynasties in China had exploited Vietnamese resources for their own benefit. In his opinion, Vietnam's historical reliance on China was a significant mistake. For a translation of Phan Châu Trinh's original writings, see Sinh, *Phan Chau Trinh and His Political Writings.*

24. Zhe, "You dian shu lue" [A tour in Yunnan], 344.

25. Chen Rongchang, a local intellectual, was known for his activities in the fields of culture and education. Xie, *Qingdai yunnan gaoben shiliao* [Documents on Yunnan from the Qing period]. Toward the end of the railway's construction, Britain increased its activities for a new railway between Yunnan and Burma. In this process, Chen became a railway rights activist, petitioning the government with other elites of Yunnan to build Yunnan's railways with native capital. Zhuang, Wu, and Li, *Dian-yue tielu shiliao huibian* [Documents on the Yunnan–Vietnam railway], 47.

26. François to Delcassé, March 30, 1903, NS 498.

27. Zhuang, Wu, and Li, *Dian-yue tielu shiliao huibian* [Documents on the Yunnan–Vietnam railway], 20–21.

28. Masaya, "Phan Boi Chau in Japan," 67.

29. Wu, "Lun yunnan duiyu zhongguo zhi diwei" [On Yunnan's place in China], 288.

30. Li, "Ji wushen yuanri benbao zhounian jinian qingzhu huishi" [Report on the New Year's Day meeting to commemorate our periodical's anniversary], 7–8.

31. Zhang, "Sijue hui xuanyan" [Manifesto of the Dare-to-Die Society], 320.

32. Chinese Youth, "He yunnan sijue hui wen" [A congratulatory message to the Yunnan Dare-to-Die Society], 321.

33. Leibold, *Reconfiguring Chinese Nationalism: How the Qing Frontier and its Indigenes Became Chinese*, 6.

34. Wells, *Political Thought of Sun Yat-Sen: Development and Impact*, 29.

35. Dirlik, *Marxism in the Chinese Revolution*, 26–38.

36. Maurice William was an American dentist and socialist thinker who refuted the economistic view of Marx in his book *The Social Interpretation of History* published in 1920. Although known for his influence on Sun Yatsen, he is rather an obscure scholar in Euro-America. For his influence on Sun Yatsen, see Shotwell, "Sun Yat-Sen and Maurice William," 19–26.

37. Sun, *San-min chu-i*, 268.

38. Lai and Trescott, "Liang Qichao, Sun Yat-Sen, and the 1905–1907 Debate on Socialism," 1053.

39. Bernal, *Chinese Socialism to 1907*, 65–66.

40. George, *Progress and Poverty: An Inquiry into the Cause of Industrial Depressions and of Increase of Want with Increase of Wealth, the Remedy*, 12.

41. George, *Progress and Poverty*, 272.

42. Henry George argued for common property, not government ownership: "We must make land common property." *Progress and Poverty*, 328.

43. Dirlik, *Marxism in the Chinese Revolution*, 33–34.

44. Xia, "Lun guomin baocun guotu zhi fa" [On the methods of people's protection of the country territories], 69–77.

45. Goswami, *Producing India: From Colonial Economy to National Space.*

46. Goswami, *Producing India*, 70.

47. Yan, "Yunnan zhi shiye" [Economy of Yunnan], 170–75.

48. Xia, "Lun guomin baocun guotu zhi fa," 71–72.

49. Dirlik, *Marxism in the Chinese Revolution*, 35.

50. "Dian du Li Jingxi zouqing chibu jiekuan banli shiye zhe" [Yunnan Governor Li Jingxi asks for government help to recover the losses of local industries], in *Yunnan zazhi xuanji* [Selections from the *Yunnan Journal*], 195.

51. Shao, "Zhongguo guomin liguo zhi genben daji" [The fundamentals of Chinese nation-building], 182–86.

52. Jia, "Yunnan yi su zhenxing canye" [Yunnan should develop its silk industry immediately], 198–201.

53. Yi, "Zhuzhong cuqian shiye yi su min kun" [Emphasis on simple industries will enrich the people], 189–91.

54. Shao, "Zhonggui guomin liguo zhi genben daji," 182.

55. Zhen, "Zhong nong zhuyi" [Agrarianism], 195. "Zhong nong zhuyi zhe" refers to the Physiocrats in modern Chinese. I translated the title of the essay as "agrarianism" because the emphasis was on agriculture and other views of the physiocratic school were not discussed in detail.

56. Zhen, "Zhong nong zhuyi" [Agrarianism], 198.

57. Yi, "Quan you mian tongbao zucheng hua shang zonghui" [On the need to establish the Chinese Chamber of Commerce in Burma], 175.

58. The Chamber was founded in 1908 with approximately 10,000 members. *Yunnan zazhi xuanji* [Selections from the *Yunnan Journal*], 733.

59. Li, "Late Qing Governors and Provincial Assemblies," 56.

60. Lee, "Local Self-Government in Late Qing: Political Discourse and Moral Reform," 35–37.

61. Lee, "Local Self-Government in Late Qing," 39.

62. Lee, "Local Self-Government in Late Qing," 39–44.

63. Lee, "Local Self-Government in Late Qing," 45–46.

64. Teng and Fairbank, *China's Response to the West: A Documentary Survey, 1839–1923*, 229.

65. Mo, "Lun difang zizhi zhi jingshen" [On the essence of local self-governance], 14–16.

66. Jeffrey G. Barlow argues that Sun Yatsen, within his anti-Manchu racialism, wanted to declare a secessionist Han state in south China. Barlow, *Sun Yat-sen and the French, 1900–1908*, 25.

67. Donald Sutton also argues that Yunnanese nationalists in Japan were not separatists. Sutton, *Provincial Militarism and the Chinese Republic: The Yunnan Army 1905–25*, 45.

68. Kuhn, "Local Self-Government under the Republic: Problems of Control, Autonomy, and Mobilization," 276.

69. Kuhn, "Local Self-Government," 271.

70. Li, "Late Qing Governors and Provincial Assemblies," 39.

71. Kang and Xu, "Qingmo xinzheng yu yunnan xinhai geming" [Late Qing New Policy and the 1911 revolution in Yunnan], 72.

72. Kang and Xu, "Qingmo xinzheng yu yunnan xinhai geming" [Late Qing New Policy and the 1911 revolution in Yunnan], 72.

73. Zhang Taiyan (1868–1936), one of the prominent figures within the Revolutionary Alliance, stood out among those criticizing the parliamentary system, as he anchored his critique in a radical idea of equality. Zhang contended that the local self-government bureaus were devised to reinforce the government's grip on local areas, a strategy that would, in his view, further sanction and legitimize the privileges enjoyed by the gentry. Wang, "Zhang Taiyan's Concept of the Individual and Modern Chinese Identity," 231–59. For Sun Yatsen's attitude toward the New Policy, see Guo, "Gemingjia yu qingmo xinzheng: shicong Sun Zhongshan dui xinzheng de taidu kan lixian zhengti gaige shibai de biranxing" [The revolutionaries and the late Qing New Policy: On the inevitability of the failure of the New Policy reforms from the perspective of Sun Yatsen].

74. Xia, "Guohui wenti zhi zhenxiang" [The truth about the National Assembly], 147. In an analysis of the late Qing rural disturbances, Lucien Bianco indicates that the fear of tax increases and military recruitment in addition to the costs of political and educational reforms were the main motives behind peasant resistance to the New Policy reforms. Bianco, *Wretched Rebels: Rural Disturbances on the Eve of the Chinese Revolution*, 130–43.

75. Wu, "Lun yunnan duiyu zhongguo zhi diwei" [On Yunnan's place in China], 281–88.

Chapter 6

1. Li, "Chinese Bourgeois Revolutionaries and the Movement to Regain Economic Rights Towards the End of the Qing Dynasty," 147–69; Rankin, *Elite Activism and Political Transformation in China: Zhejiang Province, 1865–1911*, 5–6.

2. Rankin, *Elite Activism.*

3. Rankin, "Nationalistic Contestation and Mobilization Politics: Practice and Rhetoric of Railway-Rights Recovery at the End of the Qing," 333.

4. Lee, *China's Quest for Railway Autonomy, 1904–1911: A Study of the Chinese Railway-Rights Recovery Movement*, 50.

5. Li, "Chinese Bourgeois Revolutionaries," 149.

6. Lu, "Court-Sponsored Reforms, 1895–1898," 60.

7. Edwards, "The Origins of British Financial Co-Operation with France in China, 1903–6."

8. Cao Yin, "The Yunnan–Burma Railway, 1860s–1940s: Imagining, Planning and Rejecting a Railway That Was Never Built," 298–315.

9. Bei Da, "Wuhu tengyue tielu zhi yunming" [Alas, the fate of the Tengyue railway], *Yunnan zazhi xuanji* [Selections from the *Yunnan Journal*], 414–17.

10. The company was founded in 1905 as the Yunnan–Sichuan Railway Company for the self-construction of railways, and later renamed as the Yunnan–Sichuan–Tengyue Railway to include the lines to Burma. Yun-Gui Governor Ding Zhenduo communicated the foundation of the company on July 16, 1905, in Zhuang, Wu, and Li, *Dian-yue tielu shiliao huibian* [Documents on the Yunnan–Vietnam railway], 2.

11. Telegram sent by the Yunnanese students in Tokyo to Beijing, October 13, 1905, in *Yunnan zazhi xuanji* [Selections from the *Yunnan Journal*], 422.

12. Note pour le Ministre, February 2, 1907, NS 506.

13. "Lettre des étudiantes en Europe au Vice-roi du Yunnan," *Universal Gazette*, May 4, 1907, NS 506.

14. Xue Sheng, "Dian shen tiaochen shu dian-yue lu choukuan banfa" [The Yunnan gentry proposes the methods of fundraising for the purchase of the Yunnan–Vietnam railway], in *Yunnan zazhi xuanji* [Selections from the *Yunnan Journal*], 494.

15. Des Forges, *His-Liang and the Chinese National Revolution.*

16. French translation of the telegram of Xiliang to the viceroys and governors of diverse provinces, January 2, 1908, NS 507.

17. The French Consul in Canton to Pichon, January 14, 1908, NS 507.

18. Shi Fu, "Dian-yue pangbian ji tiedao zhi shikuang" [The Yunnan–Vietnam border and the situation of the railway], 460–77.

19. The French minister in Beijing to Pichon, February 20, 1908, NS 507.

20. Note sur la question de la rétrocession du chemin de fer du Yunnan à la Chine, August 7, 1907, NS 506.

21. Note sur la question de la rétrocession du chemin de fer du Yunnan à la Chine, August 7, 1907, NS 506.

22. "The Yunnan Railway," *Peking Daily News*, May 7, 1909, NS 509.

23. Yi, "Wei dian-yue tielu gaocheng jinggao quandian" [A warning to Yunnan for the completion of the Yunnan–Vietnam railway], 515.

24. Hua Sheng, "Dian-yue tielu wenti" [The Yunnan–Vietnam railway problem], 525–27.

25. Hua, "Dian-yue tielu wenti" [The Yunnan–Vietnam railway problem], 531.

26. Hua, "Dian-yue tielu wenti" [The Yunnan–Vietnam Railway problem], 531.

27. Sun was planning to see Doumer but when Doumer was recalled to Paris, his successor Beau declined Sun's meeting request. Barlow, *Sun Yat-sen and the French, 1900–1908*, 52–55; Bergère, *Sun Yat-sen*, 116–17.

28. Bergère, *Sun Yat-sen*, 84–85.

29. J. Kim Munholland recounts that Sun, later in his memories, referred Réau as "my friend, the French consul." Munholland, "The French Connection That Failed: France and Sun Yat-sen, 1900–1908," 82.

30. Munholland, "The French Connection That Failed," 84.

31. Bergère, *Sun Yat-sen*, 178.

32. Des Forges, *His-Liang and the Chinese National Revolution*, 123.

33. The National Archives of the UK, FO 228/2639, 24.

34. Fan, "Yuenan huaqiao yu wu shen yunnan hekou qiyi" [Overseas Chinese in Vietnam and the Wushen uprising in Hekou, Yunnan], 23–31.

35. Sun, "466 gongli dian-yue tielu shang de qiwan tiao xingming" [70,000 lives on the 466 km Yunnan–Vietnam Railway], 14–18.

36. Sun, "466 gongli dian-yue tielu shang de qiwan tiao xingming" [70,000 lives on the 466-km Yunnan–Vietnam Railway], 14–18.

37. Chen, "1908 nian hekou qiyi yu zhong-fa jiaoshe" (The Hekou uprising in 1908 and the negotiation between China and France), 105–10.

38. Tixier, "La Chine dans la stratégie impériale," 261.

39. Réau to Bapst, May 20, 1908, NS 507.

40. Réau to Bapst, May 20, 1908, NS 507.

41. Réau to Bapst, May 20, 1908, NS 507.

42. The French minister in Beijing to Pichon, July 10, 1908, NS 240.

43. The report submitted by the Mengzi consul, July 1908, NS 240.

44. The Indochina governor to the Ministry of Colonies, June 6, 1908, NS 240.

45. Fan Dewei quotes from Hu Hanmin's report to Sun Yatsen, "Yuenan huaqiao yu wu shen Yunnan Hekou qiyi" [Overseas Chinese in Vietnam and the Wushen uprising in Hekou, Yunnan], 24.

46. Des Forges, *His-Liang and the Chinese National Revolution*, 115–30.

47. Des Forges, *His-Liang and the Chinese National Revolution*, 129.

48. Prince Qing to the Ministry of Foreign Affairs, May 17, 1908, NS 507.

49. Li and Shi, *Xinhai geming zai Yunnan* [The xinhai revolution in Yunnan], 55–56.

50. The Ministry of Colonies to the Ministry of Foreign Affairs, July 14, 1909, NS 694.

51. The Ministry of Colonies to the Ministry of Foreign Affairs, July 14, 1909, NS 694.

52. The French minister in Beijing to Pichon, February 22, 1909, NS 694.

53. The French minister in Beijing to Pichon, February 22, 1909, NS 694.

54. The French minister in Beijing to Pichon, February 22, 1909, NS 694.

55. Bonhoure to Veroudart, August 6, 1908, NS 694.

56. Veroudart's report concerning the claims made by the company and entrepreneurs, September 1, 1908, NS 694.

57. Veroudart's note on the company claims for recruitment costs, NS 694.

58. The compensation claim submitted by the railway company, July 15, 1908, NS 694.

59. The Franco-Chinese Convention for the repression of revolutionary movements at the Sino-Tonkin border, signed on January 4, 1909, NS 694.

60. Indochina Governor Klobukowski to the French minister in Beijing, May 24, 1909, NS 694.

61. Can Xue, "Zheren mianliu tielu zongli de miqie" [Zhejiang people's struggle to keep the head of the railway bureau]," 534.

62. Bourgeois to the Ministry of Foreign Affairs, February 10, 1909, NS 508.

63. David Todd calls the French policy of spreading its culture of luxury for imperial purposes as "champagne imperialism." Todd, *A Velvet Empire*, 123–74.

64. Che to Bourgeois, April 19, 1910, NS 510.

65. Flayelle to Getten, April 22, 1910, NS 510.

66. Flayelle to Margerie, April 26, 1910, NS 510.

67. "Faut-il prolonger le chemin de fer du Yunnan?" *Le Temps*, November 12, 1909, NS 510.

68. Ralph William Huenemann argues that the self-built railways were closely affiliated with Han nationalism. Huenemann, *The Dragon and the Iron Horse: The Economics of Railroads in China, 1876–1937*, 78.

69. Bruguière, "Le chemin de fer du Yunnan."

Epilogue

1. Speech by Henry Bourgeois, the Delegate of the Ministry of Foreign Affairs in Yunnan and the Representative of the French Government, annexed to the report by the Delegate of the Ministry of Foreign Affairs in Yunnan to Margerie, the French minister in Beijing, April 4,1910, ANOM, 47 T-P 1134/h.

2. Cooper and Stoler, "Between Metropole and Colony: Rethinking a Research Agenda," 1–56.

3. The contrast between bare life and politics refers to Agamben's distinction between *zoe* (life in the sense of biological existence) and *bios* (life in the sense of a political or social existence). In his work *Homo Sacer: Sovereign Power and Bare Life*, Agamben argues that in modern times, the distinction between *zoe* and *bios* has been blurred and led to the emergence of a new form of political power, which he terms "biopower."

4. In his discussion of the relation between nationalism and labor movements in postwar French Africa, Frederick Cooper defines the process as "the ideological journey from the peculiarity of the African to the universality of the worker." Cooper, "The Dialectics of Decolonization: Nationalism and Labor Movements in Postwar French Africa," 412.

5. Xu Guoqi, *Strangers on the Western Front: Chinese Workers in the Great War*; Mark O'Neill, *The Chinese Labour Corps: The Forgotten Chinese Labourers of the First World War.*

6. Smith, *Like Cattle and Horses: Nationalism and Labor in Shanghai, 1895–1927.*

7. Wang, Peng, and Fan, *Dian-yue tielu yu dian dongnan shaoshu minzu diqu shehui bianqian yanjiu* [The Yunnan–Vietnam railway and social change in the ethnic regions of southeast Yunnan].

8. Song, "Kangri zhangzheng shiqi zhong-fa dian-yue tielu yunshu jiaoshe lunlue" [The negotiations during the anti-Japanese war about the Yunnan–Vietnam railway between China and France], 83–88.

9. Summers, *Yunnan—A Chinese Bridgehead to Asia: A Case Study of China's Political and Economic Relations with Its Neighbors.*

10. Ding Shifu, "Dian-yue tielu de xiujian ji qi tongche hou de yingxiang" [The effects of the Yunnan–Vietnam railway during the construction and postconstruction period], 72.

Bibliography

Archival Sources

The National Archives of the United Kingdom

FO 228/2639
FO 228/2640
FO 233/123
FO 371/37

Archives diplomatiques à La Courneuve (MAE)

Nouvelle Série: Chine 148CPCOM

RELATIONS AVEC LA FRANCE

NS 194–204 Dossier General
NS 228–243 Yunnan
NS 250–251 Protection par la France de divers nationaux

INDUSTRIE, TRAVAUX PUBLICS

NS 441–444 Mines du Yunnan

CHEMINS DE FER

NS 494–510 Ligne du Yunnan

QUESTIONS SOCIALES

NS 584–589 Opium

QUESTION JUDICIAIRES

NS 599–601 Juridiction consulaire

CHINE SUPPLEMENTAIRE

NS 650 Ouvres françaises: hôpitaux à Canton et Yunnanfou
NS 655 Ouvres médicales en Chine
NS 662 Protection des Grecs et Ottomans par la France: Dossiers Particuliers
NS 689 Emigration Chinoise: Recrutement de Coolies pour le Cie du Yunnan

NS 694 Contentieux-Réclamations: Affaire de Phalong, assassinat d'un officier français du Yunnan; Indemnités; Affaire Langrone
NS 695 Réclamations de Chinois; Réclamations de Français; Dossiers divers

Archives nationales d'outre-mer, Aix-en-Provence (ANOM)
Archives municipales de Mulhouse

Published Sources

Ackerman, Evelyn Bernette. "The Intellectual Odyssey of a French Colonial Physician: Jules Regnault and Far Eastern Medicine." *French Historical Studies* 19, no. 4 (1996): 1083–102.

Agamben, Giorgio. *Homo Sacer: Sovereign Power and Bare Life*. Stanford, CA: Stanford University Press, 1998.

Altan, Selda. "Politics of Life and Labor: French Colonialism in China and Chinese Coolie Labor During the Construction of the Yunnan–Indochina Railway, 1898–1910." *International Labor and Working-Class History* 101 (2022): 77–99.

Altan, Selda. "Yirminci Yüzyıl Başında Çin'de Fransız Sömürgeciliği, Yunnan Müslümanları ve Osmanlılar [French colonialism, Yunnan Muslims, and the Ottomans in early twentieth-century China]." *Toplumsal Tarih* 323 (2020): 50–56.

Amat, Jorge, dir. Through the Consul's Eyes. Brooklyn, NY: First Run/Icarus Films, 2001.

Andrew, Christopher M. *Theophile Delcassé and the Making of the Entente Cordiale: A Reappraisal of French Foreign Policy, 1898–1905*. New York: Macmillan, 1968.

Atwill, David G. *The Panthay Rebellion: Islam, Ethnicity, and the Dali Sultanate in Southwest China, 1856–1873*. London: Verso, 2023.

Bardoux, Jacques. "M. Doumer and His Work in Indochina." *The Speaker: The Liberal Review* (1901): 613–15.

Barlow, Jeffrey G. *Sun Yat-Sen and the French, 1900–1908*. Berkeley: University of California Press, 1979.

Bei, Da. "Wuhu tengyue tielu zhi yunming" [Alas, the fate of the Tengyue railway], *Yunnan zazhi xuanji* [Selections from the *Yunnan Journal*], 414–17. Beijing: Zhishi chanquan chubanshe, 2013.

Bello, David A. *Across Forest, Steppe, and Mountain: Environment, Identity, and Empire in Qing China's Borderlands*. New York: Cambridge University Press, 2016.

Bello, David. "The Venomous Course of Southwestern Opium: Qing Prohibition in Yunnan, Sichuan, and Guizhou in the Early Nineteenth Century." *Journal of Asian Studies* 62, no. 4 (2003): 1109–142.

Benton, Gregor, and Hong Liu. *Dear China: Emigrant Letters and Remittances, 1820–1980*. Oakland: University of California Press, 2018.

Bergère, Marie-Claire. *Sun Yat-Sen*. Stanford, CA: Stanford University Press, 1998.

Bernal, Martin. *Chinese Socialism to 1907*. Ithaca, NY: Cornell University Press, 1976.

Bernard, Odile, Élisabeth Locard, and Pierre Marbotte. *Le chemin de fer du Yunnan: une aventure française en Chine: d'après les correspondances et les photographies de Albert Marie et Georges-Auguste Marbotte*. Bordeaux: Elytis, 2016.

Bianco, Lucien. *Wretched Rebels: Rural Disturbances on the Eve of the Chinese Revolution*, translated by Philip Liddell. Cambridge, MA: Harvard University Press, 2009.

Blanc, Floriane. "Vectors of French Cultural Imperialism: Training in Medicine and Pharmacy at the Schools of Hanoi and Dakar (1904–1953)." *Pharmacy in History* 52, no. 3–4 (2010): 122–33.

Bonin, Hubert, Catherine Hodeir, and Jean-François Klein. *L'Esprit économique impérial (1830–1970): Groupes de pression et réseaux du patronat colonial en France et dans l'empire*. Paris: Société française d'histoire d'outre-mer, 2008.

Bretelle-Establet, Florence. "From Extending French Colonial Control to Safeguarding National Prestige." In *Uneasy Encounters: The Politics of Medicine and Health in China, 1900–1937*, edited by Iris Borowy, 63–92. Frankfurt: Peter Lang, 2009.

Bretelle-Establet, Florence. "Resistance and Receptivity: French Colonial Medicine in Southwest China, 1898–1930." *Modern China* 25, no. 2 (1999): 171–203.

Bretelle-Establet, Florence. *La santé en Chine du Sud, 1898–1928*. Paris: CNRS, 2002.

Brocheux, Pierre, and Daniel Hémery. *Indochina: An Ambiguous Colonization, 1858–1954*. Berkeley: University of California Press, 2009.

Brown, C. F. "Mines and Mineral Sources of Yunnan." *Memoirs of the Geological Survey of India* 47 (1923).

Bruguière, Michel. "Le chemin de fer du Yunnan. Paul Doumer et la politique de l'intervention française en Chine, 1889–1902." *Revue d'histoire diplomatique* (1963).

Brunat, Paul. *Exploration commerciale du Tonkin. Report presented to the Lyon Chamber of Commerce*. Lyon: Imprimerie Commerciale Pitrat Ainé, 1885.

Brunschwig, Henri. *French Colonialism, 1871–1914. Myths and Realities*. London: Pall Mall, 1966.

Burke, Edmund. "Pan-Islam and Moroccan Resistance to French Colonial Penetration, 1900–1912." *Journal of African History* 13, no. 1 (1972): 97–118.

Can, Xue. "Zheren mianliu tielu zongli de miqie" [Zhejiang people's struggle to keep the head of the railway bureau]." In *Yunnan zazhi xuanji* [Selections from the *Yunnan Journal*], 534. Beijing: Zhishi chanquan chubanshe, 2013.

Cao, Yin. "The Yunnan–Burma Railway, 1860s–1940s: Imagining, Planning and Rejecting a Railway That Was Never Built." *Journal of Southeast Asian Studies* 54, no. 2 (2023): 298–315.

Cassel, Par Kristoffer. *Grounds of Judgment: Extraterritoriality and Imperial Power in Nineteenth-Century China and Japan*. New York: Oxford University Press, 2012.

Chan, Ming K. "Labor in Modern and Contemporary China." *International Labor and Working-Class History* 11 (1977): 13–18.

Chan, Shelly. *Diaspora's Homeland: Modern China in the Age of Global Migration*. Durham, NC: Duke University Press, 2018.

Chao, Nanzi. "Ai yue diao dian" [Grief over Vietnam and condolence for Yunnan]. In *Yunnan zazhi xuanji* [Selections from the *Yunnan Journal*], 640–44. Beijing: Zhishi chanquan chubanshe, 2013.

Chao, Nanzi. "Yuenan ren zhi haiwai xue shu" [A letter from a Vietnamese abroad written in blood]. In *Yunnan zazhi xuanji* [Selections from the *Yunnan Journal*], 627–39. Beijing: Zhishi chanquan chubanshe, 2013.

Chen, Yuanhui. "1908 nian hekou qiyi yu zhong-fa jiaoshe" (The Hekou uprising in 1908 and the negotiation between China and France). *Journal of Yunnan Nationalities University* 28, no. 4 (2011): 105–10.

Cheng, Yifang, "Dang'an jilu xia de dian-yue tielu" [The Yunnan–Vietnam railway in archival records]. *Yunnan Dang'an* 10 (2017): 40–42.

Chesneaux, Jean. *The Chinese Labor Movement, 1919–1927*. Stanford, CA: Stanford University Press, 1968.

China Imperial Maritime Customs I: Native Opium 1887. Special Series, Issue 9. Shanghai: Statistical Department of the Inspectorate General of Customs, 1888.

China Maritime Customs Decennial Reports I. Statistical Series. Shanghai: Statistical Department of the Inspectorate General of Customs, 1913.

Chinese Youth. "He yunnan sijue hui wen [A congratulatory message to the Yunnan Dare-to-Die Society]." In *Yunnan zazhi xuanji* [Selections from the *Yunnan Journal*], 320–21. Beijing: Zhishi chanquan chubanshe, 2013.

Chiovenda, Lucille. "Portrait d'un engagiste: Les premières opérations de recrutement de Francis Vetch et Paul Claudel à Madagascar et à la Réunion (1901)." In *Le travail colonial: Engagés et autres mains-d'œuvre migrantes dans les empires, 1850–1950*, edited by Eric Guerassimoff and Issiaka Mandé, 231–43. Paris: Riveneuve éditions, 2015.

Claré, Thomas. "Juger aux marges de l'Indochine: le cas des trafiquants d'opium de Lào Cai (1902–1940)." *Moussons: Recherche en sciences humaines sur l'Asie du Sud-Est*, no. 35 (2020): 83–104.

Clavel. *L'Assistance médicale indigène en Indo-chine: organisation et fonctionnement*. Paris: Augustin Challamel, 1908.

Cohen, Lucy M. "The Chinese of the Panama Railroad: Preliminary Notes on the Migrants of 1854 Who 'Failed.'" *Ethnohistory* 18 (1971): 309–20.

Compagnie française des chemins de fer de l'Indochine et du Yunnan and Société de construction de chemins de fer indo-chinois. *Le chemin de fer du Yunnan*. Paris: Impr. G. Goury, 1910.

Cooke, Nola. "A Chinese Businessman in 1860 French Cochinchina: The Making of Wang Tai (1828–1900)." *Chinese Southern Diaspora Studies* 9 (2021): 1–33.

Cooper, Frederick. "The Dialectics of Decolonization: Nationalism and Labor Movements in Postwar French Africa." In *Tensions of Empire: Colonial Cultures in a Bourgeois World*, edited by Frederick Cooper and Ann Laura Stoler, 406–35. Berkeley: University of California Press, 1997.

Cooper, Frederick, and Ann Laura Stoler. "Between Metropole and Colony: Rethinking a Research Agenda." In *Tensions of Empire: Colonial Cultures in a Bourgeois World*, edited by Frederick Cooper and Ann Laura Stoler, 1–56. Berkeley: University of California Press, 1997.

D'Agostini, Aldo. "French Policy and the Hajj in Late-Nineteenth-Century Algeria: Governor Cambon's Reform Attempts and Jules Gervais-Courtellemont's Pilgrimage to Mecca." In *The Hajj and Europe in the Age of Empire*, edited by Umar Ryad, 112–41. Leiden: Brill, 2017.

Daughton, J. P. *In the Forest of No Joy: The Congo-Océan Railroad and the Tragedy of French Colonialism*. New York: W. W. Norton, 2021.

Daughton, J. P. "The 'Pacha Affair' Reconsidered: Violence and Colonial Rule in French Equatorial Africa." *Journal of Modern History* 91 (2019): 493–524.

De Lanessan, Jean Marie Antoine. *L'Expansion coloniale de la France*. Paris: F. Alcan, 1886.

De Montjau, Madier. *De l'émigration de Chinois: Au point de vue des Intérêts Européens*. Paris: Maisonneuve et Compagnie, 1873.

Des Forges, Roger V. *Hsi-Liang and the Chinese National Revolution*. New Haven, CT: Yale University Press, 1973.

Descours-Gatin, Chantal. *Quand l'opium finançait la colonisation en Indochine: l'élaboration de la régie générale de l'opium, 1860 à 1914*. Paris: L'Harmattan, 1992.

"Dian du Li Jingxi zouqing chibu jiekuan banli shiye zhe" [Yunnan governor Li Jingxi asks for government help to recover the losses of local industries]." In Yunnan zazhi xuanji [Selections from the *Yunnan Journal*], 191–95. Beijing: Zhishi chanquan chubanshe, 2013.

Dinan, Dr. *Notice sur les propriétés fébrifuges et antipaludéennes du "Calliandra grandiflora" (Bentham)*. Tours: Imprimerie Paul Bousrez, 1906.

Ding, Shifu. "Dian-yue tielu xiujian ji qi tongche hou de yingxiang" [The effects of the Yunnan–Vietnam railway during the construction and post-construction period]. *Social Sciences in Yunnan* 3 (1982): 69–76.

Dirlik, Arif. *Marxism in the Chinese Revolution*. Lanham, MD: Rowman & Littlefield, 2005.

Doumer, Paul. *Situation de L'Indo-Chine (1897–1901): rapport*. Hanoi: F. H. Schneider, 1902.

Duan, Xi. *1910 nian de lieche: Dian-yue tielu bai nian ji shi* [The train of 1910: The 100 years of Yunnan–Vietnam railway]. Kunming: Yunnan meishu chubanshe, 2002.

Duan, Xi. *Dian-yue tielu: kuayue bianian de xiao huoche* [The Yunnan–Vietnam railway: The small train that spans a hundred years]. Kunming: Yunnan meishu chubanshe, 2007.

Dubois, Christophe. "L'Arsenal de Fuzhou et la presence militaire française au Fujian (1869–1911)." In *La France en Chine (1843–1943)*, edited by Jacques Weber, 91–102. Nantes: Presse académiques de l'Ouest, 1997.

Duiker, William J. *The Rise of Nationalism in Vietnam, 1900–1941*. Ithaca, NY: Cornell University Press, 1976.

Dupuis, Jean. *A Journey to Yunnan and the Opening of the Red River to Trade*. Bangkok: White Lotus Press, 1998.

Dutton, George Edson, Jayne Susan Werner, and John K. Whitmore. *Sources of Vietnamese Tradition*. New York: Columbia University Press, 2012.

Edwards, E. W. "The Origins of British Financial Co-Operation with France in China, 1903–6." *English Historical Review* 86, no. 339 (1971): 285–317.

Fan, Dewei. "Yuenan huaqiao yu wu shen yunnan hekou qiyi." [Overseas Chinese in Vietnam and the Wushen uprising in Hekou, Yunnan]. *Overseas Chinese History Studies* 3 (2011): 23–31.

Fan, Dewei, and Wang Liyun. "Zhou Yunxiang yu Gemingdang" (Zhou Yunxiang and Sun Yat-Sen's Revolutionary Party). *Journal of National Museum of China* 8 (2013): 119–27.

Fan, Wen. *Bisezhai*. Beijing: Beijing chuban jituan gongsi, 2018.

Fang, Guoyu, Xu Wede, and Mu Qing. *Yunnan shiliao congkan* [Collections of historical sources of Yunnan]. Kunming: Yunnan daxue, 2001.

Fauvel, Albert-Auguste. "La main-d'oeuvre chinois dans nos colonies." *Revue de Géographie* 53 (December 1903): 112–27.

Fei, Jiangjun. "Yunnan shibai zhi da yexin jia Li Wenxiu zhuan" [The story of ambitious Li Wenxiu]. *Yunnan zazhi xuanji* [Selections from the *Yunnan Journal*], 339–41. Beijing: Zhishi chanquan chubanshe, 2013.

Feuerwerker, Albert. "Economic Trends in the Late Ch'ing Empire, 1870–1911." In *The Cambridge History of China*, edited by John K. Fairbank and Liu Kwang-Ching. Vol. 1, Part 2. Cambridge: Cambridge University Press, 1980.

Foucault, Michel. *Technologies of the Self: A Seminar with Michel Foucault*. Amherst: University of Massachusetts Press, 1988.

Foucault, Michel. *The Birth of Biopolitics: Lectures at the Collège de France, 1978–79*. New York: Palgrave Macmillan, 2008.

Fourniau, Charles. "Politique coloniale ou 'politique mondiale': Doumer et le Yunnan." In *Histoires d'outre-Mer: Mélanges en l'honneur de Jean-Louis Miège*, Vol. 1, 49–73. Aix-en-Provence: Publications de l'université de Provence, 1992.

François, Auguste. *Le mandarin blanc: souvenirs d'un consul en Extrême-Orient, 1886–1904. Temps & Continents*. Paris: Calmann-Lévy, 1990.

Garnier, Francis, and Louis Delaporte. *The Mekong Exploration Commission Report, 1866–1868: A Pictorial Journey on the Old Mekong: Cambodia, Laos, and Yunnan*. Saigon: White Lotus Press, 1996.

Garnier, Francis. *Further Travels in Laos and in Yunnan*. Saigon: White Lotus, 1996.

Geddes, W. R. "Opium and the Miao: A Study in Ecological Adjustment." *Oceania* 41, no. 1 (1970): 1–11.

Geenens, Raf, and Helena Rosenblatt, eds. *French Liberalism from Montesquieu to the Present Day*. Cambridge: Cambridge University Press, 2012.

George, Henry. *Progress and Poverty: An Inquiry into the Cause of Industrial Depressions and of Increase of Want with Increase of Wealth, the Remedy*. New York: Robert Schalkenbach Foundation, 1937.

Gervais-Courtellemont, Jules. "La Grande Boucle du Yang-Tseu-Kiang." *Annales de Géographie* 69 (1904): 266–69.

Gervais-Courtellement, Jules. *Voyage au Yunnan*. Paris: Librairie Plon, 1904.

Giersch, Charles Patterson. *Asian Borderlands: The Transformation of Qing China's Yunnan Frontier*. Cambridge, MA: Harvard University Press, 2006.

Giersch, C. Patterson. *Corporate Conquests: Business, the State, and the Origins of Ethnic Inequality in Southwest China*. Stanford, CA: Stanford University Press, 2020.

Golas, Peter J. "Mining." In *Science and Civilisation in China*, Vol. 5, edited by Joseph Needham, 387–410. Cambridge: Cambridge University Press, 1999.

Goswami, Manu. *Producing India: From Colonial Economy to National Space*, Chicago: University of Chicago Press, 2004.

Guo, Ji, "Gemingjia yu qingmo xinzheng: shicong Sun Zhongshan dui xinzheng de taidu kan lixian zhengti gaige shibai de biranxing" [The revolutionaries and the late Qing New Policy: On the inevitability of the failure of the New Policy reforms from the perspective of Sun Yatsen]. The International Symposium on the Late Qing New Policy and the Xinhai Revolution, Shanghai, 2007.

Gyory, Andrew. *Closing the Gate: Race, Politics, and the Chinese Exclusion Act*. Chapel Hill: University of North Carolina Press, 2000.

He, Zhongfu. *Gebishi tielu: Yunnan ren yin yi zhibao de cun gui tielu* [An inch-gauge railway that the people of Yunnan take pride of]. Kunming: Yunnan meishu chubanshe, 2007.

Herman, John E. "Empire in the Southwest: Early Qing Reforms to the Native Chieftain System." *Journal of Asian Studies* 56 (1997): 47–74.

Hershatter, Gail. *The Workers of Tianjin, 1900–1949*. Stanford, CA: Stanford University Press, 1986.

Honig, Emily. *Sisters and Strangers: Women in the Shanghai Cotton Mills, 1919–1949*. Stanford, CA: Stanford University Press, 1986.

Howard, Joshua H. *Workers at War: Labor in China's Arsenals, 1937–1953*. Stanford, CA: Stanford University Press, 2004.

Hu, Hanmin, "Min Bao zhi liu da zhuyi [The six principles of Min Bao]." *Min Bao*, vol. 3, April 1906.

Hua, Sheng. "Dian-yue tielu wenti" [The Yunnan–Vietnam Railway problem]. In *Yunnan zazhi xuanji* [Selections from the *Yunnan Journal*], 525–34. Beijing: Zhishi chanquan chubanshe, 2013.

Hu-Dehart, Evelyn. "Chinese Coolie Labor in Cuba in the Nineteenth Century: Free Labor or Neo-slavery?" *Slavery & Abolition* 14. no. 1 (1993): 67–86.

Huenemann, Ralph William. *The Dragon and the Iron Horse: The Economics of Railroads in China, 1876–1937*. Cambridge, MA: Harvard University Press, 1984.

Irick, Robert L. *Ch'ing Policy toward the Coolie Trade, 1847–1878*. Taipei: Chinese Materials Center, 1982.

Israeli, Raphael. "The Cross Battles the Crescent: One Century of Missionary Work Among Chinese Muslims (1850–1950)." *Modern Asian Studies* 29, no. 1 (1995): 203–21.

Jia, Yuan. "Yunnan yi su zhenxing canye" [Yunnan should develop its silk industry immediately]. In *Yunnan zazhi xuanji* [Selections from the *Yunnan Journal*], 198–201. Beijing: Zhishi chanquan chubanshe, 2013.

Jiang, Ze. "Lun zhimin zhi zhonglei" [On the types of colonialism]. In *Yunnan zazhi xuanji* [Selections from the *Yunnan Journal*], 16–19. Beijing: Zhishi chanquan chubanshe, 2013.

Jung, Moon-Ho. *Coolies and Cane: Race, Labor, and Sugar in the Age of Emancipation*. Baltimore, MD: Johns Hopkins University Press, 2006.

Kam, Édith Wong Hee. *L'Engagisme chinois: révoltes contre un nouvel esclavagisme*. Saint André: Océan Éditions, 1999.

Kang, Chunhua, and Xu Xinmin. "Qingmo xinzheng yu yunnan xinhai geming" [Late Qing New Policy and the 1911 revolution in Yunnan]. In *Yunnan sheng shekejie jinian xinhai geming 100 zhounian wenji* [The anthology commemorating the centenary of the 1911 revolution], 69–82. Kunming: Yunnan daxue chubanshe, 2011.

Karl, Rebecca E. *Staging the World: Chinese Nationalism at the Turn of the Twentieth Century*. Durham, NC: Duke University Press, 2002.

Karuka, Manu. *Empire's Tracks: Indigenous Nations, Chinese Workers, and the Transcontinental Railroad*. Oakland: University of California Press, 2019.

Kawashima, Ken C. *The Proletarian Gamble: Korean Workers in Interwar Japan*. Durham, NC: Duke University Press, 2009.

Kim, Diana S. *Empires of Vice: The Rise of Opium Prohibition across Southeast Asia*. Princeton, NJ: Princeton University Press, 2020.

Kim, Ho-dong. *Holy War in China: The Muslim Rebellion and State in Chinese Central Asia, 1864–1877*. Stanford, CA: Stanford University Press, 2004.

Klein, Jean-François. "Une culture impériale consulaire? L'exemple de la chambre de commerce de Lyon (1830–1920)." In *Groupes de pression et réseaux du patronat colonial en France et dans l'empire*, 347–78. Paris: Société française d'histoire d'outre-mer, 2008.

Klein, Jean-François. *Un Lyonnais en Extrême-Orient: Ulysse Pila, "Vice-Roi De L'indochine" (1837–1909)*. Lyon: Editions Lyonnaises d'art et d'histoire, 1994.

Kuhn, Philip A. "Local Self-Government under the Republic: Problems of Control, Autonomy, and Mobilization." In *Conflict and Control in Late Imperial China*, edited by Frederic Wakeman Jr. and Carolyn Grant, 257–98. Berkeley: University of California Press, 1975.

Laffey, John F. "French Imperialism and the Lyon Mission to China." Unpublished dissertation, Cornell University, 1966.

Laffey, John F. "The Lyon Chamber of Commerce and Indochina During the Third Republic." *Canadian Journal of History* 10, no. 3 (1975): 325–48.

Laffey, John F. "Lyonnais Imperialism in the Far East, 1900–1938." *Modern Asian Studies* 10, no. 2 (1976): 225–48.

Laffey, John F. "Municipal Imperialism in France: The Lyon Chamber of Commerce, 1900–1914." *Proceedings of the American Philosophical Society* 119, no. 1 (1975): 8–23.

Laffey, John F. "Roots of French Imperialism in the Nineteenth Century: The Case of Lyon." *French Historical Studies* 6, no. 1 (1969): 78–92.

Lai, Cheng-chung, and Paul B. Trescott. "Liang Qichao, Sun Yat-Sen, and the 1905–1907 Debate on Socialism." *International Journal of Social Economics* 32, no. 12 (2005): 1051–62.

Lai, Walton Look. *Indentured Labor, Caribbean Sugar: Chinese and Indian Migrants to the British West Indies, 1838–1918*. Baltimore, MD: Johns Hopkins University Press, 1993.

Lâm, Truong Buu. *Colonialism Experienced: Vietnamese Writings on Colonialism, 1900–1931*. Ann Arbor: University of Michigan Press, 2000.

Landau, Jacob M. "Documents on Pan-Islamic Activity in France near the End of the Ottoman Empire." *Die Welt des Islams* 48, no. 1 (2008): 64–100.

Landau, Jacob M. *Pan-Islam: History and Politics*. London: Routledge, 2016.

Larson, Jane Leung. "Articulating China's First Mass Movement: Kang Youwei, Liang Qichao, the Baohuanghui, and the 1905 Anti-American Boycott." *Twentieth-Century China* 33, no. 1 (2007): 4–26.

"Le prix d'achat de l'opium." *L'Asie française: Bulletin mensuel du comité de l'Asie française*, no. 111 (June 1910): 284.

Lee, En-han. *China's Quest for Railway Autonomy, 1904–1911: A Study of the Chinese Railway-Rights Recovery Movement*. Singapore: Singapore University Press, 1977.

Lee, Robert. *France and the Exploitation of China, 1885–1901: A Study in Economic Imperialism*. New York: Oxford University Press, 1989.

Lee, Theresa Man Ling. "Local Self-Government in Late Qing: Political Discourse and Moral Reform." *Review of Politics* 60, no. 1 (1998): 31–53.

Leibold, James. *Reconfiguring Chinese Nationalism: How the Qing Frontier and Its Indigenes Became Chinese*. New York: Palgrave Macmillan, 2007.

Lenin, V. I. *Imperialism: The Highest Stage of Capitalism*. Sydney: Resistance Books, 1999.

Li, Gui. *Yunnan jindai jingji shi* [Economic history of Yunnan]. Kunming: Yunnan minzu chubanshe, 1995.

Li, Guotong. *Migrating Fujianese: Ethnic, Family, and Gender Identities in an Early Modern Maritime World*. Leiden: Brill, 2016.

Li, Fu. "Ji wushen yuanri benbao zhounian jinian qingzhu huishi [Report on the New Year's Day meeting to commemorate our periodical's anniversary]." In *Yunnan zazhi xuanji* [Selections from the *Yunnan Journal*], 7–10. Beijing: Zhishi chanquan chubanshe, 2013.

Li, Xiaoming, and Shi Yali. *Xinhai geming zai yunnan* [The Xinhai revolution in Yunnan]. Kunming: Yunnan meishu chubanshe, 2012.

Li, Zhenwu. "Late Qing Governors and Provincial Assemblies." In *China: How the Empire Fell*, edited by Joseph Esherick and George C. X. Wei, 36–65. New York: Routledge, 2013.

Li, Zongyi. "Chinese Bourgeois Revolutionaries and the Movement to Regain Economic Rights Towards the End of the Qing Dynasty." In *The 1911 Revolution—a Retrospective after 70 Years*, edited by Sheng Hu and Liu Danian, 147–69. Beijing: New World Press, 1983.

Lin, Man-Houng. "Late Qing Perceptions of Native Opium." *Harvard Journal of Asiatic Studies* 64, no. 1 (2004): 117–44.

Linder, Marc. *Projecting Capitalism: A History of the Internationalization of the Construction Industry. Contributions in Economics and Economic History.* Westport, CT: Greenwood, 1994.

Lindner, Ulrike. "Indentured Labour in Sub-Saharan Africa (1870–1918): Circulation of Concepts Between Imperial Powers." In *Bonded Labor: Global and Comparative Perspectives (18th-21st Century)*, 59–82. New York: Columbia University Press, 2017.

Liu, Mingkui, and Tang Yuliang. *Zhongguo gongren yundong shi* (The labour movement in China). 6 vols. Guangzhou: Guangdong renmin chubanshe, 1998.

Lorin, Amaury. *Paul Doumer, Gouverneur General de l'Indochine, 1897–1902*. Paris: L'Harmattan, 2004.

Lu, Xiaobo. "Court-Sponsored Reforms, 1895–1898." In *China, 1895–1912: State-Sponsored Reforms and China's Late-Qing Revolution*, edited by Douglas R. Reynolds. New York: M. E. Sharpe, 1995.

Lye, Colleen. *America's Asia: Racial Form and American Literature, 1893–1945*. Princeton, NJ: Princeton University Press, 2004.

MacMurray, John Van Antwerp. *Treaties and Agreements with and Concerning China, 1894–1919*. 2 vols. New York: Oxford University Press, 1921.

Malsagne, Stéphane. *Au cœur du grand jeu: la France en Orient: Charles-Eudes Bonin (1865–1929), explorateur diplomate*. Paris: Geuthner, 2015.

Marbotte, Pierre. *Une chemin de fer au Yunnan: L'adventure d'une famille française en Chine*. Saint-Cyr-sur-Loire: A. Sutton, DL, 2006.

Marr, David G. *Vietnamese Anticolonialism, 1885–1925*. Berkeley: University of California Press, 1971.

Martínez, Julia. "'Unwanted Scraps' or 'An Alert, Resolute, Resentful People'? Chinese Railroad Workers in French Congo." *International Labor and Working-Class History* 91 (2017): 79–98.

Marx, Karl. *Grundrisse: Foundations of the Critique of Political Economy*. New York: Random House, 1973.

Masaya, Shiraishi. "Phan Boi Chau in Japan." In *Phan Boi Chau and the Dong-Du Movement*, edited by Vinh Sinh, 52–100. New Haven, CT: Yale Center for International and Area Studies, 1988.

McClellan, James E. III. "Science, Medicine, and French Colonialism in Old-Regime Haiti." In *Science Medicine and Cultural Imperialism*, edited by Teresa Meade and Mark Walker, 36–58. Houndsmills, UK: MacMillan, 1991.

McKeown, Adam. "The Social Life of Chinese Labor." In *Chinese Circulations: Capital, Commodities, and Networks in Southeast Asia*, edited by Eric Tagliacozzo and Wen-chin Chang, 62–83. Durham, NC: Duke University Press, 2011.

McQuaide, Shiling. "Writing Chinese Labour History: Changes and Continuities in Labour Historiography." *Labour/Le Travail* 61 (2008): 215–37.

Meister, Otto. *"In den wilden Bergschluchten widerhallt ihr Pfeifen": als Zürcher Ingenieur beim Bau der Yunnan-Bahn in Südchina, 1903–1909* [In the wild mountain gorges their whistles echo: An engineer from Zurich building the Yunnan railway in southern China, 1903–1909], edited by Sylvia Agnes Meister and Paul Hugger and translated from Italian by Gabriela Zehnder with a biographical text by Ursula Meister-Cardi. Zurich: Limmat Verlag, 2014.

Miao, Chaozhu. "Fa diguo zhuyi yu dian-yue tielu" [French imperialism and the Yunnan–Vietnam railway]. *Honghe Xueyuan Xuebao* 2 (1986): 28–39.

Ministère des Affaires Étrangères. *Documents Diplomatiques: Chine, 1899–1900*. Paris: Imprimerie Nationale, 1900.

Mo, Zhihun. "Lun difang zizhi zhi jingshen" [On the essence of local self-governance]. In *Yunnan zazhi xuanji* [Selections from the *Yunnan Journal*], 14–16. Beijing: Zhishi chanquan chubanshe, 2013.

Monnais, Laurance. "Rails, Roads, and Mosquito Foes." In *Imperial Contagions: Medicine, Hygiene, and Cultures of Planning in Asia*, edited by R. Peckham and D. M. Pomfret, 195–214. Hong Kong: Hong Kong University Press, 2013.

Munholland, J. Kim. "The French Connection That Failed: France and Sun Yat-sen, 1900–1908." *Journal of Asian Studies* 32, no. 1 (1972): 77–95.

Nankoe, Hakiem, Jean-Claude Gerlus, and Martin J. Murray. "The Origins of the Opium Trade and the Opium Regie in Colonial Indochina." In *The Rise and Fall of Revenue Farming: Business Elites and the Emergence of the Modern State in Southeast Asia*, edited by John Butcher and Howard Dick, 182–95. London: Palgrave Macmillan UK, 1993.

Ngai, Mae M. "Trouble on the Rand: The Chinese Question in Africa and the Apogee of White Settlerism." *International Labor and Working-Class History* 91 (2017): 59–78.

Ngai, Mae. *The Chinese Question: The Gold Rushes and Global Politics*. New York: W. W. Norton, 2021.

Nkrumah, Kwame. *Neo-Colonialism. The Last Stage of Imperialism*. London: Thomas Nelson & Sons, 1965.

Northrup, David. *Indentured Labor in the Age of Imperialism, 1834–1922*. Cambridge: Cambridge University Press, 1995.

O'Neill, Mark. *The Chinese Labour Corps: The Forgotten Chinese Labourers of the First World War*. Melbourne: Penguin Group Australia, 2014.

Park-Barjot, Rang Ri. "Le patronat français des travaux publics et les réseaux ferroviaires dans l'empire français: L'exemple du chemin de fer du Yunnan, 1898–1913." In *L'Esprit économique impérial (1830–1970): Goupes de pression et réseaux du patronat colonial en France et dans l'empire*, edited by Hubert Bonin, Catherine Hodeir, and Jean-François Klein, 653–70. Paris: Publications de la SFHCM, 2008.

Park-Barjot, Rang-Ri. *La société de construction des Batignolles: Des origines à la première guerre mondiale, 1846–1914*. Paris: Presses de l'université Paris-Sorbonne, 2005.

Pedersen, Jean Elisabeth. "Alsace-Lorraine and Africa: French Discussions of French and German Politics, Culture, and Colonialism in the Deliberations of the Union for Truth, 1905–1913." *Historical Reflections* 40 (2014): 9–28.

Peng, Zhaorong. *San guo yanyi, bainian migui–Dian-yue tielu de lishi tuxiang* [The story of three kingdoms and the one hundred years of meter-gauge train—the historical image of the Yunnan–Vietnam railway]. Kunming: Yunnan jiaoyu chubanshe, 2010.

Perry, Elizabeth J. *Shanghai on Strike: The Politics of Chinese Labor*. Stanford, CA: Stanford University Press, 1993.

Persell, Stuart Michael. *The French Colonial Lobby, 1889–1938*. Stanford, CA: Hoover Institution Press, 1983.

Pholsena, Vatthana. "Technology and Empire: A Colonial Narrative of the Construction of the Tonkin–Yunnan Railway." *Critical Asian Studies* 47, no. 4 (2015): 537–57.

Piaud, Virginie. "Opium et intérêts français au Yunnan (1906–1937)." *La France en Chine (1843–1943)*, edited by Jacques Weber, 195–208. Nantes: Presse académiques de l'Ouest, 1997.

Pila, Ulysse. "Chambre de commerce de Lyon. Séance extraordinaire du 28 Mai 1891. Rapport de M. Ulysse Pila sur son second voyage d'études commerciales au Tonkin." 1891.

Rankin, Mary Backus. *Elite Activism and Political Transformation in China: Zhejiang Province, 1865–1911*. Stanford, CA: Stanford University Press, 1986.

Rankin, Mary Backus. "Nationalistic Contestation and Mobilization Politics: Practice and Rhetoric of Railway-Rights Recovery at the End of the Qing." *Modern China* 28, no. 3 (2022): 315–61.

Réau, Raphaël, and Philippe Marchat. *Lettres d'un diplomate en Chine au début du xxe siècle: Hong Kong, Hai Nan, Yunnan (1901–1909)*. Paris: L'Harmattan, 2011.

Réau, Raphaël, and Philippe Marchat. *Raphaël Réau: consul à Hankéou pendant la révolution Chinoise et la grande guerre: 1910–1916*. Paris: L'Harmattan, 2013.

Reins, Thomas D. "Reform, Nationalism and Internationalism: The Opium Suppression Movement in China and the Anglo-American Influence, 1900–1908." *Modern Asian Studies* 25, no. 1 (1991): 101–42.

Remer, C. F. *Foreign Investments in China*. New York: Macmillan, 1933.

Reporter. "Kan! Kan! Kan! Faguo yunnan zhi zhimin jiankang [Look! Look! Look! French colonial medicine in Yunnan]." In *Yunnan zazhi xuanji* [Selections from the *Yunnan Journal*], 361–62. Beijing: Zhishi chanquan chubanshe, 2013.

Robinson, Cedric J. *Black Marxism: The Making of the Black Radical Tradition*. Chapel Hill: University of North Carolina Press, 1983.

Rochaix, A. "La lutte contre le paludisme" [The fight against malaria]. *La Dépêche Coloniale*, June 7, 1933.

Rousseau, Jean-François. "An Imperial Railway Failure: The Indochina–Yunnan Railway, 1898–1941." *Journal of Transport History* 35, no. 1 (2014): 1–17.

Sasges, Gerard. "State, Enterprise and the Alcohol Monopoly in Colonial Vietnam." *Journal of Southeast Asian Studies* 43, no. 1 (2012): 133–57.

Shaffer, Lynda. "Modern Chinese Labor History, 1895–1949." *International Labor and Working-Class History* 20 (1981): 31–37.

Shao, Ling. "Zhongguo guomin liguo zhi genben daji" [The fundamentals of Chinese nation building]. In *Yunnan zazhi xuanji* [Selections from the *Yunnan Journal*], 179–86. Beijing: Zhishi chanquan chubanshe, 2013.

Shi, Fu. "Dian-yue pangbian ji tiedao zhi shikuang" [The Yunnan–Vietnam border and the situation of the railway]. In *Yunnan zazhi xuanji* [Selections from the *Yunnan Journal*], 460–77. Beijing: Zhishi chanquan chubanshe, 2013.

Shi, Ming. "Yunnan da shiye jia zhao laoren zhuan" [The story of the great Yunnan entrepreneur Mr. Zhao]. In *Yunnan zazhi xuanji* [Selections from the *Yunnan Journal*], 157–61. Beijing: Zhishi chanquan chubanshe, 2013.

Shi, Zhihong. *Agricultural Development in Qing China: A Quantitative Study, 1661–1911*. Leiden: Brill, 2018.

Shotwell, James T. "Sun Yat-Sen and Maurice William." *Political Science Quarterly* 47, no. 1 (1932): 19–26.

Sibeud, Emmanuelle. "Une libre pensée impériale? Le comité de protection et de défense des indigènes (ca. 1892–1914)." *Mil Neuf Cent. Revue d'histoire intellectuelle* 27 (2009): 57–74.

Singaravélou, Pierre. "L'Empire des économistes: l'enseignement de 'l'économie coloniale' sous la IIIe République." In *L'esprit économique impérial (1830–1970): Groupes de pression et réseaux du patronat colonial en France et dans l'empire*, 121–34. Paris: Société française d'histoire d'outre-mer, 2008.

Singaravélou, Pierre. *Tianjin cosmopolis: une autre histoire de la mondialisation.* Paris: Éditions du Seuil, 2017.

Sinh, Vinh. *Phan Chau Trinh and His Political Writings.* Ithaca, NY: Cornell University, 2009.

Smith, Adam. *Wealth of Nations.* Buffalo, NY: Prometheus Books, 1991.

Smith, S. A. *Like Cattle and Horses: Nationalism and Labor in Shanghai, 1895–1927.* Durham, NC: Duke University Press, 2002.

Song, Lingqian. "Kangri zhanzheng shiqi zhong-fa dian-yue tielu yunshu jiaoshe lunlue" [The negotiations during the anti-Japanese war about the Yunnan–Vietnam railway between China and France]. *Journal of Xichang College Social Science Edition* 20, no. 3 (2008): 83–88.

Stanziani, Alessandro. "Beyond Colonialism: Servants, Wage Earners, and Indentured Migrants in Rural France and on Réunion Island." *Labor History* 54, no. 1 (2013): 64–87.

Stanziani, Alessandro. "Local Bondage in Global Economies: Servants, Wage Earners, and Indentured Migrants in Nineteenth-Century France, Great Britain, and the Mascarene Islands." *Modern Asian Studies* 47 (2013): 1218–51.

Stanziani, Alessandro. "The Abolition of Slavery and the 'New Labor Contract' in French Equatorial Africa, 1890–1914." In *The Palgrave Handbook of Bondage and Human Rights in Africa and Asia*, 227–45. New York: Palgrave Macmillan, 2019.

Statistical Department of the Inspectorate General of Customs. *Treaties, Convention, etc. Between China and Foreign States.* Shanghai, 1917.

Summers, Tim. *Yunnan—A Chinese Bridgehead to Asia: A Case Study of China's Political and Economic Relations with Its Neighbors.* Oxford: Chandos, 2013.

Sun, Can. "Fan-ya tielu jianshe yu dian-yue tielu lishi wenhua baohu" [The construction of the trans-Asian railways and the historical and cultural protection of the Yunnan–Vietnam railway]. *Journal of Yunnan Nationalities University* 22, no. 4 (2005): 20–23.

Sun, Chunfu. "466 gongli dian-yue tielu shang de qiwan tiao xingming" [70,000 lives on the 466-km Yunnan–Vietnam Railway]. *Wenshi Tiandi* (2011): 14–18.

Sun, E-Tu Zen. "Mining Labor in the Ch'ing Period." In *Approaches to Modern Chinese History*, edited by Albert Feuerwerker, Murphy Rhoads, and Mary C. Wright, 45–67. Berkeley: University of California Press, 1967.

Sun, Yatsen. *San-min chu-i: The Three Principles of the People.* Taiwan: China Cultural Center, 2003.

Sutton, Donald S. *Provincial Militarism and the Chinese Republic: The Yunnan Army 1905–25.* Ann Arbor: Michigan University Press, 1980.

Teng, Ssu-yü, and John King Fairbank. *China's Response to the West: A Documentary Survey, 1839–1923.* Cambridge, MA: Harvard University Press, 1979.

Tiberi, O. "Commercial Report for 1901." *L'Echo de Chine*, March 9, 1903.

Tixier, Nicole. "La Chine dans la stratégie impériale: le role du Quai d'Orsay et de ses agents." In *La France en Chine (1843–1943)*, edited by Jacques Weber, 259–79. Nantes: Presse académiques de l'Ouest, 1997.

Todd, David. *A Velvet Empire: French Informal Imperialism in the Nineteenth Century*. Princeton, NJ: Princeton University Press, 2021.

Trang, Phan T. H. "Paul Doumer: Aux origines d'un grand projet, le chemin de fer Transindochinois." *Histoire, économie, et société* 30, no. 3 (2011): 115–40.

Trocki, Carl A. "Drugs, Taxes, and Chinese Capitalism in Southeast Asia." In *Opium Regimes: China, Britain, and Japan, 1839–1952*, edited by Timothy Brook and Bob Tadashi Wakabayashi, 79–104. Berkeley: University of California Press, 2000.

Trocki, Carl A. *Opium, Empire and the Global Political Economy. A Study of the Asian Opium Trade, 1750–1950*. London: Routledge, 1999.

Vann, Michael G. "'All the World's a Stage,' Especially in the Colonies: L'exposition de Hanoï, 1902–1903." In *Empire and Culture: The French Experience, 1830–1940*, edited by Martin Evans, 181–91. Basingstoke, UK: Palgrave Macmillan, 2004.

Villechénoux, A., and M. Louis Reynaud. "Précis d'une monographie d'un coolie terrassier Setchoannais de la province du Se-Tch'oan." *Les ouvriers des deux mondes* 111 (1912): 265–91.

Walsh, Warren. "The Yunnan Myth." *Far Eastern Quarterly* 2, no. 3 (1943): 272–85.

Wang, Hui. "Zhang Taiyan's Concept of the Individual and Modern Chinese Identity." In *Becoming Chinese: Passages to Modernity and Beyond*, edited by Wen-hsin Yeh, 231–59. Berkeley: University of California Press, 2000.

Wang, Yuzhi, and Fan Dewei. "Dian-yue tielu yu dian dongnan shaoshu minzu diqu gongyehua hudong guanxi pingshu" [The Yunnan–Vietnam railway and industrial development in ethnic regions of southeast Yunnan]. *Journal of Honghe University* 8, no. 1 (2010): 12–15.

Wang, Yuzhi, Peng Qiang, and Fan Dewei. *Dian-yue tielu yu dian dongnan shaoshu minzu diqu shehui bianqian yanjiu* [The Yunnan–Vietnam railway and social change in the ethnic regions of southeast Yunnan]. Kunming: Yunnan renmin chubanshe, 2012.

Wells, Audrey. *Political Thought of Sun Yat-Sen: Development and Impact*. Basingstoke, UK: Palgrave Macmillan, 2001.

Wilbur, C. Martin. *Sun Yat-sen: Frustrated Patriot*. New York: Columbia University, 1976.

Williams, Michael. *Returning Home with Glory: Chinese Villagers around the Pacific, 1849 to 1949*. Hong Kong: Hong Kong University Press, 2018.

Wong, J. Y. *Deadly Dreams: Opium and the Arrow War (1856–1860) in China*. Cambridge: Cambridge University Press, 1998.

Wong, R. Bin. *China Transformed: Historical Change and the Limits of European Experience*. Ithaca, NY: Cornell University Press, 1999.

Wright, Hamilton. "The International Opium Commission." *American Journal of International Law* 3, no. 4 (1909): 828–68.

Wu, Xingzhi. *Yanshen de pingxingxian—Dian-yue tielu yu bianmin shehui* (Extended parallel lines—Dian–Vietnam railway and borderland community). Beijing: Beijing daxue chubanshe, 2012.

Wu, Xingzhi. "Zuowei jiben jiyi yu ziwo yanxu de wuzhi wenhua yanjiu–Yi dian-yue tielu weilie (A research on substance culture as collective memory and self-continuance—Taking the Yunnan–Vietnam railway as example). *Nationalities Research in Qinghai* 3 (2012): 147–51.

Wu, Yi. "Lun yunnan duiyu zhongguo zhi diwei" [On Yunnan's place in China]. In *Yunnan zazhi xuanji* [Selections from the *Yunnan Journal*], 281–88. Beijing: Zhishi chanquan chubanshe, 2013.

Xia, Shao. "Guohui wenti zhi zhenxiang" [The truth about the National Assembly]. In *Yunnan zazhi xuanji* [Selections from the *Yunnan Journal*], 146–50. Beijing: Zhishi chanquan chubanshe, 2013.

Xia, Shao. "Lun guomin baocun guotu zhi fa" [On the methods of people's protection of the country land]. In *Yunnan zazhi xuanji* [Selections from the *Yunnan Journal*], 69–77. Beijing: Zhishi chanquan chubanshe, 2013.

Xia, Shao. "Yunnan zhi jianglai" [The future of Yunnan]. In *Yunnan zazhi xuanji* [Selections from the *Yunnan Journal*], 258–67. Beijing: Zhishi chanquan chubanshe, 2013.

Xie, Benshu. *Qingdai yunnan gaoben shiliao* [Documents on Yunnan from the Qing period]. Vol. 1. Shanghai: Shanghai cishu chubanshe, 2011.

Xu, Guoqi. *Strangers on the Western Front: Chinese Workers in the Great War.* Cambridge, MA: Harvard University Press, 2011.

Xue, Sheng. "Dian shen tiaochen shu dian-yue lu choukuan banfa" [The Yunnan gentry proposes the methods of fundraising for the purchase of the Yunnan–Vietnam railway], in *Yunnan zazhi xuanji* [Selections from the *Yunnan Journal*], 494. Beijing: Zhishi chanquan chubanshe, 2013.

Xue, Sheng. "Faren yu yunnan" [The French and Yunnan]. In *Yunnan zazhi xuanji* [Selections from the *Yunnan Journal*], 359–61. Beijing: Zhishi chanquan chubanshe, 2013.

Yan, Yi. "Yunnan zhi shiye" [The economy of Yunnan]. In *Yunnan zazhi xuanji* [Selections from the *Yunnan Journal*], 170–75. Beijing: Zhishi chanquan chubanshe, 2013.

Yi, Lu. "Quan you mian tongbao zucheng hua shang zonghui" [The need to establish the Chinese Chamber of Commerce in Burma]. In *Yunnan zazhi xuanji* [Selections from the *Yunnan Journal*], 175–78. Beijing: Zhishi chanquan chubanshe, 2013.

Yi, Ming. "Yunnan da shiye jia zhao laoren zhuan" [The story of Yunnan's great entrepreneur Mr. Zhao]. In *Yunnan zazhi xuanji* [Selections from the *Yunnan Journal*], 157–61. Beijing: Zhishi chanquan chubanshe, 2013.

Yi, Xia. "Wei dian-yue tielu zaocheng jinggao quan dian [A warning to Yunnan on the completion of the Yunnan–Vietnam railway]. In *Yunnan zazhi xuanji* [Selections from the *Yunnan Journal*], 514–19. Beijing: Zhishi chanquan chubanshe, 2013.

Yi, Xia. "Zhuzhong cuqian shiye yi su min kun" [Emphasis on simple industries will enrich the people]. In *Yunnan zazhi xuanji* [Selections from the *Yunnan Journal*], 189–91. Beijing: Zhishi chanquan chubanshe, 2013.

Yun, Lisa. *The Coolie Speaks: Chinese Indentured Laborers and African Slaves in Cuba*. Philadelphia: Temple University Press, 2008.

Yunnan sheng dang'an guan. *Qingmo minchu de yunnan shehui* [Yunnan society in the late Qing and early republican period]. Kunming: Yunnan renmin chubanshe, 2005.

Yunnan sheng zong gong hui gongren yundong shi yanjiu zu. *Yunnan gongren yundong shi ziliao huibian: 1886–1949* [Documents on the Yunnan labor movement: 1886–1949]. Kunming: Yunnan renmin chubanshe, 1989.

Yunnan *zazhi xuanji* [Selections from the *Yunnan Journal*]. Beijing: Zhishi chanquan chubanshe, 2013.

Zarrow, Peter. *After Empire: The Conceptual Transformation of the Chinese State: 1885–1924*. Stanford, CA: Stanford University Press, 2012.

Zelin, Madeleine. "The Rights of Tenants in Mid-Qing Sichuan: A Study of Land-Related Lawsuits in the Baxian Archives." *Journal of Asian Studies* 45, no. 3 (May 1986): 499–526.

Zhang, Chengqing. "Sijue hui xuanyan" [The manifesto of the Dare-to-Die Society]. In *Yunnan zazhi xuanji* [Selections from the *Yunnan Journal*], 320. Beijing: Zhishi chanquan chubanshe, 2013.

Zhe, Sheng. "You dian shu lue" [A tour in Yunnan]. In *Yunnan zazhi xuanji* [Selections from the *Yunnan Journal*], 342–46. Beijing: Zhishi chanquan chubanshe, 2013.

Zhen, Ge. "Zhong nong zhuyi" [Agrarianism]. In *Yunnan zazhi xuanji* [Selections from the *Yunnan Journal*], 195–98. Beijing: Zhishi chanquan chubanshe, 2013.

Zhou, Liying. *Wan qing liu ri xuesheng yu jindai yunnan shehui* [Chinese students in Japan in the late Qing period and modern Yunnan society]. Kunming: Yunnan daxue chubanshe, 2011.

Zhuang, Xingcheng. "Qiantan dian-yue tielu dui yunnan shehui jingji de yingxiang" [On the Yunnan–Vietnam railway's impact on the economy and society of Yunnan]. *Journal of Mengzi Teachers' Institute* 9, no. 3 (1992): 64–72.

Zhuang, Xingcheng, Wu Qiang, and Li Kun. *Dian-yue tielu shiliao huibian* [Documents on the Yunnan–Vietnam railway]. Kunming: Yunnan renmin chubanshe, 2014.

Zou, Rong. "The Revolutionary Army," *Contemporary Chinese Thought* 31, no. 1 (1999): 32–38.

Index

Note: Page numbers in *italics* refer to figures, maps, and tables.

Printed in the USA
CPSIA information can be obtained
at www.ICGtesting.com
JSHW080921160424
61253JS00001B/2